I0827994

MIDCOAST MAINE
in
WORLD WAR II

MIDCOAST MAINE
in
WORLD WAR II

Margaret Shiels Konitzky

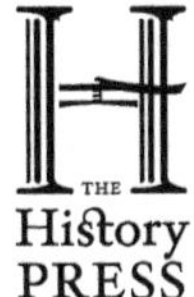

Published by The History Press
Charleston, SC
www.historypress.net

Front cover, top, left to right: Two older men and two women working at Hyde Windlass, 1943. *Maine Maritime Museum, BIW Collection*; Radar School parade in dress whites in front of Walker Art Building, Commencement 1945. *Bowdoin College Archives, Brunswick, Maine*; *bottom, left*: Mrs. Virginia Keefe christening Coastal Transport APC68 at Hodgdon & Goudy & Stevens Shipyards, East Boothbay, July 20, 1943. *Boothbay Region Historical Society.*

First published 2018

ISBN 9781540228918

Library of Congress Control Number: 2017963236

This book is dedicated to my parents, John Michael and Ruth Besson Shiels, for their unwavering love, support and belief in me. Thank you for always being there, always listening and always loving. This is for you.

CONTENTS

PREFACE

This book began with a talk I developed several years ago for the first *Wings Over Wiscasset* air show, which featured World War II planes, music and a veterans' discussion. The town manager decided the homefront also needed to be represented, and she volunteered me to do that. As the site manager of two nineteenth-century historic houses in town, a period of furious extracurricular research followed, nineteenth century by day and the 1940s at night and on weekends. The talk was well received despite the audience having to struggle to hear over the airplane engines. After the talk, I went back to my office and filed it all away. Then something interesting began to happen. Through the Historic New England Speakers Bureau, a service the nonprofit regional heritage organization offers to anyone looking for a speaker on a historical subject, the requests for my World War II homefront talk kept coming. And coming. To make the talks more interesting, I did a little more research for each of the communities I spoke to, each time learning about a different facet of 1940s New England life that I then wove into the talk. Every time, the audience included people who had been children or young adults during the war who now wanted to share their memories.

Most people know the basics of life on the World War II homefront—pulling together, working war jobs and dealing with rationing—but few understand the reality of hardships, toil and stress that Americans lived in from 1941 through 1945. Each community experienced the war years in a slightly different way. Those who lived through it never forgot the experience.

The research for my talks in Maine, Massachusetts and New Hampshire laid the groundwork for this book, which has given me the opportunity to dig deeper locally, finding new stories and friends along the way.

The aim of this book is to give the reader a sense of what life was like in these communities during the war, who lived here and how they got through it. To understand that, you need to know the context of what was going on in the war at the time, some of which has been forgotten over the years. When possible, I have included the ages, location, family situation and livelihood of the people I mention to give the reader a sense of who they were as individuals and in the context of their town, and to allow for comparisons to today. I hope the balance of context and detail does justice to the story.

My primary source materials were local newspapers and personal interviews. Personal and family information comes primarily from Ancestry.com and local town directories. Business information comes from directories, advertisements and the annual Maine Registers. Secondary sources are listed in the bibliography. Chapter titles came from the music of the 1940s, which boosted morale all over the world and has endured as a uniquely American art form that I have loved and listened to for years.

ACKNOWLEDGEMENTS

This book could not have been written without the support and assistance of many generous individuals and the staffs of several local historical organizations, including Robin A.S. Haynes and Peter Goodwin at the Sagadahoc History and Genealogy Room at the Patten Free Library; Nathan Lipfert at Maine Maritime Museum; Larissa Vigue Picard, Stephanie Ruddock and Rachael Jeffers at the Pejepscot Historical Society in Brunswick; David Hackett at the Harpswell Historical Society; Barbara Rumsey and Margaret Tew at the Boothbay Region Historical Society; Ron Orchard at the Southport Historical Society; and Bob Bouchard at St. John's Church, All Saints Parish, Brunswick. Thank you all for your research assistance, encouragement and willingness to share your deep knowledge of local history. Thank you, Pam Brackett and David Cherry at the Wiscasset Public Library, for always helping when I need something and Jay Robbins for sharing your wonderful family document. Calvin and Marjorie Dodge generously gave me hours of time at their kitchen table, sharing their fabulous collection and memories of Damariscotta and Newcastle. Dr. Charles Burden, Maine maritime and Bath history buff, Sue Fitzgerald and Kerry Nelson researched and presented talks to the Bath Historical Society on Bath's grocery stores and downtown in the 1940s that were an invaluable source of information. Rupert White provided a boy's-eye view of one of the most exciting local events of the war in a presentation given to the Pejepscot Historical Society and shared stories and memories of Brunswick life during those years. Thank you, Charlie,

Sue, Kerry and Rupert, for preserving and sharing those memories. Thank you, Lin Snow, for your wonderful books and your willingness to offer counsel and share great stories. Thank you to the Woofenden family—Todd, George and Randall Woofenden—who, through unexpected family connections, shared family photos and accounts of their grandparents and great-grandparents in Bath. Thank you to Sarah Sherman Brewer for capturing the memories of people in Boothbay and Southport before we lost them. Thank you, Ron Orchard, for sharing memories of Southport. Thank you to Laurie Smith, who started this whole thing. Thank you to my Brunswick parents—Nancy and Ed Langbein—for your support and enthusiasm for all my historic (and life) endeavors. Thank you to my wonderful in-laws, Sally and the late Don Reed, for your support, love and encouragement. And most of all, thank you to my husband, Gus, for your love, patience, help and understanding during the writing of this book.

INTRODUCTION

The world of the 1940s was very different from today. It was a more innocent, less complicated time in many ways, but not necessarily an easier one. Mainers had always had to work hard. Families were larger and ethnic identities felt more closely. Many people had family who had emigrated from Europe or Canada just a few years or a few decades earlier. Others had built lives, worked the same jobs and lived in the same houses or at least the same town for generations. Most people in Maine didn't have much in the way of material possessions, but they didn't consider themselves poor. There was no television, computer, Internet or mall. People got their news from the radio and the newspapers. The wealthy and working classes lived parallel but very different lives within the same small towns. Summer residents, known locally as summer people, came back every year to what they considered their second home, but most had little or no interaction with the people who lived there and kept the communities running other than the Mainers who took care of their boats and houses or who served them in stores and restaurants.

Women's roles in society were basically the roles they had played for centuries. Women were expected to marry, have children and, if economically feasible, stay home to care for their families. Some women worked, went to college and had careers, but the majority of American women, particularly in rural areas, did not. Those expectations were reflected in the media of the time, where the way women were discussed and addressed is dramatically different from what we are used to in the twenty-first century.

Midcoast Maine is made up of rocky coasts, small towns, rural villages, one larger town and one city. Each has its own unique character and personality. Bath, the only midcoast city, was always grittier, more industrial and completely dependent on the maritime-related economy to survive. The pivotal role of Bath Iron Works (BIW) in the city's development is undeniable, and its success supported the many small businesses and civic and cultural organizations of the community. Bath came out of the Depression before any of its neighbors, but having experienced the dramatic boom and bust of World War I, its residents knew wartime prosperity doesn't last. As BIW waxes and wanes, the city's economy does the same. Brunswick has been the intellectual capital of Maine since the turn of the nineteenth century through the presence of Bowdoin College and the men and women associated with it, many of whom left their mark on its rich culture. Throughout the twentieth century, the mix of town, gown, mill and base resulted in a thriving yet historic downtown and a more diverse population and economy than almost anywhere else in Maine. Brunswick welcomed them all and was better for it. Life in Boothbay and Boothbay Harbor revolved around tourism, fishing and boats and had done so since the early nineteenth century. Whatever else is happening in the world and the economy, that cycle continues. Small circles of hardy and hardworking locals keep things running and maintain strong ties to traditions and one another, but tourists and summer residents always return, and the local economy depends on them. Topsham was a mix of mill town and farms, closely tied to Brunswick economically and socially. The mills and some of the countryside are gone now, but the historic village and its character remain. Harpswell remains rural, a quiet place where life has revolved around fishing, farming and family, taking in stride the seasonal influx of town and city folk who escape there to relax. Damariscotta is and was a hardworking, self-sufficient small town with services, arts and amenities that have enabled a steady, loyal, independent, family-centric population to absorb and welcome incomers. The peninsula towns and villages are made up of a combination of fishermen, merchants and professionals and are invaded every year by summer residents and tourists in numbers just slightly less than in Boothbay and Boothbay Harbor. Each has its own slightly different culture but with very similar hubs of gossipers who always know who is doing what with whom and where.

World War II brought everyone together in civilian defense activities, war work and, most importantly, in the strong belief that we were all in it together and everyone had a part to play.

As a fellow historian kept reminding me, so many of these people had nothing, yet they kept giving, year after year. They gave their money, their time and their energy to the war effort, their families and their communities. They did their bit, and more.

Chapter 1

WHITE CHRISTMAS

The signs were everywhere that war was coming. In 1933, the U.S. Navy began giving Bath Iron Works (BIW) orders to build more destroyers. By 1940, the yard had delivered eleven new ships and was one of the leading shipyards in the nation.[1] A build-up was underway. Newspapers and the radio pronounced the bad news from Europe and Asia. Japan successfully invaded China and gradually extended its hold over the country. In the spring of 1940, the Nazis conquered Denmark, Norway, Belgium and the Netherlands. In June, France fell. In July, the Battle of Britain began.

Knowing that the majority of Americans were still opposed to the United States entering the war, but recognizing the necessity of assisting our ally in its time of greatest need, President Franklin D. Roosevelt (FDR) signed the Lend-Lease agreement on September 2, 1940, trading old destroyers to Great Britain in exchange for leases on land in Newfoundland and the Caribbean to be used for American military bases.[2] That agreement triggered even more orders for BIW-built destroyers.[3] On September 16, 1940, FDR reinstated the U.S. Selective Service (or draft). On September 27, 1940, Germany, Italy and Japan signed the Tripartite Agreement to fight any country joining the Allied powers in war. After nine months of escalating German U-boat attacks on British and Canadian merchant ships, the president declared an unlimited national emergency on May 27, 1941, telling Americans that the United States had to join the Battle of the Atlantic. "The war…is coming very close to home.…It would be suicide to wait until they are in our front yard.…Old-fashioned common sense calls for the use of a strategy that will

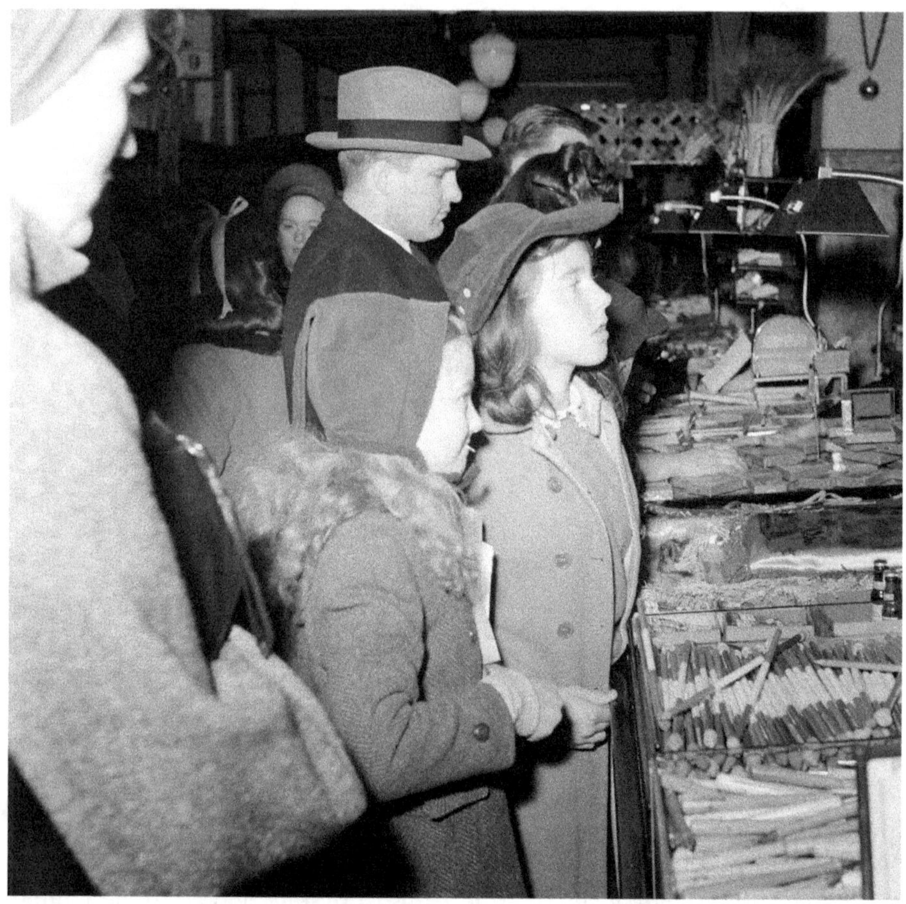

Girls shopping at F.W. Woolworth's Five and Ten Cent Store in Washington, D.C., December 1941. *John Collier, Photographer. Library of Congress.*

prevent such an enemy from gaining a foothold in the first place."[4] This was the declaration that America was preparing for war.

On Saturday, December 6, 1941, American main streets were busy with holiday shoppers. But behind the holiday cheer lurked a jittery uneasiness. Moviegoers watched newsreels of Hitler's advances and the suffering of the Belgians and the Dutch. At home, Americans listened to Edward R. Murrow's radio reporting from London during the Blitz and helped make "Bundles for Britain" care packages. The attack finally came, but not where people expected it.

On December 7, the Japanese attack on Pearl Harbor shocked the nation and hurled the country into life at war.

The headline of the *Bath Independent* on December 11 read, "Pearl Harbor, Hawaii Stronghold, Bombed by Japanese"[5] in the same font size as "City Council Passes Order to Buy Two-Way Radio for Police Force" and "Annual Planning Meeting Dromore Farm Bureau Held."[6] In contrast, the *Brunswick Record* sounded a call to action with a front-page editorial entitled "Am I Doing *All* That I Can?" The editorial eloquently captured the simultaneous strength and uncertainty of the moment:

> *This is the question that every man and woman in this community must ask himself or herself in this hour of our country's trial. All has been said that needs to be said about the need for national unity. Action—and action only—is what is needed now. The dogs of war are unleashed; they are at your throat and mine. We must fight—fight savagely and brutally to destroy the invaders who are murdering American people like you and me. Men of military age and sound body—enlist today! Men and women who cannot join the military forces—sign up today for Civilian Defense. Inquire—until you find out—where the right registration point is in your town and then register....Offer your services now—today. Fellow citizens of Brunswick, Topsham, Harpswell, Freeport and Bowdoinham! Have unbounded faith, show high courage and work with redoubled enthusiasm! And be sure that you are doing all that you can.*[7]

Next to that passionate exhortation was an article designed to reassure and strengthen resolve titled "Community Calm in War—Citizens Resolve to Do All in Their Power to Help."[8] To further that calm resolve, a week later, the paper asked preachers to use a conversational rather than inflammatory tone in their sermons and services.[9]

The following Saturday, just as the season's first snowstorm began, an army unit of black soldiers arrived unexpectedly at the armory in Brunswick.[10] The men were assigned to guard the approaches to the Carlton Bridge, railroad lines and other key points.[11] They had been dispatched with such secrecy and haste that no one had made any arrangements to house or feed them.[12] The men set up their cots in the armory and arranged to take their meals at the nearby Miss Brunswick Diner on Pleasant Street.

Brunswick immediately made the soldiers welcome. Brunswick Hardware Company sent them a radio. The Red Cross and American Legion post collected furniture, games, magazines and other items for their off-duty recreation. The unit arrived in full winter uniforms, but some well-meaning townspeople assumed that the black soldiers were from the South and

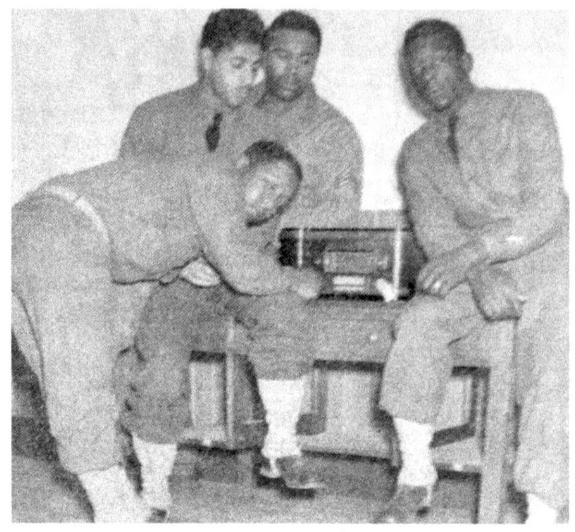

Four soldiers from the U.S. Army detachment sent to guard the Carlton Bridge listening to the radio at the Brunswick Armory, December 19, 1941. *Brunswick Record.*

commiserated with them about the weather. The soldiers laughed as they explained that they came from upstate New York, including several from Buffalo who claimed the winters there were worse than they were in Maine. Money was raised to give the men a good Christmas dinner, since military units on detached duty had only a small daily allowance. Enough money was raised to give them not only a Christmas but also a New Year's dinner and a carton of cigarettes for each man.[13]

Another part of the unit, stationed in Bath, was given a similar welcome. The soldiers there arranged to take their meals at Central Café on Center Street. The *Bath Independent* of January 8, 1942, reported that they, too, had received a radio from a local hardware store (Gediman's), along with an iron, a coffeepot and an ample supply of coffee, cream and sugar to go with it.[14] Local children wanted to help, too. The eighth grade class of Central Grammar School donated "cooked food" organized and distributed by fifteen-year-old Anna Day. Anna was the middle child of seven of Perley Day, a ship stager at BIW, and his wife, Cora.[15]

Despite or perhaps in some ways because of the official outbreak of war, Christmas 1941 was the best in years for local merchants. Wartime shortages had not yet begun. More people were employed, and most had more money in their pockets than they had for decades. There was a slight lull during the week immediately after Pearl Harbor, but even then, sales were higher than they had been in 1940.[16] There was a determination on the part of most to make the holidays the best they could be, a part of American life the war would be fought to preserve.

Chapter 2

WE'LL MEET AGAIN...DON'T KNOW WHERE, DON'T KNOW WHEN

Answering the Call

After December 7, enthusiastic young men rushed to enlist. Men and boys flooded draft registration stations. As a little boy in Newcastle, Calvin Dodge remembered seeing truckloads of soldiers drive by bound for Eastport, where they would be shipped overseas. He remembered waving to them and some of them waving back.[17]

Roland Bernier of Bowdoin had just turned twenty-one and was eager to join the fight. He went to work as usual on Monday, December 8, at Tondreau's Market on Maine Street in Brunswick, where he was an assistant meat cutter. Immediately upon arriving, he told his boss he wanted to go to Portland to enlist. Roland was the eldest of five children of Frank and Genevieve Bernier. Frank, forty-five, was a World War I veteran and a floor helper at Cabot Mill. He and Genevieve met and married in France in 1918. Genevieve, a French citizen, followed Frank to the United States in 1919 after the end of World War I. The Berniers heard the news of Pearl Harbor with dread, knowing that their son would enlist as soon as he could. Older voices persuaded Roland to wait at least until he was told where to report.[18]

Those instructions were communicated via radio and newspapers. In Brunswick, draft registration took place in the high school gym. Every week, the newspapers published lists of who should register, who had enlisted and who was called up. Everyone knew someone who had enlisted or was drafted. High-spirited recruitment campaigns created excitement, but newspaper

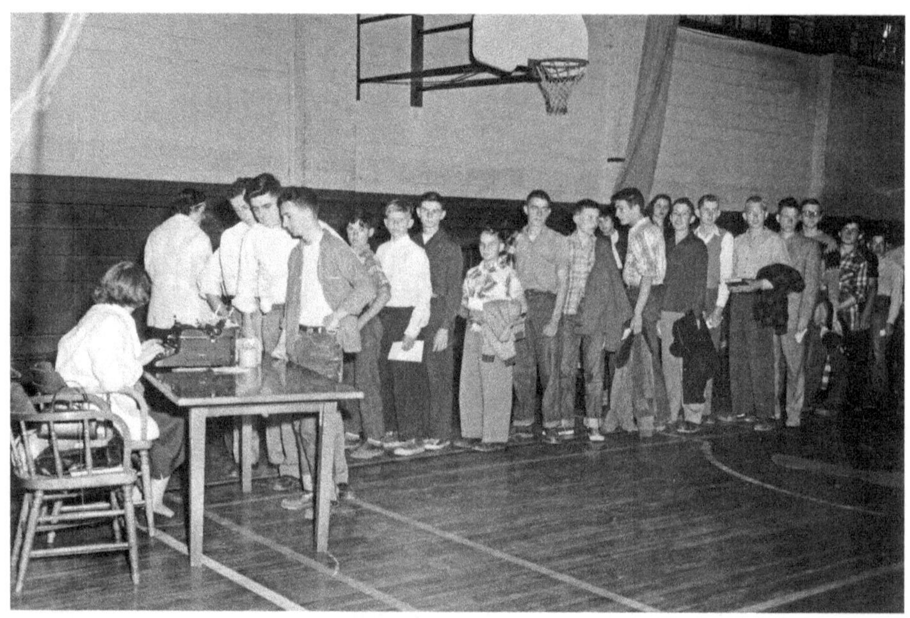

Boys lined up to register for the draft in the Brunswick High School gym, December 1941. *Pejepscot Historical Society.*

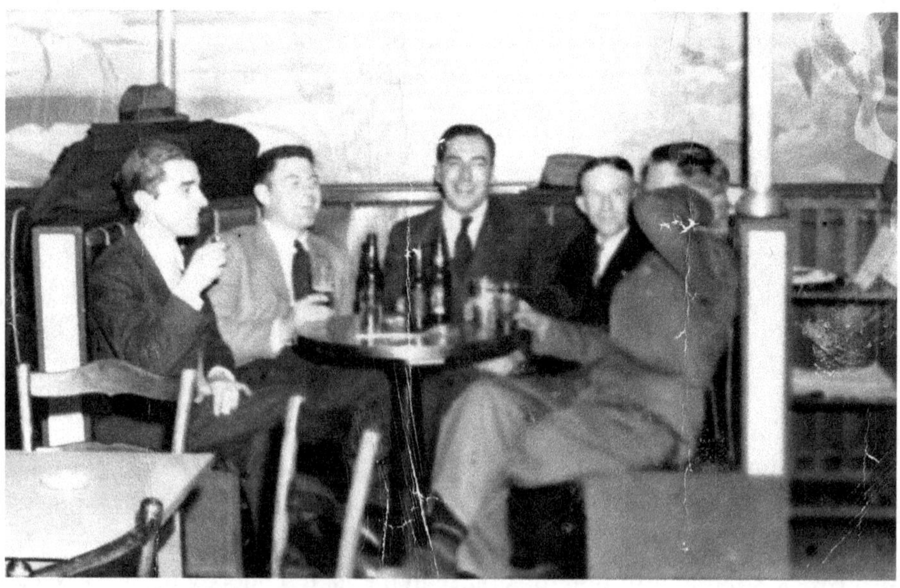

Left to right: William Tomkins, James Stevens, Frank H. Cummings Sr., Lewis Burnham and Doug Hodgdon from East Boothbay sharing some laughs in Portland before their induction physical. *Boothbay Region Historical Society.*

accounts of Japanese victories in the Pacific and Nazi advances in Europe sobered the excitement with reality. Families like the Berniers with draft-eligible sons, husbands and fathers steeled themselves to do what needed to be done.

The registration process was not without its humorous moments. When forty-five- to sixty-four-year-olds were registered in April 1942, one man had no proof he had been born. After much discussion, he used his World War I discharge papers to determine the year but had no idea of the exact date.[19] A seventy-two-year-old man insisted on registering and almost cried when he was told he could not. The man insisted on getting a receipt to show that he wasn't a draft dodger. Brunswick town clerk John W. Riley told him to send anyone who bothered him to the town office and the town would provide proof that he had done his duty. A local businessman found that he was being registered by his own secretary. Since she knew all the information needed for the registration forms, he sat back and read the morning paper.[20]

For the families of men and women who enlisted, anxiety became a constant. By October 1942, Pauline and George Lowery on Barter's Island had five sons in the army plus Pauline's brother in the navy.[21] Pauline, forty-one, was a retired teacher, and George, forty-two, was a fisherman, as were their sons. The Lowery boys made up one-third of the Barters Island men in service. Marie Fortin was a sixty-year-old widow working at Cabot Mill in 1941. She and her husband, Joseph, emigrated from Canada in 1896 and became U.S. citizens. By 1920, they had ten children plus Joseph's son by a previous marriage. The family lived in a pretty 1894 three-bedroom house on Bowker Street in Brunswick, behind Bowdoin College. Joseph, who worked as a brake man at the railroad yard, died sometime between 1930 and 1940, leaving Marie to manage the family. Their son Roger, twenty-three, a millworker and star of the Cabot Mill baseball team, enlisted immediately after Pearl Harbor. Roland, twenty-five, worked at BIW before joining the marines in 1942, followed that same year by brothers Christian, twenty-four, and Paul, nineteen, both of whom joined the army. Marcel, eighteen and a hotel bellboy, enlisted in the army in January 1943. Marie became the first Brunswick mother with five sons serving in the armed forces.

Guy and Ruth Toothaker, thirty-nine and thirty-seven, respectively, of Jordan Avenue in Brunswick, had four sons in the navy. Guy was a florist. Their youngest son, Donald, seventeen, enlisted in March 1942. Within months, he was taking flower orders from his shipmates and sending them back to his father in Brunswick, who delivered them through the Florists' Telegraph Delivery Service (the first out-of-town floral delivery service, now known as FTD, Inc.).[22]

Families of servicemen and women bought official war flags to hang in their windows. The flags showed a blue star for each family member in service, thereby announcing the family's patriotism and sacrifice. An advertisement in the *Boothbay Register* asked, "Have You a Man in the Service of Our Country? Son? Husband? Father? Employee? (Daughter? Sister?)"[23] Milton and Lena Giles of Boothbay Harbor also had five sons in the service. Lena's daughter remembered her mother writing letters and sending care packages to each of them, plus her four nephews.[24] The army and navy honored (and promoted) "Five Star Mothers" like Marie, Pauline and Lena as examples of homefront strength and sacrifice. A gold star indicated someone in the family had died in the service of their country.

For veterans of World War I, dread and resignation were added to the mix of emotions felt by draftees. Ezra Webber, a forty-eight-year-old World War I veteran, enlisted in May 1942.[25] His letters to his sister Sue in Wiscasset reflected a mature man's seriousness about the war and life. He wrote about arrangements he made to put his affairs in order and how he didn't have the energy for this war the way he had in 1917. Ezra also told a story about giving a French woman two cakes of soap. The grateful woman returned and offered Ezra a bottle of 1937 champagne and her daughter's hand in marriage! Ezra thanked her but declined, explaining that he was already married. Ezra learned that her husband, another veteran of World War I, had recently died in the fighting.

Ezra spent his war in Europe, while his son was stationed in the Pacific. In most of his letters, Ezra said he hadn't heard from Alden, twenty-two, who enlisted in June 1942. Their letters missed each other more often than they connected. Alden also wrote to his aunt Sue, but in contrast to his father's letters, Alden's had a much lighter younger man's tone. After starting each letter with a joke like, "Well, I'm still alive," he wrote about bad food, unfamiliar weather and strange animals like the Philippine water buffalo. He also told his aunt about things like jungle rot and crotch itch.

Not all men were cut out for military service. On the night of March 11, 1942, Peter Watts Jr., a soldier from Fall River, Massachusetts, decided he wasn't going overseas. Watts went AWOL and stole a car in Wiscasset, where he drove off the road and was arrested. He escaped, stole a second car in Montsweag and headed for Bath, where he hit another car on the Carlton Bridge. Watts then vaulted over the rail of the bridge, a twenty-foot drop, hitched a ride and stole a third car, a 1941 Chevrolet convertible. He was finally captured by the Maine State Police in Bath.[26] The September 17, 1942 *Brunswick Record* reported that another two deserters, one from Brunswick and the other from Portsmouth, New Hampshire, were arrested in Bowdoinham and held in the Brunswick Police Station. The men had broken out of the Fort Levett guardhouse in August and taken jobs cutting pulp wood near Bowdoinham. They were caught when the Brunswick man was seen in town and recognized.

MIDCOAST WOMEN GO TO WAR

America was calling women to serve, too. The traditional role for women in wartime was nursing, and the armed forces needed a lot of nurses. Midcoast women answered the call. Ellen Dolloff of Bath became a navy nurse in 1935. She was stationed at Pearl Harbor the day of the bombing and, in 1943, received a citation for outstanding ability in the performance of duties under fire.[27] Evelyn Libby of Boothbay Harbor enlisted in the army. The July 2, 1943 *Boothbay Register* announced that First Lieutenant Libby had been recognized as one of twenty-nine outstanding nurses enrolled in the first U.S. Army Nurses Corps School in Great Britain. Ruth Williams, Brunswick High School class of 1923, also became an army nurse. The February 17, 1944 *Bath Independent* reported that Ruth had completed the first course in a special training program "somewhere in England." Class participants had to have demonstrated outstanding ability and leadership while serving in the European Theater of Operations. The course included 119 hours of "drill, rendering mine and booby traps harmless, making river crossings, interpreting military maps, making military sketches" and other activities necessary to field soldiers. Ruth's two brothers and sister were also in the army.

Only graduates of nursing schools were accepted as nurses in any of the armed forces. This made military nursing out of reach for young women whose families couldn't afford nursing school. War jobs in industry paid better, required less red tape to enter and offered on-the-job training paid for by the federal government. In 1943, a federal nurses training program was launched to enable women of all economic strata to serve. The U.S. Cadet Nurse Corps offered free training, uniforms, a small monthly stipend and a career that could continue after the war.[28]

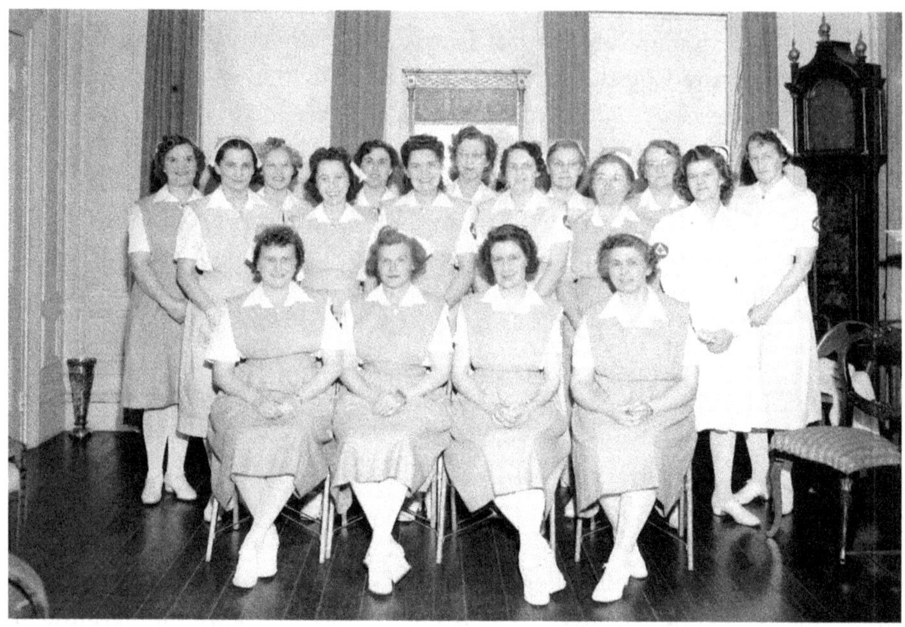

Volunteer nurses' aid training graduation at the Loyall Sewell Residence, 963 Washington Street, Bath, January 25, 1944. *Photographer Otis. N.E. Card, Richard Card Collection, Sagadahoc History & Genealogy Room, Patten Free Library.*

Meanwhile, homefront nurses were busy covering for hospital staff who had enlisted. Virginia McDougall, twenty-four, was married and had just given birth to her first child in 1941. She was the only surgical nurse at St. Andrews Hospital in Boothbay Harbor during the war, working day and night for one dollar a day. Virginia brought her baby daughter with her to work, and the lab crew looked after her until Virginia was done. There was only one doctor at the hospital, Dr. Philip Gregory, thirty-two. Each day, he did surgery in the morning, followed by house calls and then clinic hours. Like Bath and Brunswick, Boothbay Harbor was overwhelmed with military men and war workers, and the hospital had only thirty beds. Virginia remembered hauling patients on hand litters upstairs to their rooms because there was no elevator.[29]

After almost a year of heated debate over women's abilities and proper place in society, Congress passed a bill establishing a Women's Army Auxiliary Corps (WAACs) in May 1942. Their commanding officer, Oveta Culp Hobby, was a thirty-seven-year-old newspaper and PR executive from Texas. She was given the rank of colonel but only paid as much as an army major.[30] Within two months, the first contingent of women officer candidates entered the WAAC training camp in Iowa. Colonel Donald Faith, commander of the WAAC Fort Des Moines Provisional Army Officer Training School, said:

> *The auxiliary corps will have a 52-hour week of training, which does not include time out for making beds, cleaning quarters and home work. This isn't a jamboree of funny business, nor is it a feminist movement, he declared. The auxiliary must first learn to live harmoniously together and the sky is the limit for those who apply themselves. The highest rank authorized to date for the women who will take over the Army's noncombatant chores to release fighting men is equivalent to a captaincy in the Army.*[31]

So the sky was the limit for women in the army, but only so far as a captaincy! In 1943, the WAACs became the Women's Army Corps (WAC) with full army benefits.[32]

Thirty-nine-year-old Olive Stratton, a longtime summer resident of Southport, was working as a saleswoman in her father's car dealership in Malden, Massachusetts, when war broke out. She enlisted, went through basic training and officers' candidate school in Des Moines and was commissioned an officer in October 1942. When the Boothbay paper mistakenly listed her rank as captain, she wrote back to correct them. She explained that her rank was the equivalent of a second lieutenant but clarified that there were no captains in the WACs yet.[33] Olive was the first woman to appear in the newspaper's honor roll of hometown people in the service. Years later, she remembered the difficulty WACs faced in getting uniforms. Manufacturing and distributing women's uniforms was not a priority for the army, so sometimes the women were issued men's gear instead.[34] This problem would also occur when women entered the war production workforce.

It's difficult to compile a full list of midcoast women who enlisted in the military in World War II. Military records for women are not as readily accessible as the records for men, often because their names changed when they married. Midcoast WACs included Bath public schoolteacher Elizabeth Pinkham, twenty-three, and divorced single mothers Hilda Somes, thirty-nine, from Newcastle, whose son Robert, nineteen, was in the navy, and Marion Chaney of Bath, forty-seven, mother of six, whose youngest son, Philip, twenty-two, was in the coast guard. Emma Moulton, forty-two, enlisted in the army the same day her daughter Elizabeth, twenty-three, enlisted in the marines. Virginia Dall, who had been driving a taxi for

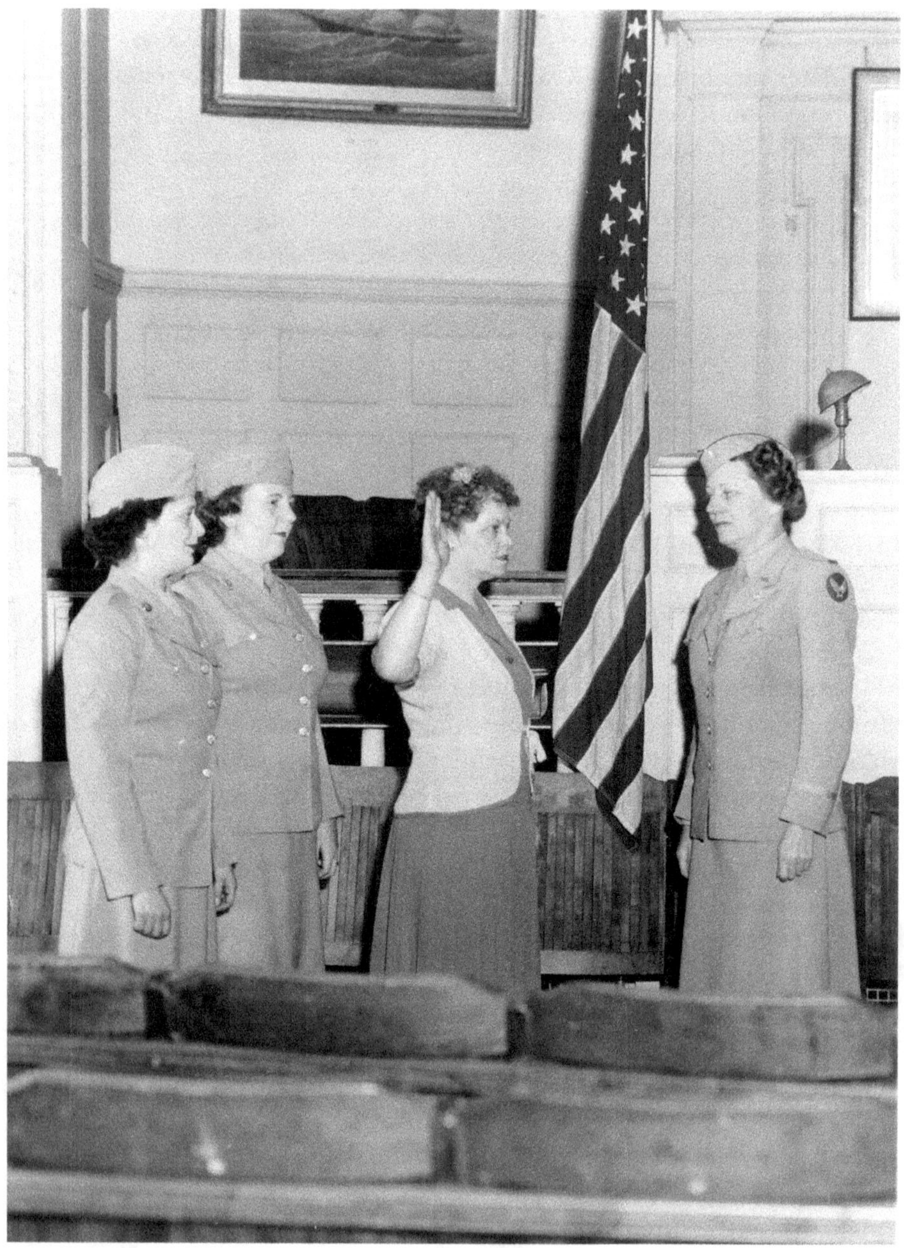

WAC induction at Bath City Hall, September 7, 1944. *Left to right*: Private First Class Elizabeth Rich, Private Alice Donovan, Mrs. Hilda Somes and Lieutenant Helen Pease. *Sagadahoc History & Genealogy Room, Patten Free Library.*

Freeman's Taxi Service while her husband, Ed, worked at BIW, enlisted in 1944. Emma, Elizabeth and Virginia were also from Bath. Kathleen Archibald from Brunswick enlisted at the age of eighteen. By March 1943, her parents, George and Ida, had three sons, a daughter and a son-in-law in the armed services.[35] No doubt their worry increased as much as their pride.

Lieutenant Dorothy McKenna, WAC, did a recruiting tour of the midcoast in May 1943. She inspired Lillian Gray, twenty-two, of East Boothbay to leave her job at the local Depositors Trust Bank and enlist. Lillian trained at Daytona Beach and served as a radio operator in the 204th Army Air Force, including some missions as a radio operator on C-47 transport planes.[36] Walpole's Harriet Haley, twenty-two, worked as a housekeeper in Damariscotta, and Wiscasset's Phyllis Reid, nineteen, worked as a telephone operator before enlisting. Another group of Lincoln County girls enlisted in 1944, including Lilla Granger, twenty-three, of Boothbay; Martha Greenleaf, twenty-nine, of Boothbay Harbor; Marjory L. Colby, thirty-seven, a widow from Dresden; and Connie Sherman, twenty-four, of Southport.[37]

The WAVES were established in April 1942 as the women's branch of the U.S. Naval Reserve.[38] WAVES stood for Women Accepted for Volunteer Emergency Service. Their first commander was Naval Reserve lieutenant commander Mildred Macafee, president of Wellesley College.[39] Unlike the WAC, which required only that the enlistee be over twenty-one and of good health and character, navy enlisted women had to be ages twenty to thirty-five and have a high school or business diploma or equivalent experience. Officer candidates had to be twenty to forty-nine, with a college degree or at least two years of college work plus two years' professional or business experience. Donna Stinson Doe of East Edgecomb graduated as an ensign in 1943 at the age of twenty-one.

The navy regulated all aspects of the WAVES' physical appearance. Each enlistee was given four uniforms designed by American designer Mainbocher at the request of Josephine Forrestal, wife of the assistant secretary of the navy and a former fashion writer for *Vogue* magazine. The uniforms included summer grays, summer dress whites, working blues and dress blues. Consensus at the time was that the WAVES had the best uniforms of the women's services. Navy regulations specified that WAVES should wear their hair short, but they were encouraged to wear feminine hairdos. The uniform regulations were specific, and frequent surprise inspections were standard procedure.[40]

Unlike the WACs, WAVES were not permitted to serve overseas. Instead, they were assigned to one of nine hundred stations across the country,

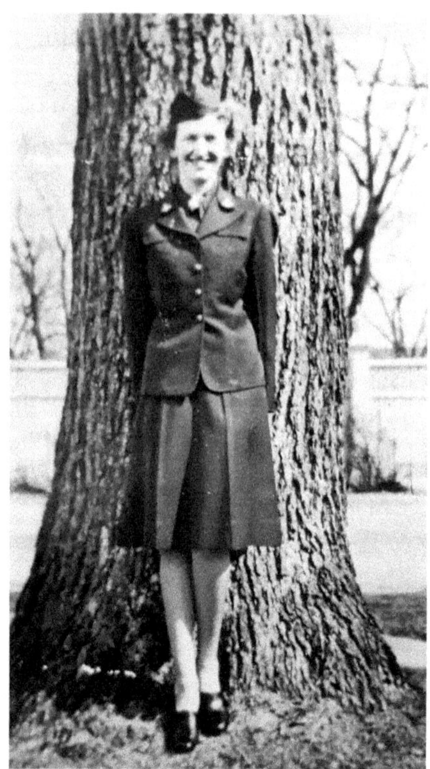

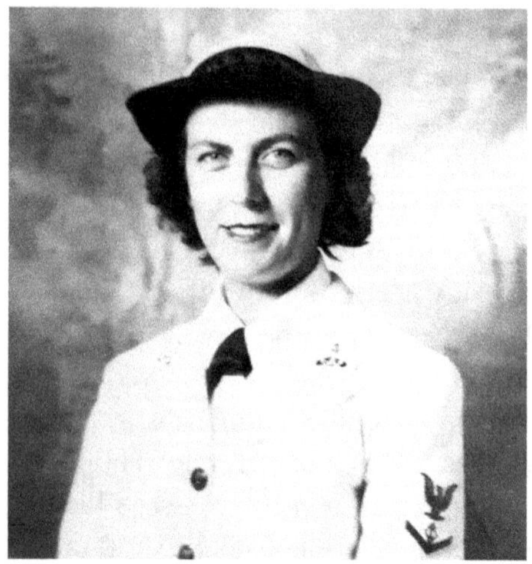

Above: Genevieve Hodgdon in WAVES uniform, 1943. *Wiscasset Public Library*.

Left: Kathryn Perkins in WAC uniform, 1943. *Wiscasset Public Library*.

where they were used to fill a variety of jobs, including administration, cryptography, communications, intelligence and supply management.[41] Elizabeth Sayward, twenty, of Boothbay Harbor, was a legal secretary when she enlisted in the WAVES in the summer of 1942. Bath's Jean Dennison, twenty, and Jean Danforth, twenty-seven, and Genevieve Hodgdon, twenty-one, from Woolwich, enlisted in 1943.[42] Esther Barnes of North Harpswell trained as an aviation machinist mate.[43] Sylvia Paine, twenty-three, from Boothbay Harbor, and Pearl Brewer, twenty-two, from East Boothbay, enlisted together. Sylvia went to officers' training school at Hunter College and was stationed in Washington, D.C.[44] Pearl became a seaman first class.[45] Helen Martin of Southport, twenty-two, was working at the Bethlehem-Hingham Shipyard in Hingham, Massachusetts, when she enlisted. Wiscasset's Kathryn Perkins, twenty-nine, was a stenographer who became a stock keeper petty officer second class. Boothbay's Bernice Cunningham enlisted in 1944 after working as a secretary at a shipyard in Camden, Maine. She trained on IBM keypunch machines before being assigned to posts in Philadelphia and Quonset Point, Rhode Island.[46]

Other branches of the service also established women's corps. The coast guard SPARS (based on their motto *Semper Paratus*, "always ready") were established in November 1942 with the same requirements as the WAACs. Evelyn Larrabee, twenty-three, whose widowed father, Erwin, lived in Boothbay, enlisted in the SPARS in March 1943. The Women's Army Air Force (WAAFs) was never an official branch of the military; they remained a civilian auxiliary despite their heroic service. The marine corps established their women's reserves in January 1943. The women were called marines. Beth Trott, twenty, a high school algebra teacher from Bath, was one of only two Maine women selected for Marines Officer Training at Camp Lejeune, North Carolina.[47]

Over the course of the war, women proved themselves in harrowing and difficult conditions. In 1944, both General Dwight D. Eisenhower and General George Marshall gave speeches emphasizing the contributions women were making to the war effort and urging women to enlist.[48]

Chapter 3

ANCHORS AWEIGH

Midcoast Shipyards

America had to crank up the war machine in a hurry. That meant revving up boatyards, machine shops and more. Wartime marketing often called defense workers "production soldiers" to reinforce their vital role in the war effort.[49]

The largest employer in the midcoast was BIW. The BIW "family" included Hyde Windlass, a manufacturer of precision deck machinery, located next to the shipyard, and later, the South Portland Shipbuilding Corporation, a joint venture of BIW and Todd Shipbuilding. To further facilitate production, a new fabrication facility, the Harding Plant, was built in East Brunswick between July and December 1940.[50] By the spring of 1941, BIW had 4,150 workers, 70 percent of whom lived in Bath.[51] Two years later, the workforce had grown to 12,042, with 75 percent of the workers commuting from out of town.

BIW was led by an effective, seasoned senior management team. William Stark "Pete" Newell and Archibald Main had worked together for over fifteen years building the yard back up after the first ironworks went out of business in 1925. Older managers and production workers deferred or returned from retirement. Their most experienced employees included foremen George "Bert" Dickinson from Dresden, who had joined the old ironworks in 1891,[52] and Frank Bowker, who joined in 1896.[53] An influx of new, younger talent filled the middle management ranks in the mid- to late 1930s. The BIW management team had the right people for the job the war required. They passed their tradition of hard work, skill, pride in your work and strong Yankee patriotism to the thousands of wartime newcomers.[54]

Increased productivity demanded more working hours. On Christmas 1941, the *Bath Independent* reported that BIW was eliminating the traditional noon-hour break in favor of an eight-hour day with multiple shifts, and "Men Can Now Dine on Company's Time Either from Cafeteria Service or from Own Lunch Boxes."

The company had to figure out a way to transport workers from ninety-four communities in a sixty-mile radius to and from work, for every shift, every day.[55] Midcoast Maine had no public transportation system. U.S. 1 was the only road that could sustain any type of heavy traffic. Many roads were still unpaved, and keeping even paved roads plowed during Maine's heavy winter snows was a challenge. New workers lived farther away because they couldn't find nearby housing and then had difficulty getting the extra gas and tire rations they needed to keep their cars running. First, the company instituted a ride-sharing program. Many people signed up, but the wear and tear on older cars and inability to get spare parts made the plan unsustainable. BIW's personnel department could no longer handle managing the large workforce *and* getting them to and from work. They needed their own public transportation system.

Transportation specialist Edward F. Edgren was hired in November 1942 to lead a new transportation department, which he broke into divisions. The Rationing and Employee Service Division was responsible for managing the transportation needs of every employee, matching passengers with drivers and making sure drivers had available parking. BIW established its own ration board to expedite gas and tire rations. Drivers got the tires, gas coupons and spare parts they needed *while they were at work*, so no productivity was lost. The Bus Division worked with Congress to pass a law allowing the navy to lease buses to the company under navy contracts. This gave BIW higher gas and tire rations and greater access to parts and repair services. The Bus Division operated a garage in a former car dealership in downtown Bath to keep the buses running, occasionally using the shipyard machine shop to make scarce or unavailable parts.

Thirty-seven buses were in operation by March 1943.[56] The ride was not comfortable. The seats were hard and roads were bumpy. The buses were poorly heated and without air conditioning. When buses got stuck in the snow or mud, horses, oxen or farm tractors were used to pull them out. If the passengers were lucky, there was a tow truck or a snow plow nearby to help. Some workers endured six hours a day commuting to and from their jobs.[57]

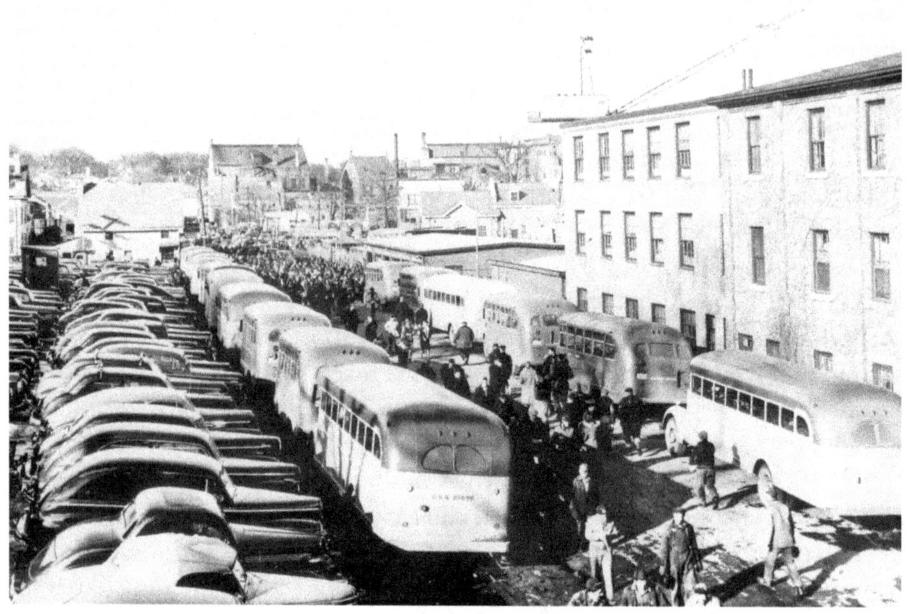

Buses and cars waiting to transport workers at shift change, BIW, 1943. *Maine Maritime Museum, BIW Collection.*

By 1945, BIW was launching a new destroyer every seventeen days—a 70 percent reduction in production time from 1941.[58] The company received several Army-Navy "E" for Excellence Awards, the highest recognition given to a company for performance during the war. The BIW workforce was exemplified by Cecil Whalen, featured in the September 26, 1943 BIW *Bulletin*. Cecil, fifty-three, was married and the father of seventeen children, ages six to twenty-eight. He and his wife, Mabel, had moved with thirteen of their younger children to Bowdoinham to work for BIW. Four Whalen sons were in the service, all strapping young men over six feet, one inch tall when they enlisted. Chandler was in the navy. Cecil Jr., Ronald and Bertram were in the army. The only time Cecil Sr. missed work was when he had to go and tell his wife that Cecil Jr. had been killed in North Africa.[59] BIW built seventy-six destroyers for the war effort, more than any other American shipyard,[60] only seven of which were destroyed by the enemy.[61]

Even small boatyards went into war production. From 1942 to 1944, the *Brunswick Record*, *Boothbay Register* and *Lincoln County News* were full of navy ship launchings from midcoast boatyards. Even Freeport relaunched its small boatbuilding industry and built four barges for the military.[62] Harry

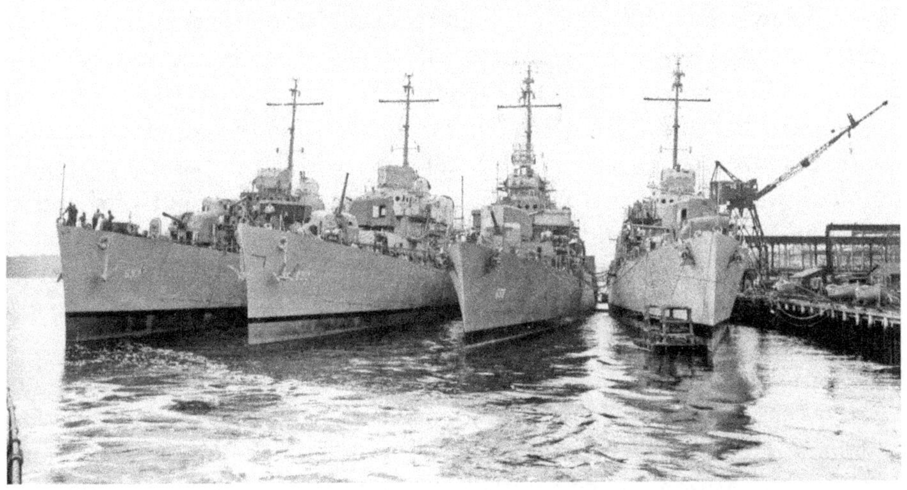

Four BIW destroyers with workers on board, with manager and navy officer watching from the bridge of the destroyer closest to dock. *Maine Maritime Museum, BIW Collection.*

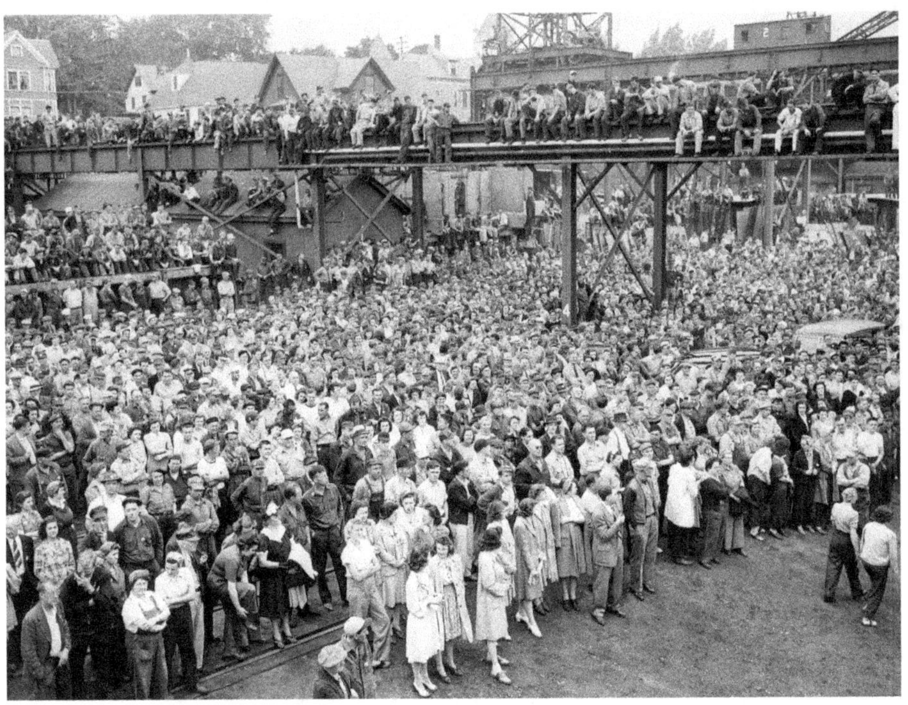

One shift comes out to watch a launching at BIW, 1943. *Maine Maritime Museum, BIW Collection.*

Marr's boatyard in Damariscotta built two wooden minesweepers and five coastal transport boats between 1940 and 1944.[63] The Gamage Shipyard in South Bristol built eight boats for the war effort.[64]

Samples Shipyard in Boothbay Harbor had been in business for over one hundred years, and owners Frank Sample Sr. and Frank Sample Jr. made sure they were ready for war work. Frank Jr. bought a second yard and a railway in March 1939 and won a contract for three minesweepers in 1940. By December 1941, he had constructed a large new building with three additional shipways. The first Sample minesweeper launched in February 1942, then another in March. In July, Sample bought Lewis Garage on Commercial Street for office and storage space, freeing up space in the shop.[65] The yard's excellent work and increased capacity won contracts for additional minesweepers and six 534-ton Maricopa Class rescue tugs, the first of which was launched in 1943. These boats were 143 feet long and carried a crew of thirty-three men.[66]

Samples Shipyard won an Army-Navy "E" for Excellence Award in November 1942. The award ceremonies for these accolades were a big deal, whether they took place at BIW or the smaller yards. Governor Sumner Sewall, Rear Admiral W.T. Culverius Jr. and Brigadier General Thomas Troland attended the ceremony at Samples.[67] A *Boothbay Register* article about the ceremony noted that the vessels were built "under the supervision of…oldtime Maine wooden shipbuilders…Benjamin Rand [67] and Gilbert

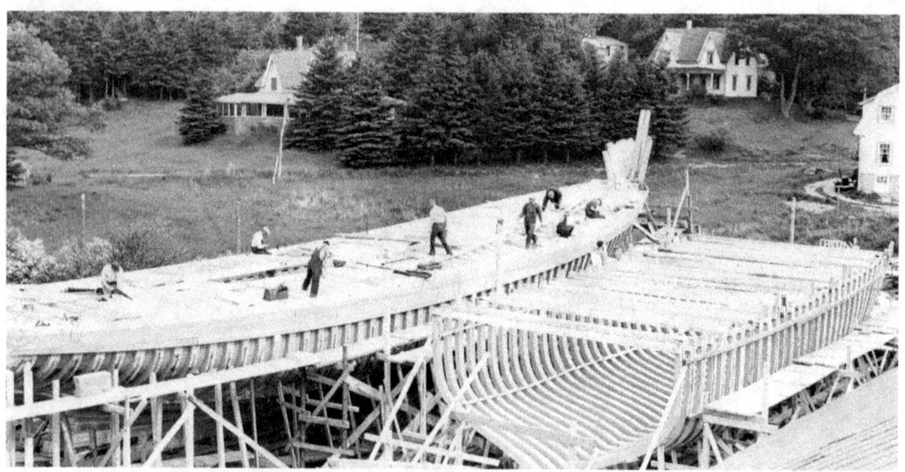

Two minesweepers under construction at Marr's Shipyard, Damariscotta, 1942. Notice the scale and proximity of nearby houses. *Courtesy of Calvin and Marjorie Dodge.*

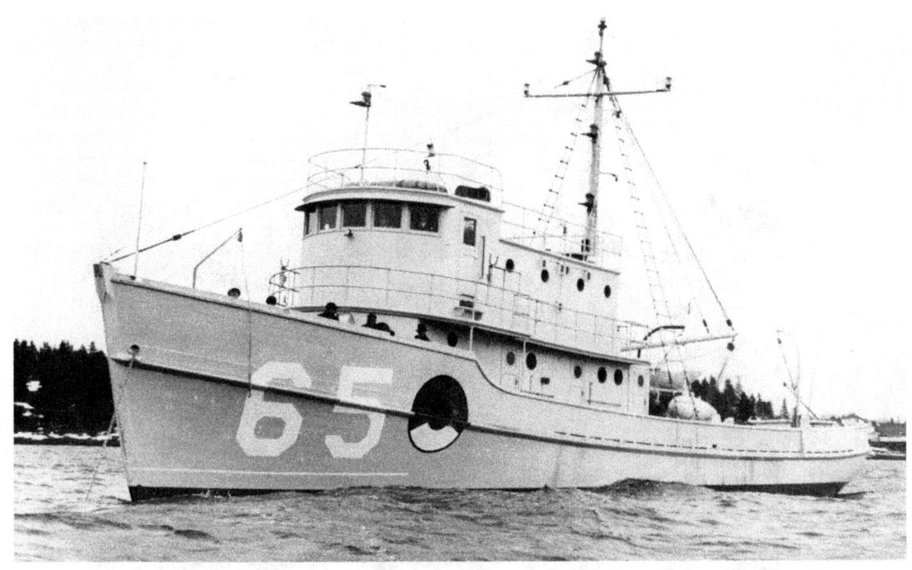

One of eight wooden minesweepers built at Harvey Gamage Shipyard, South Bristol, 1940–44. *Boothbay Region Historical Society.*

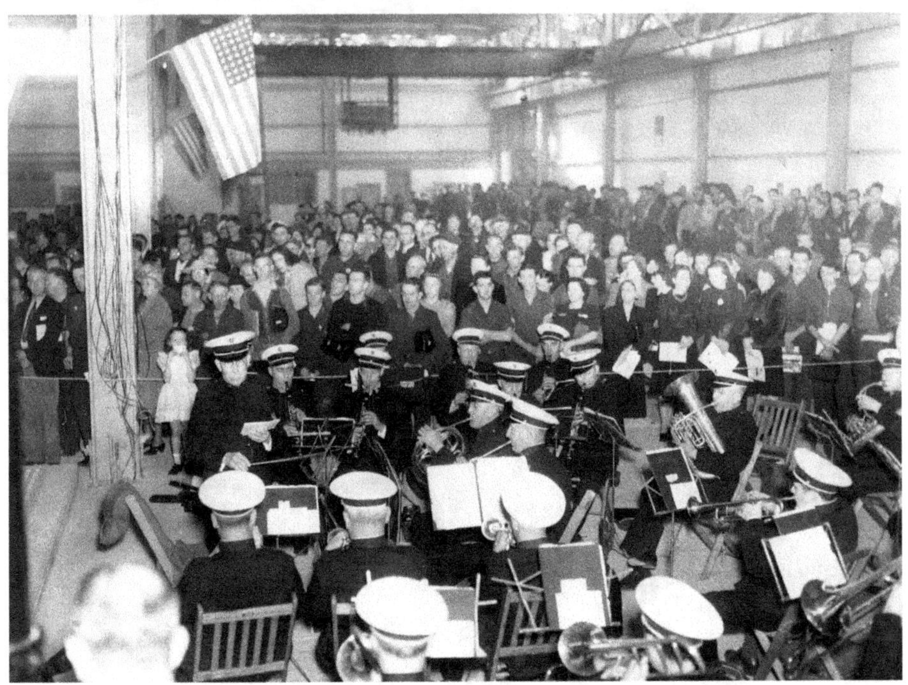

BIW band and audience at Hyde Windlass Army-Navy "E" Award presentation, September 23, 1942. *Maine Maritime Museum, BIW Collection.*

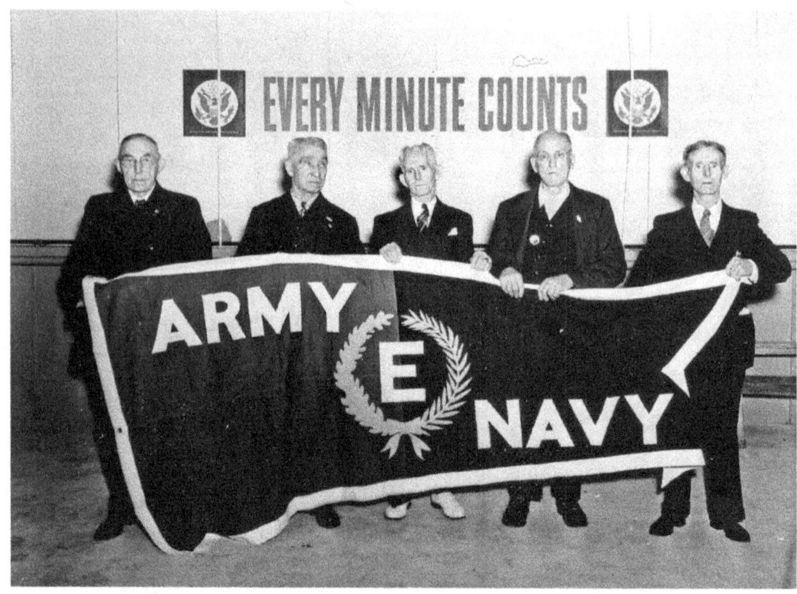

Above: Fifty-year service award honorees at Hyde Windlass Army-Navy "E" Award presentation, September 23, 1942: Napoleon A. Lemoine, Alonzo B. Thayer, Sidney McPherson, Stewart McPherson, James W. Gillespie, Fred A. Bowey and James T. Bonney. Two are missing from the photo. *Maine Maritime Museum, BIW Collection.*

Below: Goudy & Stevens crew working on APC67: J. Arthur Stevens in hat, Jig Jacobsen in white sweatshirt, Irving Jones at right. June 13, 1943. *Boothbay Region Historical Society.*

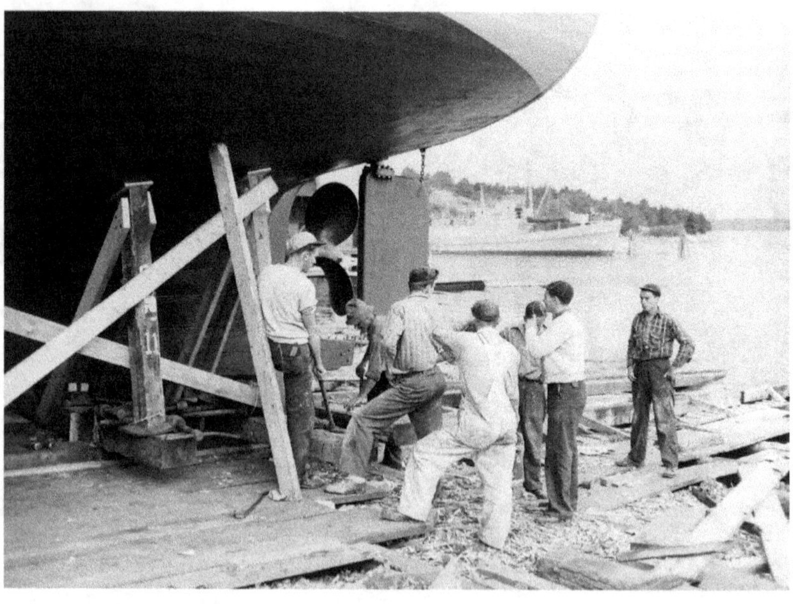

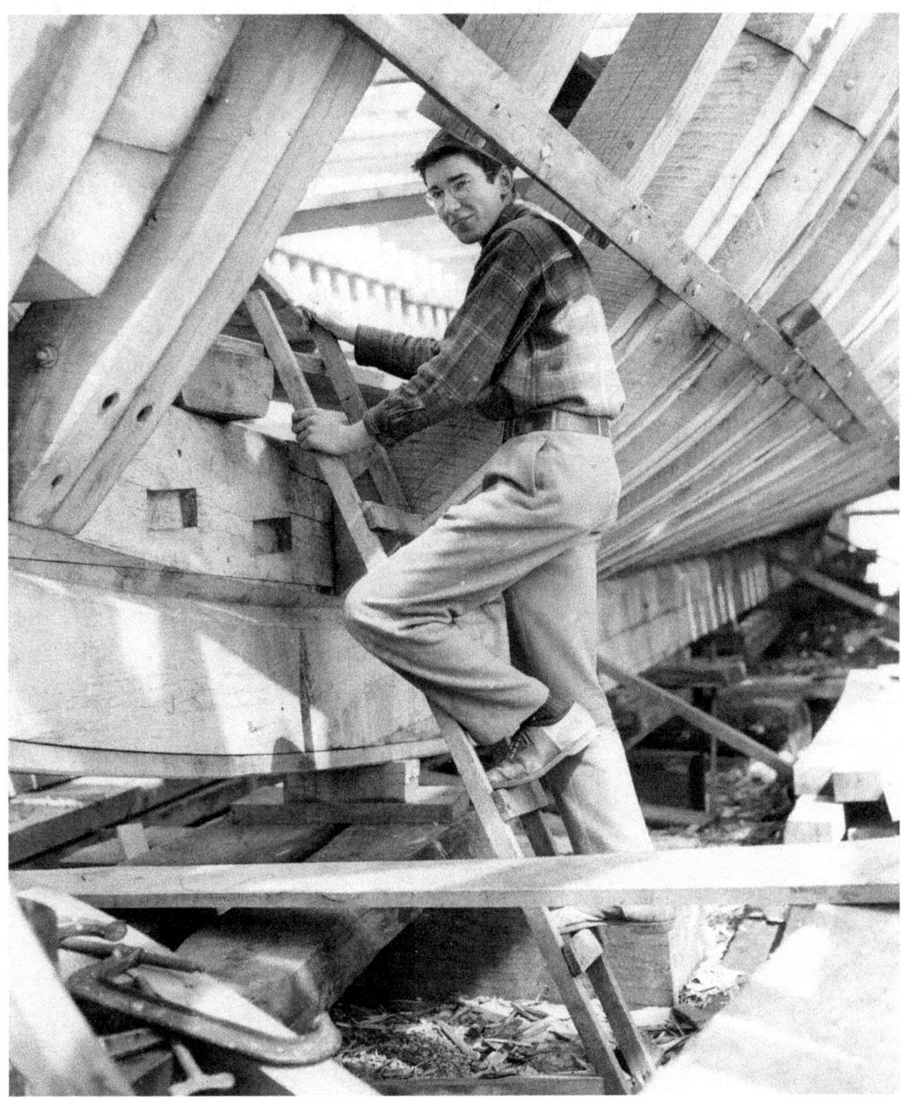

George Hodgdon Jr., seventeen, at boatyard, 1941. *Boothbay Region Historical Society.*

Haggett [40], both of Boothbay Harbor."[68] At its peak, the Sample yard employed 765 men and women.[69]

Hodgdon Brothers shipyard and Goudy & Stevens shipyard in East Boothbay were separated by only a few feet of water, so they decided to work together for war production. In April 1942, they were awarded an Army-Navy "E" Award for two 97-foot minesweepers. Contracts for ten 103-foot coastal transport boats followed.[70] The Goudy & Stevens yard was destroyed by fire in 1944 but quickly rebuilt. Together, they employed 190 men and women during the war.[71]

Frank and Henry Rice started a boatyard in East Boothbay in 1892. Frank left and went out on his own. He returned in 1903, and Rice Brothers was incorporated. They received a navy contract in 1942 for two 110-foot wood and steel sub-chasers. Additional contracts for eleven 136-foot motor minesweepers followed. Each could hold a crew of 36 men. In 1944, they won a navy Certificate of Achievement. Rice Brothers' largest workforce during World War II was 390 workers.[72]

Reed and Reed Boatyard in Boothbay Harbor built thirty plane-rearming boats for the navy. These thirty-three-foot, four-ton boats were used to deliver ammunition to seaplanes. The yard also built ten seven-ton buoy boats.[73] The smallest of the Boothbay-area yards, it employed forty men and women at its maximum production.[74]

Chapter 4

SWING SHIFT SALLY

Women Take on New Jobs

Women working outside the home was not new for midcoast Maine. Mills had employed women since the early nineteenth century. In the 1940s, the Cabot Mill workforce was largely men and women of French Canadian descent. Laurie Caron, whose mother and grandmother also worked at the mill, started at age sixteen working in the weave room making parachutes. She remembered "the noise, the hot, steamy days," but said, "you got used to it."[75] Throughout the war, the mill advertised "Girls Wanted, Working Age, 16 Years or Over, Good Opportunity for the future and to be paid while learning."[76] Working with vocational guidance counselors in the high school, they recruited male and female students to work three to four hours a day while they were still in school.[77]

Women also worked in family-owned stores and restaurants. When their husbands went into the armed forces, the women took over their jobs. Harriet Orchard, thirty-five and a mother of two, delivered groceries for her father's grocery store in Southport.[78] Violet Merrill, thirty-three, took over Webber Studio photographers at 98 Maine Street in Brunswick when her husband, Stephen, was called up.[79] She advertised that the studio was still open for business and that she was assisted by Betsy Winchell Morss. Betsy, twenty-eight, was married to Robert Dillingham Morss, a Bowdoin graduate and photographer working in England for a publishing company. Betsy joined him in March 1939 but returned to Maine the following October with their infant daughter, born ten days after England declared war on Germany. The war was very close and personal to both women.

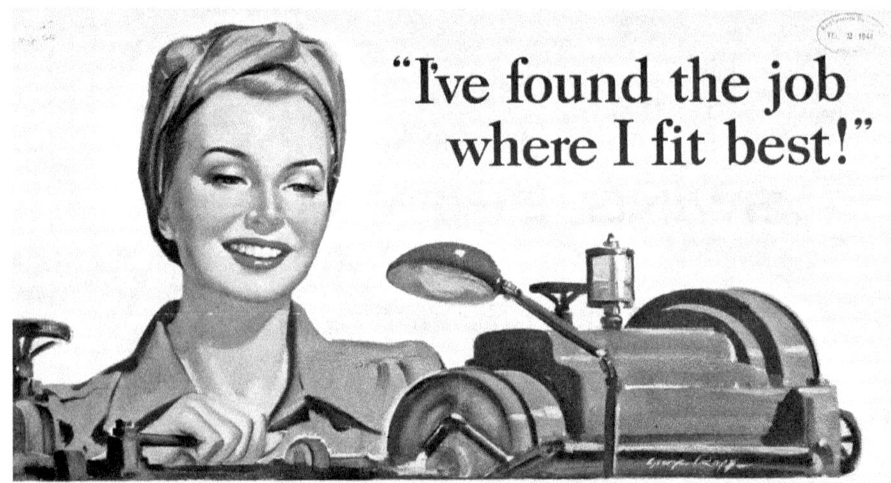

"I've found the job where I fit best," OWI poster, 1943. *Library of Congress.*

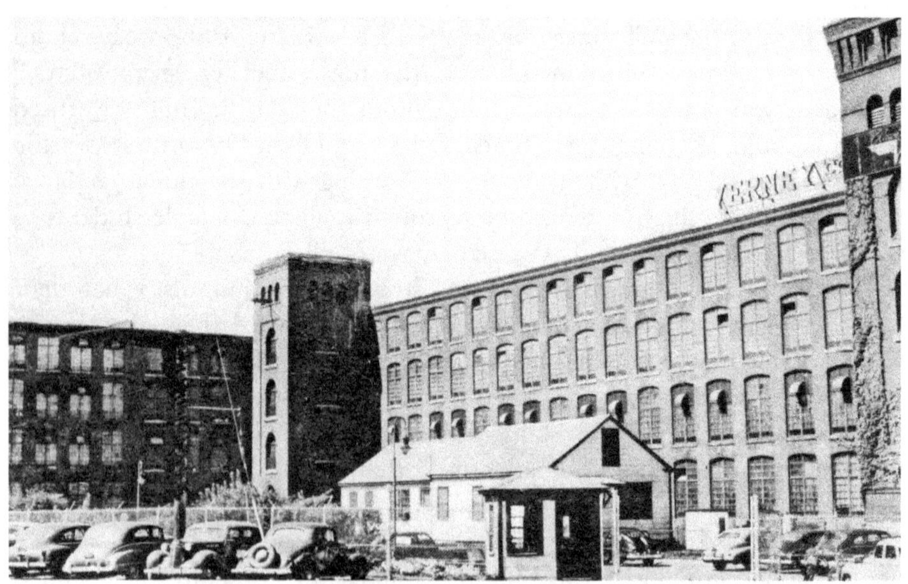

Postcard of Cabot Mill in the 1940s. *Author's collection.*

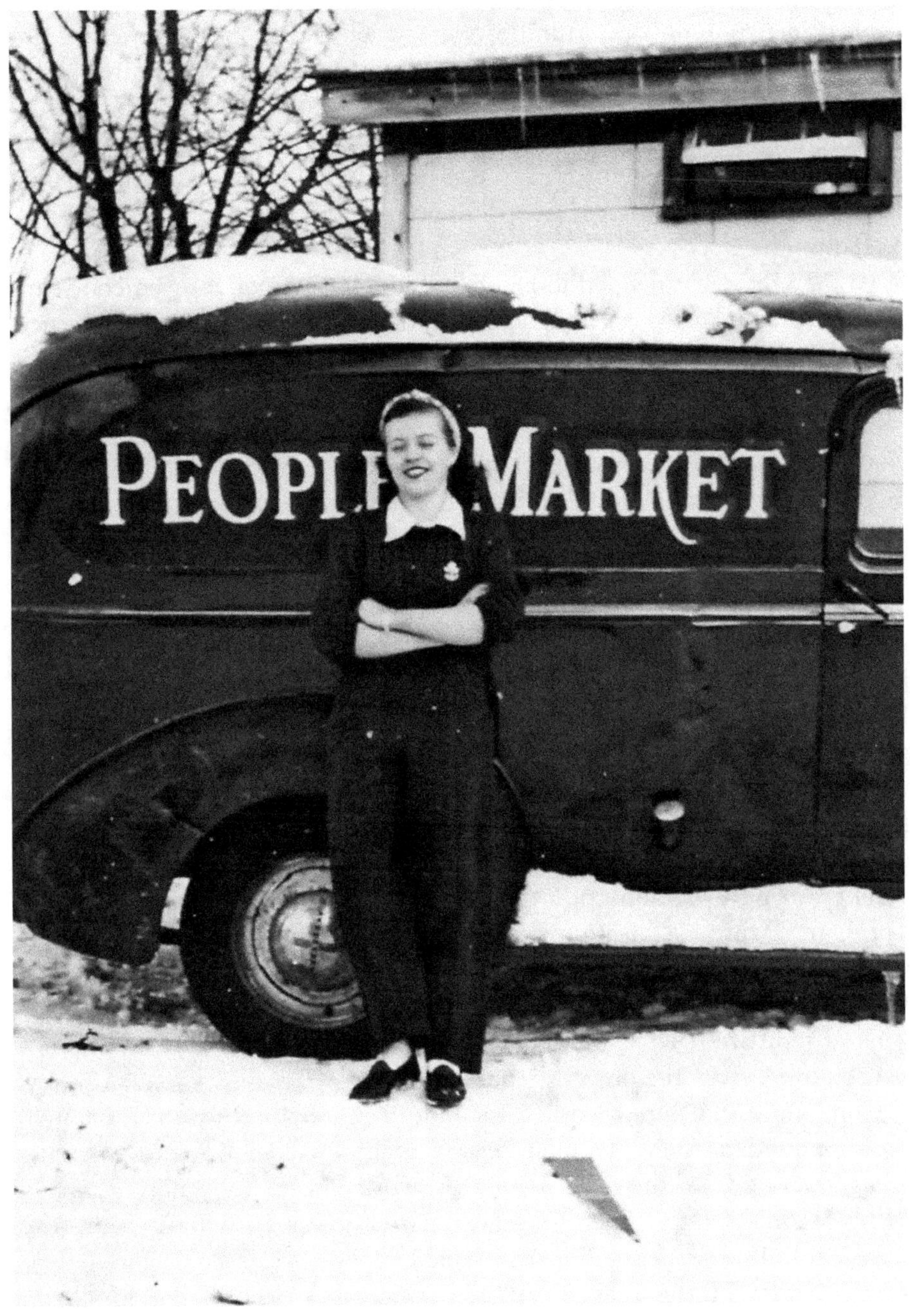

People's Market truck with Frances Southard, store clerk, 1943, Bath. *Courtesy of Kerry Nelson from Richard Lemoine.*

Jobs and training opportunities were available everywhere. The War Manpower Commission training facility in Quoddy trained girls to be mechanics, sheet metal workers, welders, aviation engineers, aircraft mechanics and radio operators.[80] The National Youth Administration offered young women training in industrial clerical work, typing and shorthand. The girls received room and board for courses in Dexter that lasted two to three months.

Women did what needed to be done. Shirley Bittinger, a seventeen-year-old junior at Brunswick High School, took over the job of delivery truck driver for Brunswick Cleaners and Dyers when owner Emile "Pinkie" Bouchard couldn't find a man to do it.[81] Emile Tondreau wasn't as progressive. In July 1943, he was still advertising for "any young men" to volunteer as delivery drivers to replace his driver, who had gone into the military.[82] The front page of the October 8, 1942 *Brunswick Record* featured "Girls Who Have Taken Over Men's Work Recently." The article included a photo of Lorraine Lariviere, nineteen, described in her yearbook as one of the smallest and daintiest members of Brunswick High School's class of '42, delivering telegrams for Western Union.[83] Also pictured were Lucille E. Jackson driving the delivery truck for Curtis IGA market and Gertrude Paradis running the movie projector at the Pastime Theater. Lucille, twenty, was working as a clerk in the grocery store when she stepped in to drive the truck when the male driver went to work for BIW. Gertrude, also twenty, was the daughter of French Canadian immigrants and one of just a few female camera operators in Maine.[84]

The war gave women opportunities they might not otherwise have had. Topsham's Mary E. Johnson, twenty-two, joined the *Brunswick Record* staff as a news reporter, replacing Leonard Cohen, who joined the military.[85] Brunswick lawyer Jean Bangs became Maine's first female assistant attorney general in April 1943.[86] Bertha Cullinan was the first Brunswick police matron to be given the power to make arrests.[87]

Companies that hired women for industrial jobs had to make changes to accommodate them. Women needed bathroom facilities and changing areas separate from the men. Uniforms, work clothes and safety gear had to be modified and resized. Most women working in defense industries wore coveralls and heavy hairnets, called snoods, to protect against their hair catching in the machinery. The December 1942 *Wiscasset Gazette* announced, "Recently the directors of the Bath Iron Works, after thoughtful consideration, decided to go co-educational. A large number of women and girls are now being employed. You should be here to see them all dressed up

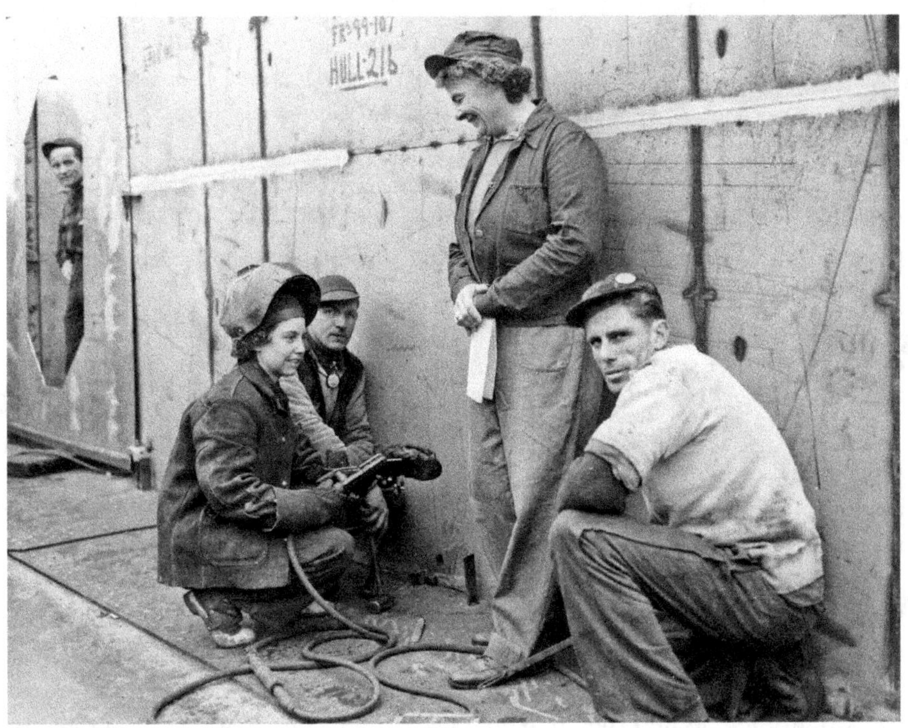

A BIW crew working on the USS *Cogswell*, a Fletcher Class destroyer, launched in June 1943. *Maine Maritime Museum, BIW Collection.*

in their snappy overalls and carrying a dinner pail on their way to work! We are proud of the girls!"

Clothing companies saw opportunity in the new market of women war workers. Vanity Fair marketed a special line of women's underwear called "Line-of-Duty Undies." Made of rayon jersey, they were inexpensive, washed and packed easily and were available in "fresh cool colors," including Tea Rose.[88] Senter's department stores advertised, "So Proudly We Hail Women at Work—You're doing a man's job and doing it well. Choose the correct work clothes," to sell heavy cotton and blue denim coveralls.[89] Brehaut's advertised a "Victory Workers" jumpsuit.[90]

Other businesses developed new services to meet the needs of working women. The Personal Finance Company advertised "Loans to Women in men's shoes," illustrated by a woman wearing large oversize shoes:

> *We realize the problems of women…today…and we've arranged our loan service to meet their needs. There's no need to worry about "people*

> *knowing." They won't because loans are made on your own signature....If you need $25 to $250 or more, for any worthy purpose, come in and see us today. Quick, lunch-hour service. We'll be glad to serve you.*[91]

It's hard to know if they meant that a woman could keep the loan secret from her husband or from nosy neighbors, but the fact that they specify that the woman herself could sign for the loan indicates that it was something new or at least uncommon.

Department stores and banks started encouraging women to shop by mail or phone. Senter's ad said, "NGL [no gas left]. Cheer up. You can do your shopping by mail or telephone."[92] First National Bank recommended, "For Efficiency, Pay Household Bills by Check," showing a woman sitting at a table with a checkbook open before her.[93] Brunswick Savings Institution advertised, "MINUTES ARE PRECIOUS...BANK BY MAIL," with a drawing of a woman in uniform behind the wheel of a vehicle checking her watch.

Managers learned that women work and think differently from men. One plant manager said, "It's a funny thing about women, they are more conscientious than men on the testing machines....Nothing gets by them until it's right....They take orders easily, have the patience of Job and are more frank than men. When they make an error, they come tell me."[94] Managers reported that women were more accepting and willing to do whatever was needed. Foremen found that most women were quicker to learn than the men available, exhibited a greater interest and were more anxious to know "why" and "how."[95]

Women learned they had transferrable skills that could be useful in industrial work, including sewing, cooking and time management. Industrial pattern-making utilized sewing skills. Making sand cores or molds used baking skills. Women who had never envisioned themselves working in industry found that not only *could* they do it, but they could do it well. One housewife-turned-ship-fitter summarized, "It's really simple to build a ship....You get your plan, cut out your pattern, prefabricate it, fit it together, and launch it. Men have always made such a job out of it!"[96]

The first women hired for production jobs at BIW were hired as welders. Laura Burpee, twenty-seven, of Bath and Verna Genthner, thirty-two, of Waldoboro began welding school in September 1942 at the same sixty cents an hour that men in training were paid. They were guaranteed equal pay for equal work once they joined the production force.[97] Laura had worked in a clothing factory with her husband before she joined BIW. Verna was married to an oil truck driver and mother of a thirteen-year-old daughter.

She had worked in a button factory. For both women, the shipyard job paid better and allowed them to do their bit for the war effort.

The Wiscasset women at BIW traveled to work on a bus they called the "Brown Bomber."[98] Nadine Dow, eighteen, and Jean Reid and Elaine Moore, both seventeen, were the youngest. Elaine's father was a welder at the shipyard. Verna Southard, a drugstore clerk, and Mildred Morris, a waitress, were both twenty, single and living with their parents. Mabel Macafee and Elaine Dow were also twenty and were married. Elaine's husband was a Newcastle schoolteacher. Mabel had a two-year-old daughter and lived with her parents. Madaline Jones, twenty-six, was married to a grain mill truck driver. May Sherman, thirty-six, was married and continued to volunteer for the Red Cross and the Wiscasset Congregational Church while she worked at BIW. At sixty-four, Frances Grover, a farmer's wife, was the oldest of the Wiscasset bus group.

BIW began publishing a company newsletter in 1943 to strengthen morale and inspire teamwork. The company made a point of highlighting

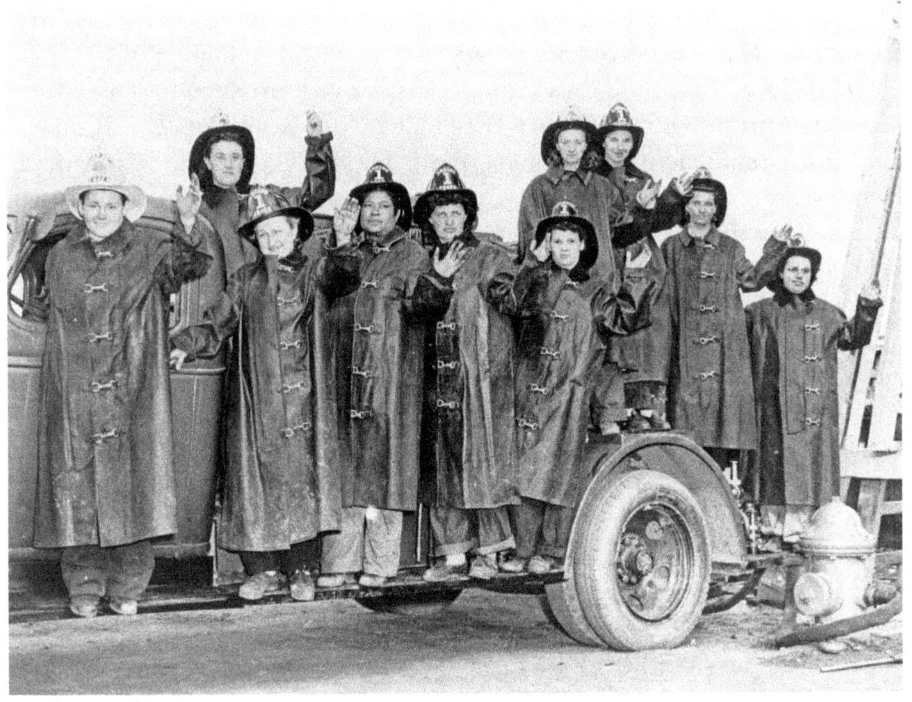

Todd Bath Iron Shipbuilding Fire Department, circa 1942. *Maine Maritime Museum, BIW Collection.*

the contributions of women. Blanche H. Smith of Bowdoinham, sixty-five, was a ship fitter. At five feet tall and ninety-nine pounds, she had raised six children, trained racehorses and driven a truck hauling horses and cattle for the government before coming to work at BIW.[99] Grace Dodge of Boothbay, eighteen, worked at BIW from 1941 until December 1945, first as a pipe coverer and then a welder. She also volunteered as a plane spotter and helped her brother in the First National grocery store in her spare time.[100] Edna Mae Waning, fifty, of Newcastle, joined BIW in 1943 as a riveter. Her husband, son, daughter-in-law and two nephews also worked there.[101]

At Samples Shipyard, Donna Andrews remembered that she and Beverly Farnham, both nineteen, were the first women in the pipe shop. "We were threading bolts and it was a really hard job."[102] Muriel Lowe, nineteen, lived with her widowed father and brother in Boothbay Harbor when she joined Samples, where her brother worked as a ship fitter. Priscilla Giles, seventeen, remembered working on the ATR7 and ATR8 Auxiliary Tug Rescue boats and wearing coveralls and a snood.[103] Clara Reynolds was nineteen and lived in South Berwick before she came to work at Samples. Lulu Watts was forty, a Boothbay Harbor native and a single mother of one daughter.

Other local businesses also hired women for production jobs. Rice Manufacturing, owned by Henry Rice (one of the owners of Rice Brothers Shipyard), manufactured airplane parts for Lockheed and Grumman. Henry's son Donald, forty-two, managed the business and hired about ten women. Gertrude Lewis was sixteen and the youngest of six children living with her parents in Boothbay Harbor. Pauline Hardwick, twenty-three, was married and lived with her husband, their one-year-old son and her in-laws in Boothbay. Edna L'Hostis, forty, was the mother of two young daughters and wife of a machinist in a shipyard.[104]

Cecil Pierce of Southport, thirty-four and married with two children, anticipated the war and started several businesses to do war production. He opened a marine engines repair shop called Marine Services in Boothbay Harbor. The government needed parts, and through connections, Cecil became a preferred supplier of aircraft turnbuckles.[105] He subcontracted with Reed Brothers Shipyard to install engines and electronics systems in the thirty plane-rearming boats they built. Pierce opened a second small machine shop that did work for Hodgdon and Goudy & Stevens Shipyards in East Boothbay when they were building minesweepers. When his male staff enlisted or went to work at BIW, Cecil hired and trained local women to do the work.

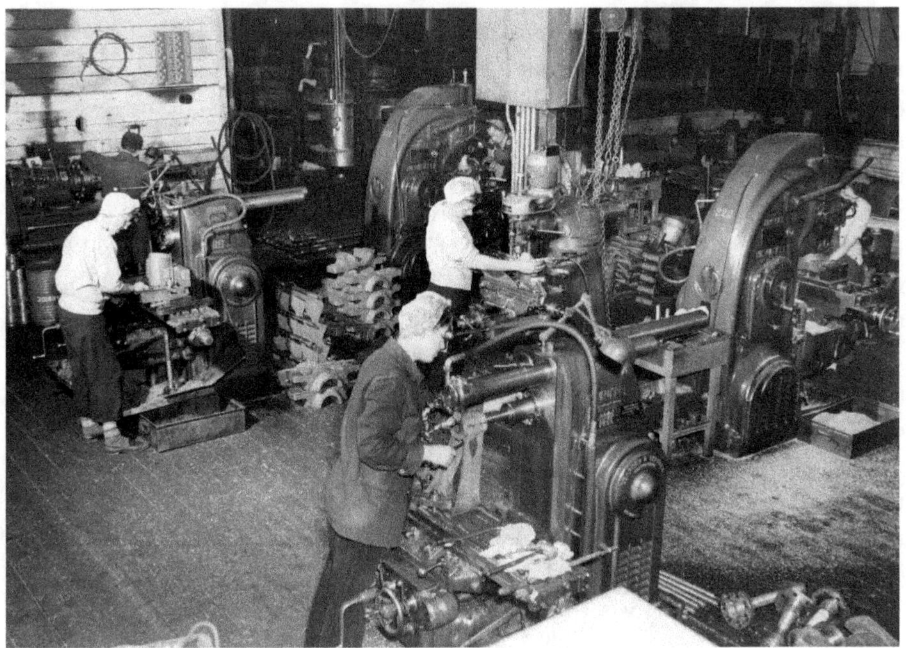

Four women working on small lathes at Hyde Windlass Co., 1943. *Maine Maritime Museum, BIW Collection.*

Wendell Rand of Southport, forty, was the machine shop foreman whose crew grew to include thirty women.[106] The women worked eight-hour shifts, with two shifts running each day. Franny Childs was only fifteen when she came to work at the machine shop. She was one of five children, and her father was a fingerprint expert. Cecil Pierce's daughter Evelyn was a year younger than Franny. She worked in the shop on Saturdays and during school vacations during the war. Evelyn remembered being so tired at the end of one shift that she could barely stand, so she sat down. Her father "came along and said, 'What are you doing?' so she replied 'Dad, my legs are tired.' He quickly pointed out that no one else was taking a break and I'd better get back to work. It was the longest 15 minutes of my life."[107]

The rest of the women in the shop ranged in age from twenty to sixty.[108] Many were already working outside the home when they came to work at Marine Services. Peggy Giles, twenty, was single and energetic. In addition to her machine shop job, she was a volunteer plane spotter at the observation post on Fisher's Hill in Boothbay Harbor, helped in her father's grocery store and still had the energy to go to dances with her friends.[109] Anna Perkins, twenty-three, worked in a drugstore in Bath before the war. Muriel Greenleaf, twenty-four, lived with her mother, brother and grandmother and worked as a maid before working at Pierce's. Agnes Lowe Dunton, twenty-five, was married to a lawyer. She worked as a dental nurse before the war and took the machine shop job when her husband of thirteen months, Frank, enlisted in December 1942. Grace Gaudette from Southport was also twenty-five. Her husband, Norm, was a grocery clerk who enlisted in April 1943. He was killed in action on November 11, 1944, in France. Violet Smith, forty-three, was a widowed schoolteacher living in Southport with four of her five children. Her daughter Thelma remembered her being "so weary and lame from working at Cecil Pierce's machine shop" that she was slow to wake, even on the day in 1943 when a pilot kept diving low over their house trying to alert people to a house fire nearby.[110] Etta Lewis, sixty, was the oldest of the women. She and her husband, Joseph, were both born in Russia but raised in the United States. They married in Bath in 1906 and had four grown children and one grandchild by 1940.

Working women's lives during the war years were much more difficult than their male counterparts', especially those who were married with children or who were taking care of relatives. These women had to run their households at a time when very few stores were open at night and none on Sundays. Children walked to school and came home for lunch. Most men, even those whose wives now worked, didn't do housework or cook. A 1943 article in *Harper's* magazine told the story of one woman who worked all night and got home from the late shift just before her children left for school.

> *She....went shopping so that she could get rationed meat...before it sold out for the day. She sent the kids off, ate breakfast, cleaned the kitchen and got to bed about 10 am. At 11:30, the alarm rang to warn her that the kids were about to get home from school for lunch. She went back to bed when they left and slept until they arrived home again around 3:00. Then she cleaned house, did laundry and cooked dinner. The family ate when her husband got home from work at 6:00. Afterwards, Alma took another nap before leaving for work at 10 pm.*[111]

Chapter 5

ANY BONDS TODAY?

Financing the War

Uncle Sam needed money to fund the massive war effort. Historically, countries paid for war by borrowing from bankers and imposing heavy taxes. While the U.S. government did impose a 5 percent "Victory Tax" on Americans' earnings, the FDR administration wanted Americans to contribute voluntarily. They knew that funding the war through voluntary contributions made a powerful contrast to the totalitarian regimes we were fighting against. Contributing to a common cause, knowing that your small contribution went directly to help the troops overseas, helped raise morale. Washington turned to Madison Avenue and Hollywood to deliver the message.

The marketing campaign to sell war bonds was a uniquely American blend of patriotism, capitalism and salesmanship. The message was that it was not just your patriotic duty to buy bonds or stamps, it was also a good investment. Actors, singers, dancers, composers and musicians all helped sell war bonds through benefit performances and concerts. Music publishers put war bond messages on sheet music. Newspapers and magazines featured cartoons and ads along with emotional stories of people who heroically bought war bonds despite personal hardship and messages from servicemen overseas stressing the importance of funding the war. The "Buy Bonds" message was heard at the beginning and end of every radio program. Judy Garland, Mickey Rooney, Rita Hayworth, Bob Hope, Bing Crosby, Frank Sinatra, Bette Davis, Marlene Dietrich and Betty Grable toured the country putting on shows and appearing on radio programs selling bonds. Norman Rockwell's *The Four Freedoms* toured the country, selling $132 million in war bonds.

You lent money to the government to pay for the war through your purchase of war bonds. The $25.00 bonds were the most popular. They sold for $18.75, and when they matured over ten years, the government paid you $25.00. If you couldn't afford the $18.75, you could buy $0.10 savings stamps that you put in a treasury-approved stamp album until you reached the required amount. Even children got the message. Schools across the country held savings stamps campaigns. Movie cartoons encouraged children to buy war stamps. They heard it straight from Bugs Bunny, Superman and Captain America!

The first big bond drive was in the spring and summer of 1942. Volunteers went door to door, rewarding purchases with stickers to display on your window. Brunswick's bond committee had a booth in the town hall next to where people registered for sugar rationing.[112] Brunswick Girl Scouts sold stamps in Woolworth's as part of "Retailers for Victory Month."[113] At another booth in Curtis IGA market, Girl Scouts dressed up as Revolutionary War heroine Molly Pitcher. The message was that every girl could be a modern Molly Pitcher.[114] Saul Hayes ran the Strand Theater in Boothbay Harbor, where he held Bank Night every Wednesday. Everyone in the audience got a ticket for a drawing at the end of the night for a cash prize of $100 to $150. Ronald Orchard remembered that the Strand was standing room only on Wednesdays.[115] Saul and his wife, Lucy, were Russian immigrants whose Yiddish-speaking parents brought them to the United States when they were very young. Saul and Lucy became citizens and moved to Boothbay Harbor before 1920. Like so many immigrants across the country, they wholeheartedly supported the war effort, volunteering wherever they could.

Working Americans were encouraged to contribute at least 10 percent of their income to help fund the war effort. BIW, Central Maine Power, Cabot Mill and other companies set targets for employee contributions and participation. The Brunswick office of Prudential Insurance Company was honored for its 100 percent participation.[116] Workers could buy war bonds or stamps through a new process—automatic deductions from their paychecks. BIW had large signs tracking how much each department gave and progress to date toward the latest bonds goal. Every BIW newspaper had a story about one man and one woman and their contribution to the war effort, measured by the number of family members in the armed services, number of children at home and how much of their wages they were pledging to buy bonds.

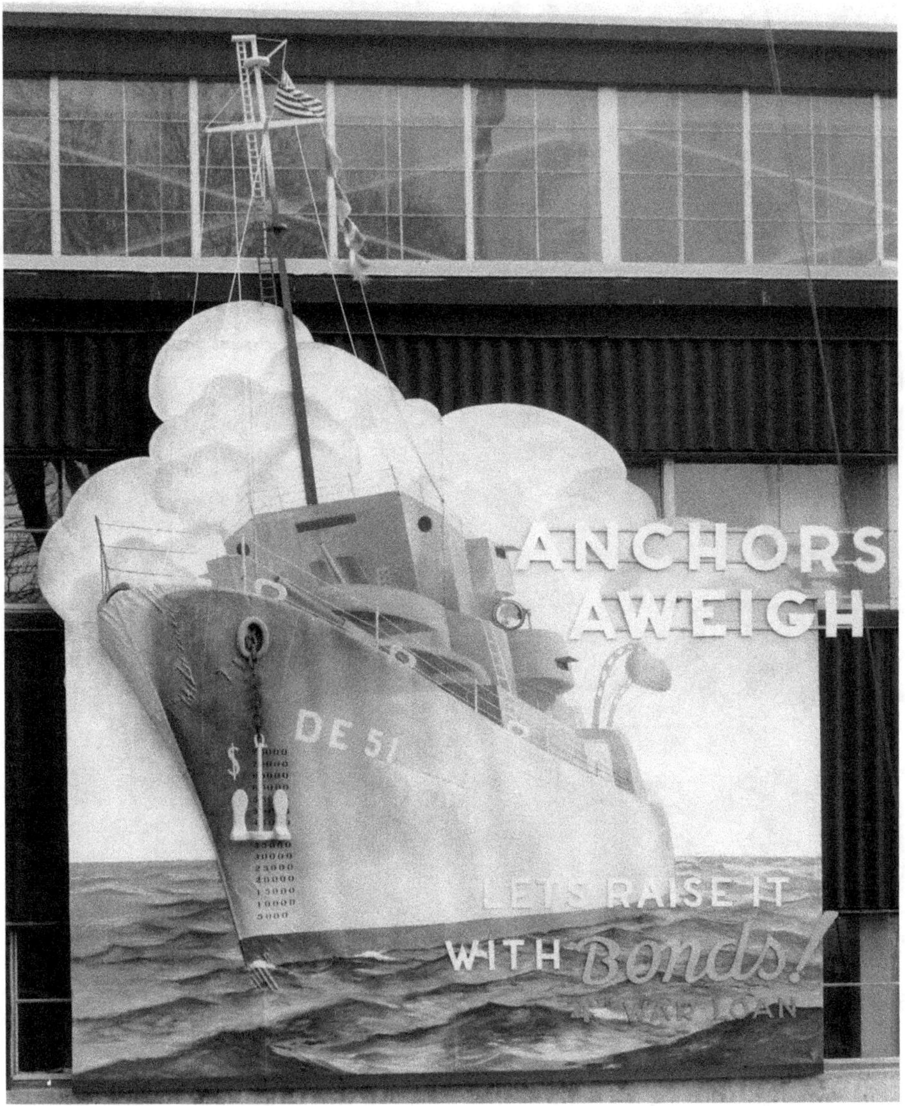

Fourth war bond drive sign made by Clifford Russell and installed at Hyde Windlass Co., February 16, 1944. *Photographer Otis. N.E. Card, Richard Card Collection, Sagadahoc History & Genealogy Room, Patten Free Library.*

July 31 and August 1, 1942, were War Bonds Dollar Days. Shoppers signed a book in retail stores to participate in a drawing to win a $25 bond. September was "Theaters for Victory" month. In November, women working in stores and offices and professional women were given

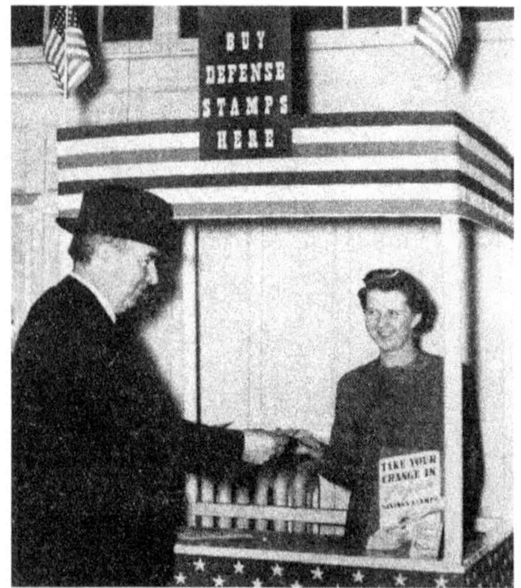

Left: War defense stamps booth at Senter's store, Brunswick, with Lucienne LeClair selling stamps to John Riley. Brunswick Record, *March 12, 1942*.

Below: Beta Sigma Phi sorority selling war bonds at the Bath Opera House on Centre Street, 1942. *Photographer Otis. N.E. Card, Richard Card Collection, Sagadahoc History & Genealogy Room, Patten Free Library.*

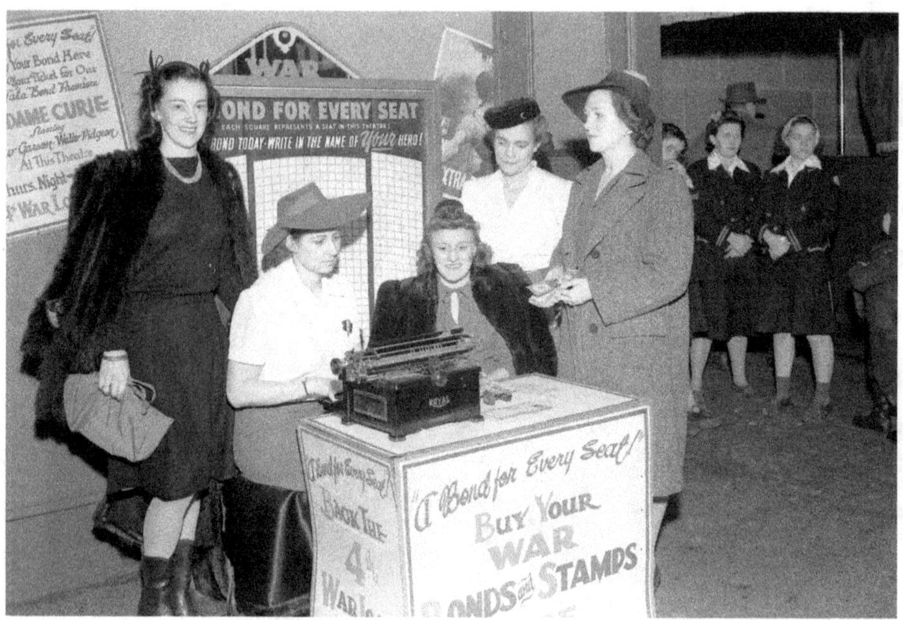

armbands and encouraged to sell war bonds in the "Minute Women" campaign.[117] Brunswick High School students alone bought $4,514 in war stamps in 1942.[118]

The second war bond drive was from April 12 to May 1, 1943. Every $900 raised bought a jeep for the army.[119] St. John's and Hawthorne elementary schools and Brunswick High School raised enough to buy twenty-one jeeps.

In July, a New England Liberty Ships War Drive, under the auspices of Franco-American fraternal and social organizations, raised money to build three liberty ships to be named after prominent Franco-Americans.[120] A separate Victory Fund Committee was formed in Brunswick to target companies and wealthy individuals for higher-denomination bond sales. This committee was made up of businessmen and community leaders, including Kenneth Sills (president of Bowdoin College), Reverend William Dauphin (pastor of St. John's Church), Emile Tondreau (grocery store owner), Harold Treworgy (president of both Brunswick Hardware Co. and Treworgy Furniture Co.), John W. Riley (president of Brunswick Savings Institution), Allen E. Morrell (president of Brunswick Coal Co.), John L. Baxter (of H.C. Baxter Bros. canned foods) and Edward W. Wheeler (attorney and justice of the peace).[121]

Community leaders and bond committees gradually realized that there were too many competing fundraising efforts. People were tired of constantly being asked for money and confused by all the different appeals. By late 1943, it was getting harder for towns to meet their bond quotas. The new message was "we're all in this together," stressing that as weary as everyone was on the homefront, the men overseas were even

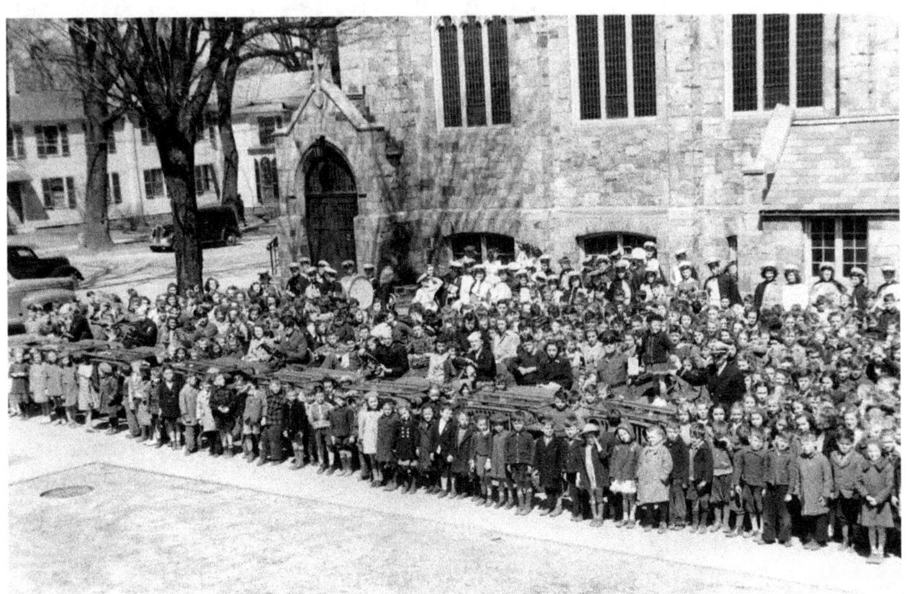

St. John's schoolchildren and St. John's band outside the church building with the seven jeeps they helped purchase with bond stamps. Jeeps are driven by soldiers and sailors, 1945. *Courtesy of Bob Bouchard.*

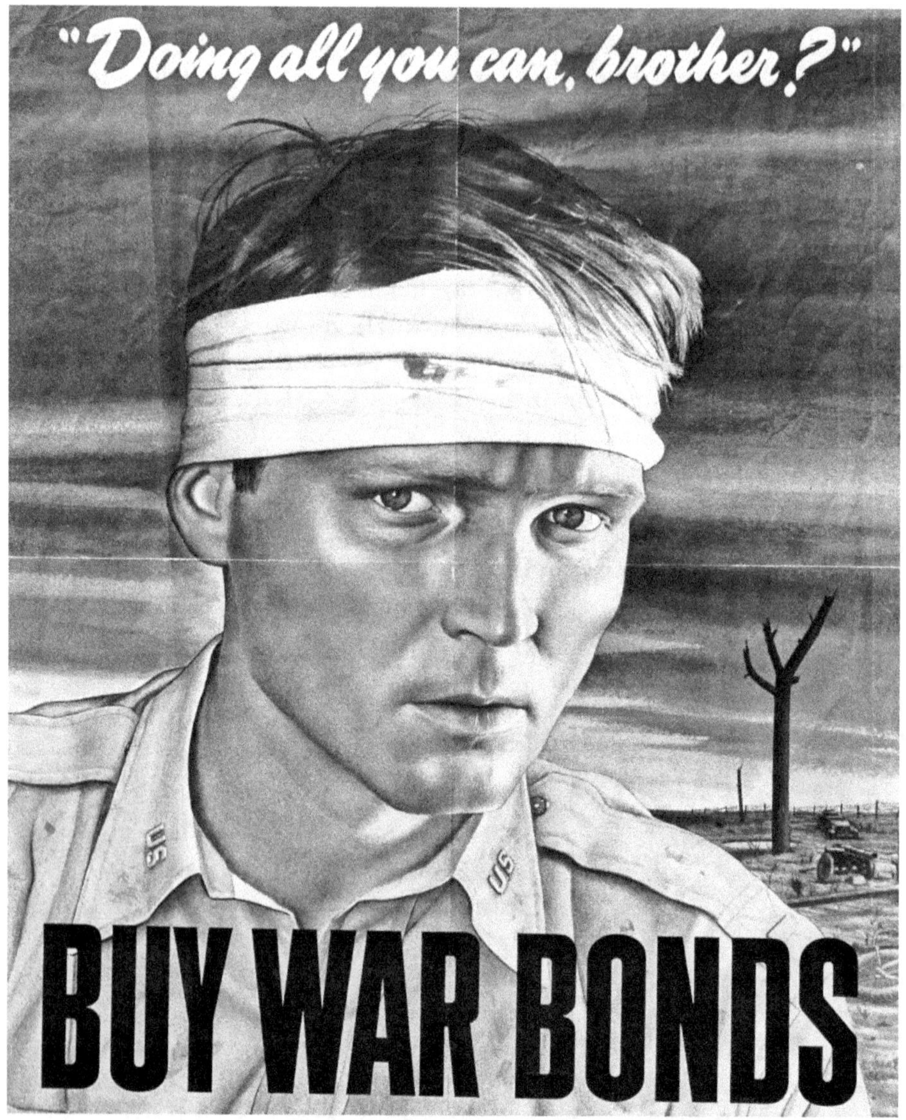

"Doing all you can, brother?" Robert Smullyan Sloane, artist. U.S. Treasury Department poster, 1943. *Northwestern University Library, images.northwestern.edu.*

more exhausted, and they were still fighting and dying. The War Fund reorganized as the Community Chest, combining the financial appeals of the United Service Organizations (USO), Red Cross and fifteen other war relief agencies. President Sills of Bowdoin was named Cumberland County chairman. Committees included merchants and businessmen like

Alfred Senter in Brunswick and L.L. Bean in Freeport. The Community Chest promised to do only two appeals a year, one for the Red Cross in March and another for the general War Fund in October.

The third bond drive was from September 9 to October 1, 1943. Brunswick Naval Air Station personnel worked with the army air force Meteorology and Engineering Schools at Bowdoin to help publicize the drive. Navy planes flew over Brunswick and dropped leaflets, while the Bowdoin army schools held a parade. The Cumberland Theater held a special Navy War Bond Night, with navy men and women selling bonds to audiences. Bowdoin College, the military schools there and Brunswick Naval Air Station (BNAS) personnel contributed generously to bond drives throughout the war, both in dollars and in volunteer time.

Eight war bond drives were conducted from 1942 to 1945. By the end of the war, eighty-five million Americans had purchased $185.7 billion in bonds—over $2,000 per person—when the average income was $2,000 per year.[122]

Chapter 6

WHAT A DIFFERENCE A DAY MAKES

Bowdoin College and the War

On December 8, 1941, the navy ordered all officers to wear full uniform in public.[123] Suddenly, men in uniform were everywhere, including the three hundred men already at Bowdoin College in the Navy Radio Training School. Marines took over guard duty at BIW in Bath and East Brunswick. Military guards were posted at the Central Maine Power Generating Plant and the pumping station of the Brunswick and Topsham Water District. Calvin Dodge remembered that when the army came to Damariscotta, it seemed like the town turned from "a seasonal place to a year-round place overnight."[124]

Brunswick, Maine, had been a college town since 1804 and a mill town since 1809.[125] Now, it became a military town as well. At Bowdoin College, President Kenneth Sills held a special chapel service the Tuesday morning after Pearl Harbor, where he advised undergraduates to continue attending classes until called into service, but it was impossible to hold back the tide of men willing and able to go. Their country needed them. The challenge was to adapt the college to the needs of the war without sacrificing its identity and values.

President Sills urged Bowdoin men to finish their degrees and use what they had learned to advance the nation's cause, and the college made changes to help them do that. In January 1942, he announced that courses would be shortened to accelerate completion of degree programs, and commencements would be held accordingly.[126] The Memorial Day commencement class was half the size it had been the previous year.[127] In

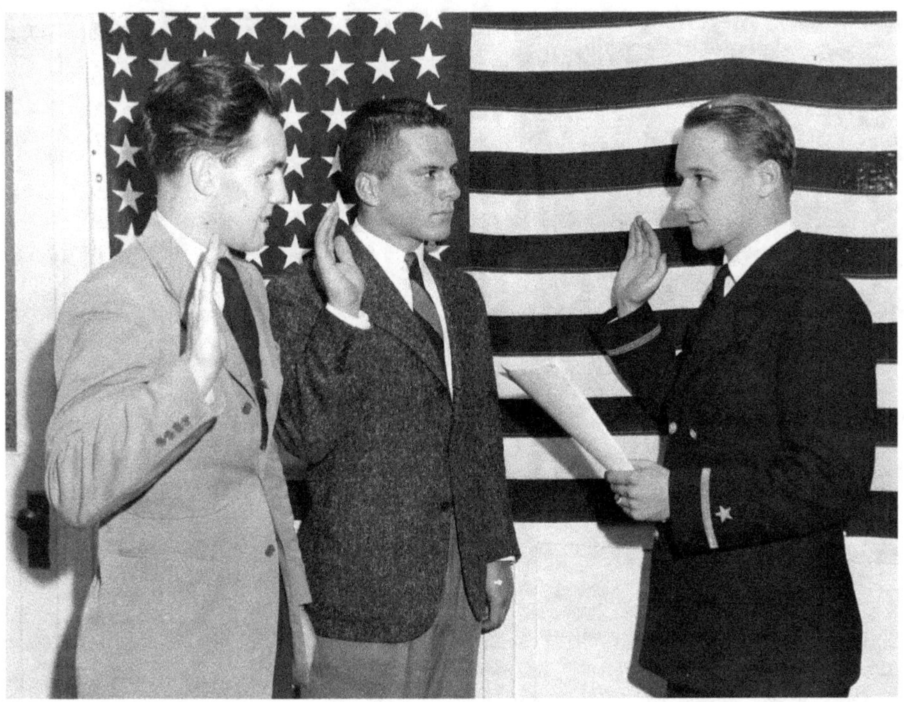

William Henry Elliott (Bowdoin, 1944), *left*, being sworn into the navy, 1942. *Courtesy of the George J. Mitchell Department of Special Collections & Archives, Bowdoin College Library, Brunswick, Maine.*

September, sixteen men graduated with commencement ceremonies that were described in the *Brunswick Record* of September 3, 1942, as "brief and simple" but still including an academic procession and music so students and families could still share the full experience. Bowdoin held winter, spring and summer commencements throughout the war.

In November 1942, President Sills announced that in addition to the navy, Bowdoin would also be the site of an army air corps meteorology school. Two hundred army officers arrived on campus in January to begin their training. Another two hundred army men arrived for engineering training six months later. All these new military students had to be housed and fed. One of the college dormitories was turned over to the navy for its use. Hyde Hall and the Delta Upsilon fraternity house were turned over to the army.

On December 12, 1942, First Lady Eleanor Roosevelt came to Bowdoin College. About 200 people greeted her at the train station, where students had brought a car to transport her to campus. Given a choice between

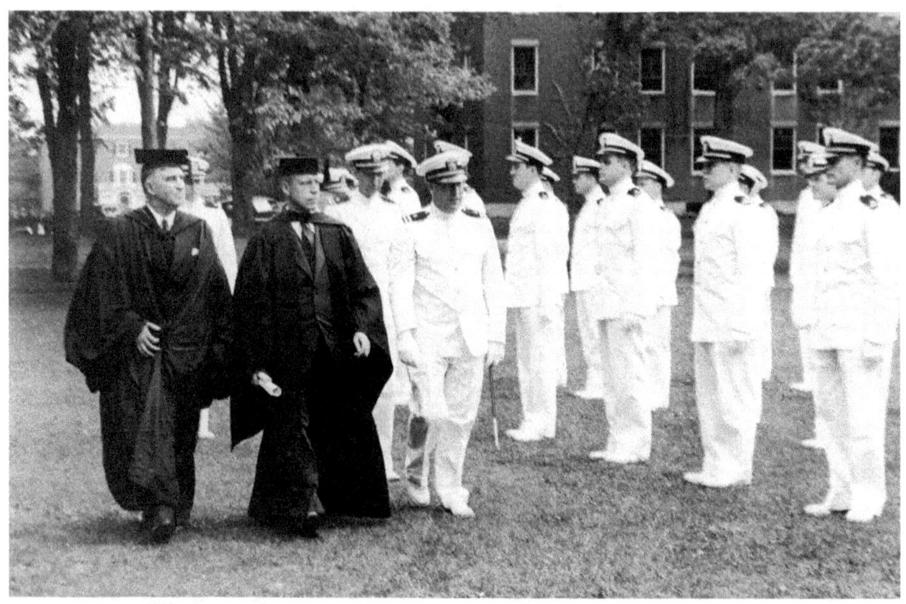

Informal portrait of President Sills at the inspection and review of alumni at the August commencement of 1942. *Courtesy of the George J. Mitchell Department of Special Collections & Archives, Bowdoin College Library, Brunswick, Maine.*

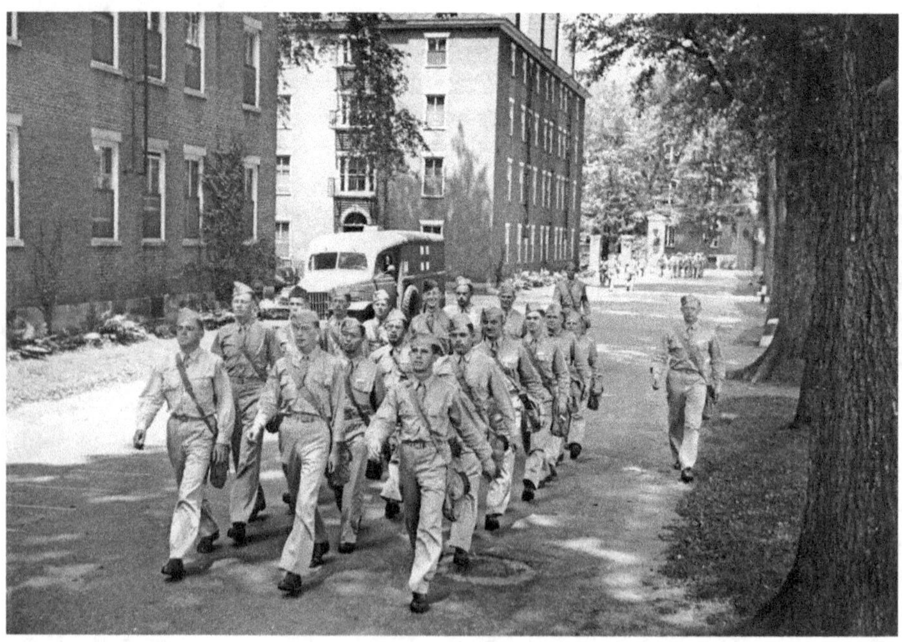

USAAF tech training detachment, 1943. *Courtesy of the George J. Mitchell Department of Special Collections & Archives, Bowdoin College Library, Brunswick, Maine.*

the young men's car and that of her Secret Service detail, Mrs. Roosevelt gleefully chose the students'. Invited by members of the Bowdoin chapter of Delta Upsilon fraternity, the first lady spoke to a student-only crowd of 1,200 at First Parish Church, sharing observations from a recent trip to England. After the talk, she mingled with students and faculty before saying that she wanted to "spend some time with the boys who invited me."[128] Fraternity members crowded into the living room, where, behind closed doors, Mrs. Roosevelt answered their questions for an hour. She wrote about how much she enjoyed her visit in her "My Day" column on December 14, 1942.

As undergraduates enlisted and were called up, new military students arrived. The college, which normally had a student body of around six hundred, saw the number of civilian students decrease and the number of military students grow until the military students were almost double the civilian undergraduates.[129] Professors in the navy, army and army air corps reserves were also called up for duty. Fifty-two-year-old Professor Thomas Curtis Van Cleve, a medieval and English constitutional history scholar, was one of several Bowdoin faculty members who had served in World War I and reenlisted when hostilities broke out in 1941.

The exodus of so many faculty and staff from campus just as hundreds of military students arrived eventually led the all-male college to hire retired professors, alumni and even, in February 1943, its first women faculty members.[130] Marguerite Little, forty-seven and a mother of three teenagers, was hired to teach physics in the meteorology school. She had been assisting her husband (a lieutenant commander in the navy and physics professor) with teaching navigation prior to her hiring. Marguerite was a Radcliffe graduate with an MA from Boston University and additional postgraduate work at Vassar, where she taught for three years. Marion Holmes, forty-five, was the wife of a Bowdoin mathematics professor and mother of four children under the age of twelve when she was hired to teach mathematics. Marion was a graduate of Bates College with an MA from Harvard. Ruth Yeaton Junkins was fifty-one and had a physics degree from Mount Holyoke and an MA from Cornell. She taught at both Mount Holyoke and Vassar before being hired to teach physics to both meteorology and college students.

The whole campus was involved in the war effort. Students volunteered for the Red Cross and were the first participants in blood drives. Professors and alumni who were ineligible for the draft remained at work and volunteered in civilian defense efforts along with their wives. Music and theater professor Frederic Tillotson continued teaching, leading the glee club, giving concerts and directing and acting in Masque and Gown theater productions. He and

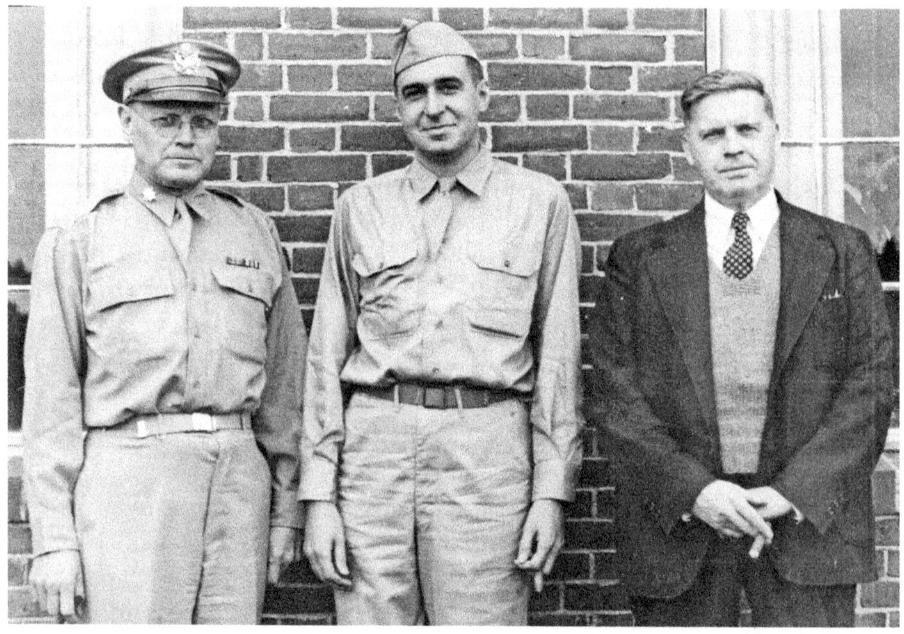

Three Bowdoin professors. *Left to right*: Thomas C. Van Cleve, Albert "Jim" Abramson and Charles H. Livingston, 1943. *Courtesy of the George J. Mitchell Department of Special Collections & Archives, Bowdoin College Library, Brunswick, Maine.*

his wife, Marjory; Morgan and Amy Cushing; Mary and Bruce White; and others also opened their homes to families needing housing while their men attended Bowdoin.

The navy and army men and their families played a very active role in the community while they were at Bowdoin. They volunteered for civilian defense and participated in air raid drills. When army engineering students arrived fresh from boot camp in late summer 1943, the timing was fortuitous. Local farmers very much needed the help of those healthy young men, some of whom had grown up on farms. The August 19, 1943 *Brunswick Record* reported that six men were already "mucking out beans for the Fenimore brothers in Bowdoinham," and seven more were cutting hay on local farms. They reported that the men were eager to help and enjoyed the work. Women whose husbands were enrolled in classes at Bowdoin or assigned to BNAS also volunteered and contributed hours of service to their adopted community. The war years were the beginning of the inclusion of military families into the Brunswick community.

Chapter 7

AMERICAN PATROL

Coastal Defense and Brunswick Naval Air Station

The military men assigned to Bailey Island, Fort Baldwin, Damariscotta, Kresge Point, Boothbay, Damariscove Island, Wiscasset and Southport were assigned to defense efforts that, although largely forgotten today, were a critical part of American homeland defense at the beginning of the war. These were the Coastal Picket Patrol and the Coastal Beach Patrol.

THE COASTAL PICKET PATROL

The U.S. Navy had to defend the waters and coastline from Iceland to the Caribbean with a force already stretched by Lend-Lease and convoy protection. In the summer of 1941, the commodore of the Cruising Club of America, New York yachtsman Alfred Stanford, began trying to convince the navy that yachtsmen and pleasure boats could actively help with coastal defense. Fleet Admiral Ernest King strongly resisted the idea, even though he knew the navy did not have the resources to protect East Coast shipping lanes against growing U-boat attacks. While American shipyards scrambled to produce the smaller patrol boats, the coast guard bought motor and sailing yachts, fishing boats and small freighters and converted them for use in coastal defense.[131] Jack Stover, eleven, son of a coast guardsman stationed at Damariscove Island, remembered the coast guard taking beautifully varnished yachts and pleasure boats and painting them with flat gray paint for use as patrol boats.[132]

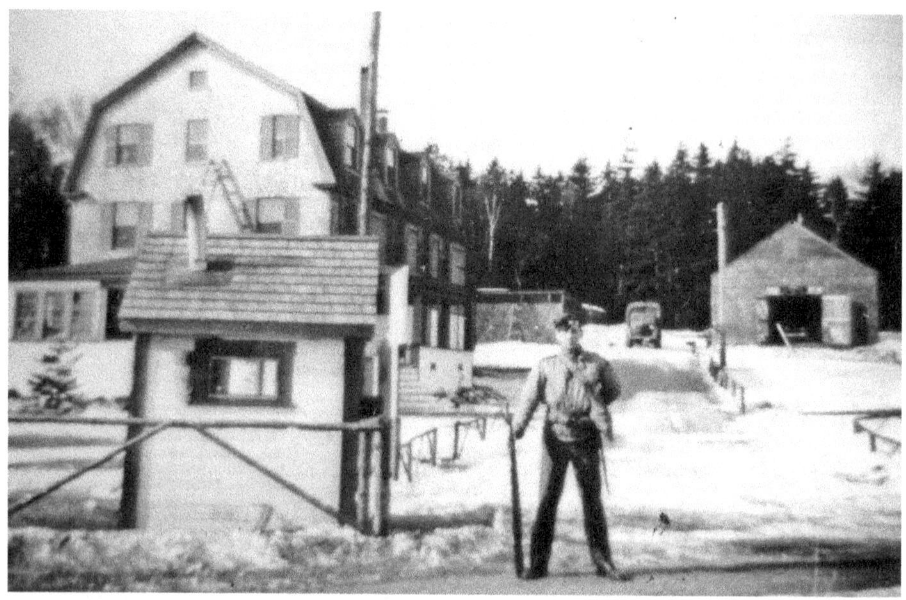

Entrance to Bailey Island navy base with guard, 1941. *Harpswell Historical Society.*

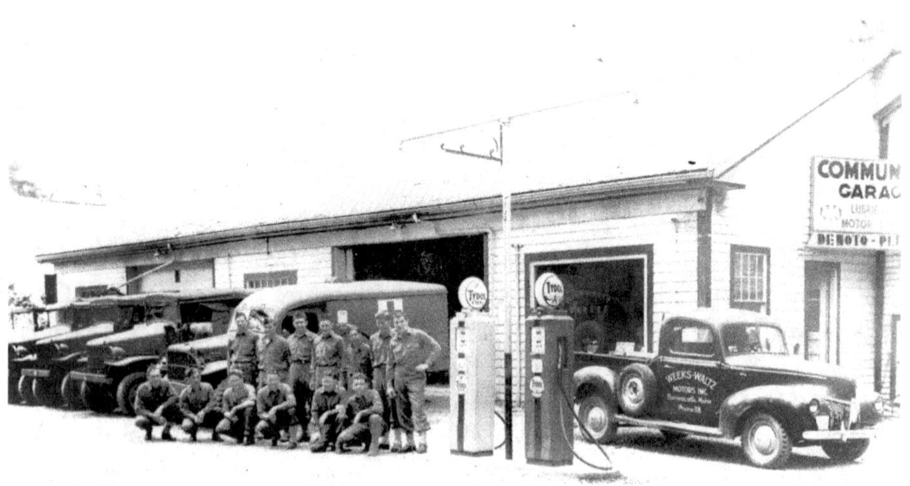

Company C, 181st Infantry, U.S. Army, in Damariscotta in front of Weeks and Waltz garage, which they commandeered for their equipment. *Courtesy of Calvin and Marjorie Dodge.*

"He's Watching You" poster, Glenn Ernest Grohe, artist. Office for Emergency Management Division of Information, 1942. *Northwestern University Library, images.northwestern.edu.*

January 1942 was the beginning of eight desperate months of losses of Allied merchant men, ships and cargoes along the Atlantic and Gulf coasts. Without long-range radar on either side, German submarines could refuel as needed from their own tanker submarines in the middle of the Atlantic, where neither the British nor the Americans could see them. That gave them almost unlimited attack range. This was the time of the "wolf pack."[133] Seven to nine German submarines in a group would target a merchant ship or convoy. When the first "wolf" struck, all attention would be on him, leaving the others free to surface and attack any ships nearby. Merchant seamen who survived the torpedo attack and were seen floating or swimming in the water were gunned down by U-boat crews.

German submarines sank eighty-two ships off the East Coast in the first four months of 1942.[134] Those ships were carrying just under 500,000 gross tons of badly needed oil, coal, food and supplies to the Allies. At night, people on American beaches saw flashes of light and heard explosions that they knew were not thunder and lightning. All along the coast, fishermen and pleasure boaters reported seeing oil slicks, bits of charred lifeboats, empty life buoys and dead fish and birds killed by oily waters. On June 15, 1942, two large American freighters were torpedoed by a U-boat in full view of a crowd of bathers on Virginia Beach.[135] German grand admiral Karl Doenitz gave an interview to a German war correspondent in the summer of 1942, saying, "Our submarines are operating close inshore along the coast of the United States of America, so that bathers and sometimes entire coastal cities are witnesses to the drama of war, whose visual climaxes are constituted by the red glorioles of blazing tankers."[136] Official sources said as little as possible about what was happening, not wanting to cause panic, but sinkings witnessed by Americans onshore or reported by the Germans could not be denied.

In May 1942, Admiral King finally authorized the U.S. Coast Guard Auxiliary to take over and organize the Coastal Picket Patrol.[137] The coast guard opened a recruiting office in Portland and used local newspapers to get the word out that men and boats were needed, saying, "The Coast Guard now operates every size of ship afloat from the thirty-eight-foot picket boat… to the enormous ocean-going converted passenger liners.…Its large seagoing cutters and patrol planes not only protect life and property afloat, but they must also now combat the submarine menace to our vital sea lanes."[138]

The Coastal Picket Patrol consisted of small yachts, motor and converted fishing boats manned by civilian sailors whose job was to patrol the coastline out to the fifty-fathom curve, where the waters of the coast become the

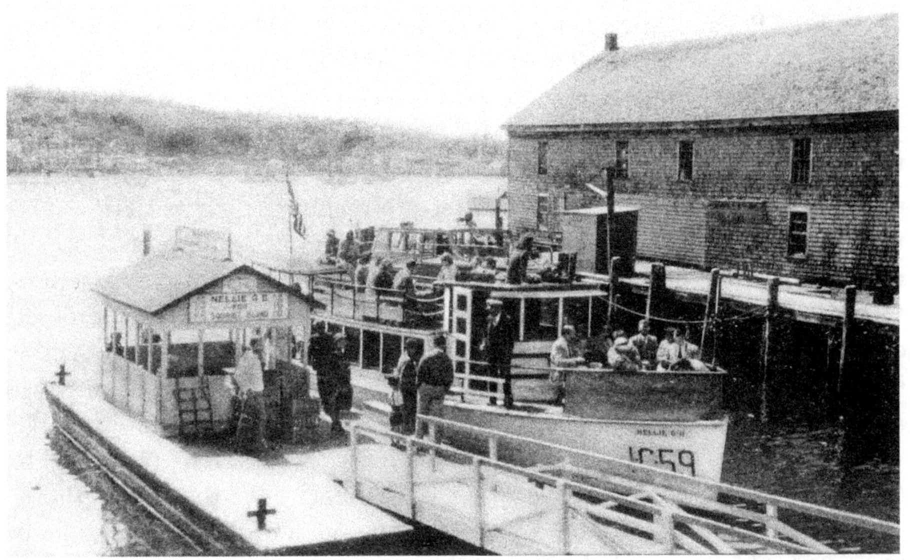

Postcard of the Nellie G with a U.S. Navy number on its bow, circa 1942. *Boothbay Region Historical Society.*

Atlantic Ocean.[139] Their mission was to "observe and report the actions and activities of all hostile submarine and air forces and to attack and destroy enemy submarines when armament permits."[140] Fifty- to one-hundred-foot sailboats were the most effective because of their long cruising range and the legendary ability of New England sailors to handle the vessels in bad weather. Each vessel was given a U.S. Army Interceptor Command grid chart that divided a two-hundred- to three-hundred-mile offshore area into fifteen square-nautical-mile sections. A fleet of forty-five- to sixty-five-foot yachts and powerboats, many of them two-masted schooners, patrolled the coast of Maine. Where practical, the boats were equipped with at least four two-hundred-pound depth charges, one .50-caliber machine gun and a radio set. The coast guard called the auxiliary the Corsair Fleet, but their more popular nickname was the Hooligan Navy.[141]

The Hooligan Navy was composed of yachtsmen, fishermen, "college boys, adventurous lads of shore villages, Boy Scouts, beachcombers, ex-bootleggers and rum-runners—almost everyone who declared he could hand, reef and steer—and many who could not."[142] They ranged in age from seventeen to sixty-four. Men rejected for military service due to age or physical defects like poor eyesight or even missing limbs were accepted.

Humphrey Bogart, Arthur Fiedler and Governor of Maine and World War I Flying Ace Sumner Sewall were members of the Hooligan Navy.[143]

The auxiliary crews were too poorly armed to do any real damage to a submarine. All they had were pistols, hunting rifles and old World War I guns. Their true value was in giving the navy additional eyes and ears at sea. U-boats had to surface to recharge their batteries. The Hooligan Navy listened for submarines using hydrophones dropped into the water.[144] Crews on sailboats could hear submarines better than those on motorboats, where sounds were drowned out or couldn't be differentiated from those of a submarine. Musicians turned out to be the best at hearing U-boat propellers because of their ability to distinguish sounds.[145] Another way to detect a submarine was "the unmistakable stench"[146] of its diesel fuel. The problem was whether to report it. If the sailors broke radio silence, they told the U-boat they were there. The enemy could then shoot them or submerge and flee, knowing their location had been made.[147] It took brave men to make that call so far from anyone who could help them if things went bad.

THE COASTAL BEACH PATROL

The Coastal Beach Patrol's job was to observe and report any enemy vessels operating in coastal waters or any attempts by the enemy to land, and to stop anyone trying to communicate from land with an enemy at sea. They worked in conjunction with the FBI and were given communications equipment to relay messages and send reports. It seemed farfetched to think that the Germans or the Japanese would try to land on the East Coast until June 13, 1942, when four German saboteurs landed on Long Island, New York, and were later captured. Within a month, beach patrols became well armed and an almost constant presence on the midcoast. A recruiting article appeared in the August 7, 1942 *Boothbay Register* titled "Draft-Ineligible Men Asked to Sign Up for Patrol Duty." In Damariscotta, a group of older men, including Ben Duce, Verne Battese and Jake Day, signed up.

Beach patrols were usually two men on foot or in small boats, armed with rifles or pistols and flares. Sometimes they were accompanied by trained guard dogs. An organization called Dogs for Defense worked with dog owners and the military to supply selected dogs to the army, navy and coast guard. *The Boothbay Register* of November 13, 1943, had an article on the

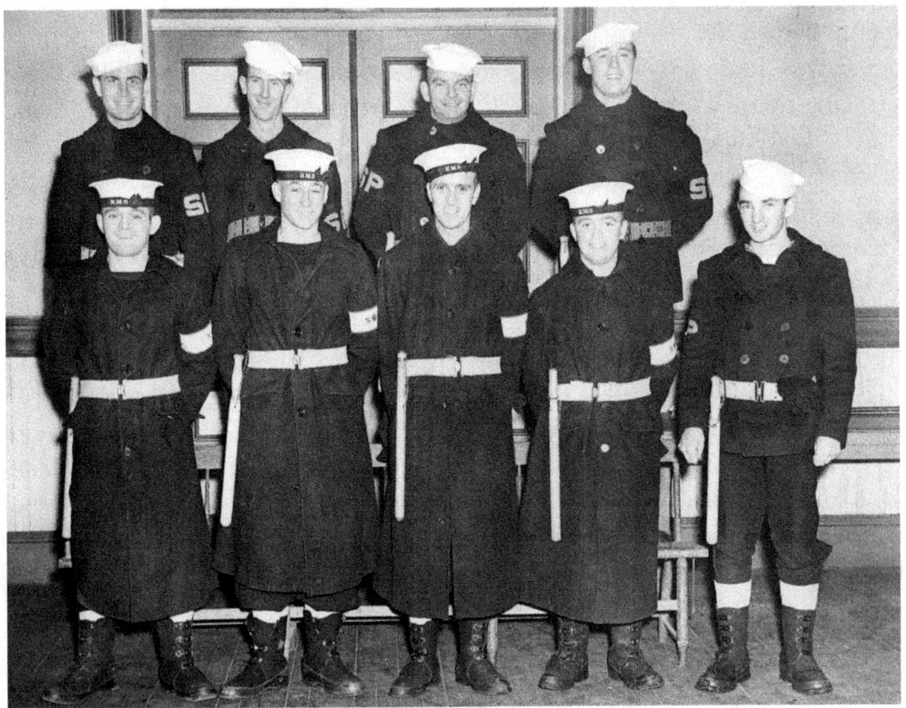

Brunswick Naval Air Station Shore Patrol, circa 1945. *Pejepscot Historical Society.*

service and gave instructions on the process for volunteering your dog. The patrols also helped police the coast and assisted with rescues.

The coastal patrols created strong memories for local children. Jean Luther Thompson of Southport said that the army coastal patrol regularly drove a weapons carrier down to Southport to check the shore roads. Her mother would give them lemonade in summer, hot cocoa in the winter and sometimes even a home-cooked meal, while her grandfather regaled them with stories.[148] But sometimes, the locals weren't that supportive. Leslie Brewer, a young fisherman in his twenties, was out looking for herring when he found a coast guard patrol boat tied to the Cedarbush Buoy with its crew sound asleep. He cut the boat adrift and never did hear where they wound up.[149]

It's easy to discount the effort of the Coastal Beach Patrols because of what *didn't* happen, but the patrols did find pieces of charred boats, torn and bloody life vests and occasionally even bodies or body parts washed up on shore. These were packaged up, delivered to the army or navy and never mentioned to the general public. Coast guardsman Eugene Stover, thirty-eight, was stationed at Damariscove. Jack Stover remembered his father bringing home a large black bundle that he wouldn't talk about or let them touch. The bundle was put on a coast guard truck the next day. Jack later learned that it had been a German life raft.[150] Jean Huskins Chenoweth, a schoolgirl in West Boothbay during the war, remembered "air raid sirens going off, blackouts at night with the shades drawn and lights out, the dull thud of depth charges exploding offshore.…One day…a boy at school brought in a human skull that had washed up on the beach, presumably from a German on a submarine that exploded."[151]

Patrol boats were kept on the Sheepscot and Androscoggin Rivers. British pilots training in Brunswick did practice bombing on Mile Beach at the end of Georgetown Island. A crash boat was kept at Five Islands wharf to rescue accidentally downed pilots, who needed rescuing fairly frequently. Leslie Brewer remembered being kept out of the restricted area but still hearing the loud and frightening noise of the planes overhead.[152]

Flotilla 208 of the auxiliary, composed of men from Damariscotta, Newcastle, Bristol and South Bristol, was responsible for checking all vessels entering or leaving Boothbay, Boothbay Harbor and East Boothbay. A flotilla was a group of ten boats, each with a captain and crew of four or five men.

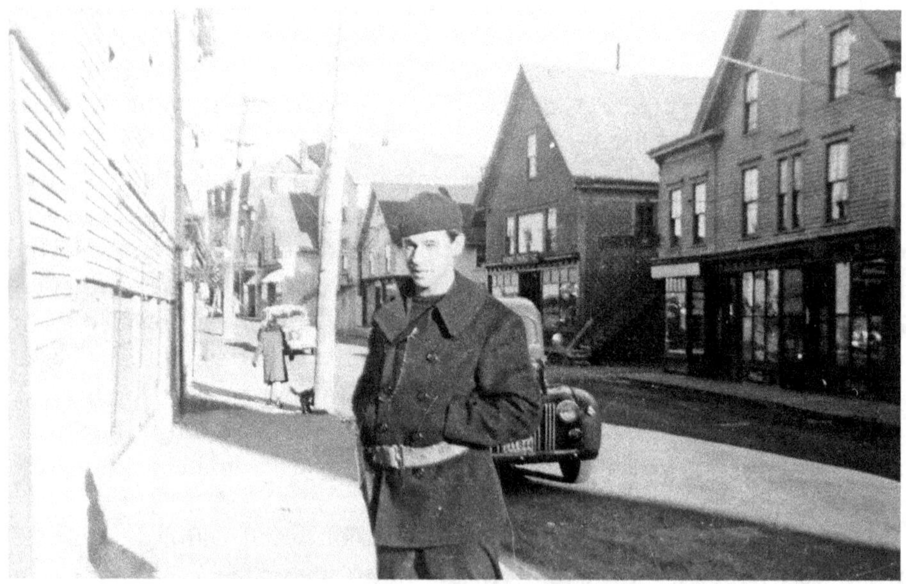

Navy Shore Patrol sailor in Boothbay Harbor, 1941. *Boothbay Region Historical Society.*

The men were given uniforms, rifles and automatic pistols. They trained in first aid, signaling and navigation at the coast guard building on McKown Hill. Their patrol boats docked at the Shell Dock in Boothbay Harbor. Many of the men of Flotilla 208 worked nine-hour shifts at Samples or Gamage Shipyards in addition to their Coastal Picket shifts, which consisted of one twelve-hour shift two nights a week.[153]

Civilian boats had to fly signal flags identifying themselves whether they sailed on the coast or a river. Boat owners had to get a license from the coast guard. License rules included no enemy aliens, cameras or firearms and no persons without coast guard identification on board unless the captain could vouch for them as itinerant guests. A permit from the captain of the port was required for a boat to leave the inland waters of the United States, which included rivers, lakes, wetlands and reservoirs. No one was allowed to operate a boat at night except "when absolutely necessary on legitimate business…[or at any time] within 100 feet of a Navy or military establishment, shipbuilding plant, power plant, oil or freight dock unless on legitimate business."[154]

Charlie Hull, a coast guardsman stationed at Damariscove early in the war, remembered a night when he had just finished investigating what he thought was a fire alarm near Pierce and Hartung Hardware Store. Finding nothing there, he was about to turn around when he heard Milton Seavey, officer in charge of Damariscove Island,

> *…bellowing through a bull horn…"Get that boat over here!" Milton jumped aboard with a machine gun. He then instructed me to head the boat through the inner pass and to open her up full throttle, because a suspicious vessel had been reported near Samples Shipyard. It was a very dark night… and I was afraid Milton and I would be up on the rocks if we weren't careful. Luckily, we made it through without a scratch, only to discover a fishing boat from Gloucester, Massachusetts had come in with her running lights on.…* [They had] *tied up at Samples Shipyard and were quite surprised, to say the least, to be met by the Coast Guard and machine gun fire as they came into town.*[155]

Coast guardsmen on patrol were the first to discover a fire at the Goudy & Stevens boatyard in East Boothbay on Sunday, January 9, 1944, a few days after a blizzard had cut off access to and from the region.[156] They helped keep the blaze from spreading to nearby buildings, but the shipyard was destroyed.

Fishermen had to apply for new licenses. They were issued identification cards, photographed and fingerprinted by the coast guard. Captains were often given deferments because they were older and working an essential job, but the young men in their crew were drafted. This severely hampered the fishing fleet and reduced fish supplies at a time when people needed the additional food. Coast guard and navy personnel were assigned to both fishing boats and yachts to supplement crews. They received training in sailing and working on small boats that proved invaluable later in the war when they were transferred to landing craft.[157]

Fishing boat captains were given personal indicator numbers and issued two-way voice radios with sealed frequencies accessible only to the coast guard and the Radio Marine Company, which had a secure wire to the U.S. Army Interceptor Command.[158] Those were the only radios allowed on board. If anyone saw something suspicious, he was supposed to use the radios to call in the report. One Phippsburg fisherman devised a clever way to work around the restriction to communicate with his wife, Manela, at home. Alvin Brewer, thirty-one, used homing pigeons. His wife's job was to call the local fish wholesaler and tell them how many barrels they needed to bring to the dock for Alvin's catch. Alvin said:

> *When I had a good set* [of pigeons], *I would write a note to Manela, telling her to call the Juliano Brothers, affix it to the bird's leg and release it. When the military put in a radar station on Morse's Mountain in Sebasco, it interfered with the pigeon's minds. After that, all they could do was fly around and around in circles. They could no longer find their way home, and I lost my source of communication with the mainland.*[159]

With their deep knowledge of the waters they fished, fishermen could be valuable observers and "were less likely to mistake a school of fish for a submarine."[160] The opposite of this was one observer at an Aircraft Warning Service (AWS) post in South Bristol who reported a submarine in John's Bay. Investigated by the Damariscove coast guard, it turned out to be a school of blackfish.[161] A report to the Bailey Island coast guard station of puffs of steam or smoke rising from the ocean and headed east turned out to be a whale.[162] Few fishermen called in any reports. Those who did tended to wait until they were returning to shore out of fear of being fired upon by whoever they were watching, since Nazi submarine crews were known to kill any survivors in lifeboats or in the water.[163]

Many fishermen told stories of seeing submarines. Leslie Brewer told the story of cod fishing on Great Ledge off Woolwich and seeing a submarine and its periscope surfacing:

> *I got the hell out of there as fast as I could, and reported the incident to the Coast Guard. That night the depth charges started going off in the river and the concussions from them cracked the plaster in the ceiling of my house. A day or two later I returned to the same spot and saw a lot of oil floating on the surface of the water.*[164]

Leland Snowman, a Southport fisherman in his early thirties, reported seeing a German submarine surface when he was lobstering near Seguin Island. He must have been far enough away not to have been unduly frightened or else he decided it was the better part of valor to stay still and watch. He reported the incident to the coast guard when he returned to shore.[165]

Charlie Hull remembered hearing stories from men on draggers and seiners that Nazi submarines were surfacing among the fishermen and threatening crews that they would sink their vessels if they didn't hand over diesel fuel. When improvements in Allied radar made Nazi refueling in the Atlantic impossible, the submarines could only operate off the East Coast for about forty days before running out of fuel. Hull remembered being told the Germans were offering between three to five dollars a gallon for any diesel fuel that fishing boats would sell them.[166]

Word got around Boothbay that some fishing boats had added extra fuel tanks in their fish holds. They would get fuel at different ports until they had several hundred gallons, presumably enough to make it worth their while to risk selling it to the enemy. The Damariscove station received orders to sound the fish hold of every fishing vessel passing through the area. A rod inserted into the hold would easily tell the coast guard if the fisherman was hiding something. At least one vessel, a seventy-five-foot dragger from Down East, was captured with extra fuel tanks on board. The boat was brought into Boothbay Harbor and put under guard until the customs agents could come and question the crew the next day. This was one stubborn crew, however, and someone on board cast off the lines and they tried to sneak away.[167]

> *My friend, John Foss, was on duty and had watched the escape attempt. He picked up a machine gun and walked to the end of the wharf and*

said, "Alright boys, bring her back in." There was no response to the order, so John touched off the gun. The crew soon had a change of heart and returned to the wharf. The next morning the customs officials showed up and took the Captain and crew away, presumably charging them with aiding and abetting the enemy in a time of war.[168]

Fishermen are known for their stories, and there is little official documentation of Nazi submarines spotted off the Maine coast. However, the documented volume and success of Nazi activity off the Atlantic coast, particularly in the first six months of 1942, combined with multiple reports of unexplained oil slicks, explosions and bursts of light at night, lend veracity to the fishermen's stories. By fall 1943, the coast guard had enough cutters and smaller boats being built to replace the auxiliary vessels. On October 1, 1943, the auxiliary was virtually disbanded, and coast guard personnel took over the work of the Hooligan Navy.

The Civil Air Patrol

The Civil Air Patrol (CAP) was a group of civilian pilots, mechanics and flying enthusiasts who saw that the military did not have the resources for effective anti-submarine warfare and knew they could help by giving them eyes in the air.[169] None of their pilots could claim a draft deferment to participate, so every pilot and plane was an additional resource for the navy. CAP pilots flew their own planes, paid for their own gas and supplies (using their own rations) and found or built their own hangars.

The CAP did reconnaissance, fire patrol, rescue work and whatever the navy or coast guard needed done. From September 1, 1942, through August 29, 1943, CAP pilots flew anti-submarine patrols along the Maine coast day and night, seven days a week, in all kinds of weather. Because CAP planes (marked with a white pyramid so they could be easily identified from water or land) flew lower and slower than military planes, they could see more. Pilots risked their lives flying hundreds of miles over the ocean in planes too small to be armed, in which only a pilot, observer and radio set could fit. They risked being shot down by an enemy plane or submarine when all they could do was report the sighting to someone who could respond. CAP planes helped escort Boston-to-Halifax convoys during the bitterly cold winter of 1942–43. Their search and rescue efforts for crews from downed aircraft or sunken vessels who otherwise would have died in the icy waters of the Atlantic saved hundreds of lives.[170]

The CAP was never even an auxiliary part of the armed services, but since they were armed and authorized to attack enemy submarines, they were the only American civilian defense unit to see active service against the enemy. There were two CAP bases in Maine, Portland and Bar Harbor, but fields throughout the midcoast were used as needed.

BRUNSWICK NAVAL AIR STATION

Brunswick had a small airfield that was used by civilian pilots and the Bowdoin College Civilian Pilot Training Program. In 1941, the British Royal Navy Fleet Arm selected Brunswick as the site of its new Vought Corsairs, Grumman Avengers and Grumman Hellcats pilot training facility. A member of the first squadron assigned there wrote a tongue-in-cheek account about the unit's formation and activities:

> *Give credit where credit is due. Right from the start THEIR LORDS OF THE ADMIRALTY decided to treat the squadron as a secret weapon and arranged for it to be sent to BRUNSWICK, MAINE, U.S.A., a sparsely populated area where revolutionary flying might go un-noticed, new styles of aerial warfare be practiced and be unknown to the enemy, and where no outside interests of drink or women would interfere with the serious work of these young aviators.*[171]

In 1942, the decision was made to expand the airport into a U.S. Naval Air Station by combining the existing acreage with land owned by Bowdoin College and part of the Brunswick Town Common. The navy also purchased land from local homeowners.[172] The November 19, 1942 *Brunswick Record* announced that the new base would be one of the largest on the Atlantic coast, with two six-thousand- to seven-thousand-foot runways and accommodations for 1,500 enlisted men and 150 officers.

The base offered new opportunities for civilians as well. The February 25, 1943 *Brunswick Record* reported a widespread rumor that "phenomenal wages" were being offered at the air station for civilians to work digging up a local cemetery because the navy wanted that land. The rumor wasn't true, but not everyone in town completely trusted the navy to play fair with local

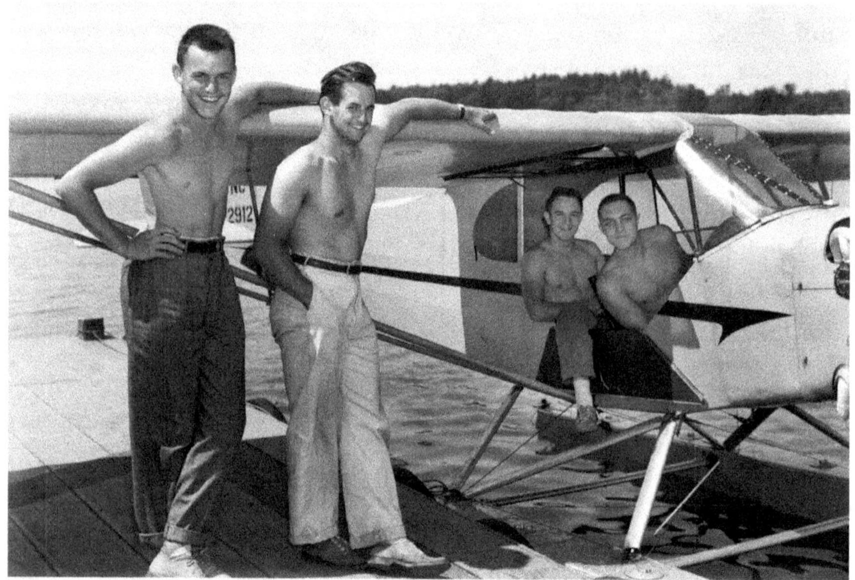

Left to right: William Bloodgood, Certificate of Honor, Bowdoin, 1942; Stanwood Fisher, Bowdoin, 1941; Edgar Curtis; and Stanley James, Bowdoin, 1941, in the Civilian Pilot Training program at Bowdoin College, 1940. *Bowdoin College Archives, Brunswick, Maine.*

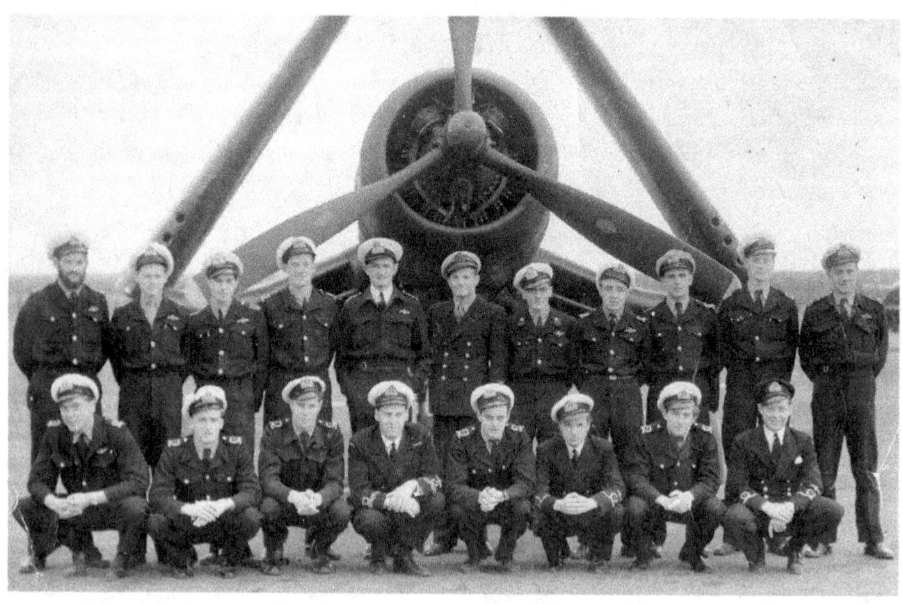

Royal Navy 1845 Squadron at Brunswick Naval Air Station, July 1943. *Courtesy of Peter Dunn, Australia@War, www.ozatwar.com.*

landowners. It *was* true that over three hundred new jobs became available for administrative, clerical, secretarial and other work. Telephone operators, firefighters, storekeepers, messengers, inventory supervisors, foremen, mechanics, riggers, joiners, painters, electricians and pipefitters were all needed. Local businesses immediately profited from the construction and deployment of navy men to the base. Restaurants especially thrived from the influx of new people without access to kitchen facilities.[173]

Others were not as happy with the new developments, especially the people who complained about the noise of low-flying planes overhead. Calvin Dodge remembered his excitement as a little boy when the Royal Navy flew practice strafing missions over the backyard of their home in Newcastle. Sometimes the planes flew so low that he could see the pilot wave to him.[174]

Brunswick Naval Air Station was commissioned on April 15, 1943, with John C. Alderman as its first commander. Commander Alderman appeared on a local radio program on March 14 to answer questions about the new station, as people were directed to call it, and was very well received. Alderman was a war hero who had received the Navy Cross for bravery. While in command of the USS *McFarland* in the Battle of Guadalcanal, he delivered much-needed gasoline to Henderson Field under fire and returned his ship to Hawaii even after thirty feet of its stern was blasted away.[175] Navy Undersecretary James B. Forrestal, Maine Senator Ralph Brewster and Governor Sumner Sewall all attended the commissioning ceremonies. Alderman especially endeared himself to the Bath/Brunswick community when he married his fiancée, Nancy Randolph Wall of Los Angeles, in the Bowdoin College Chapel on July 15, 1943. The Honorable Rupert H. Baxter of Bath, whose daughter Lydia was a close friend of Miss Wall, gave away the bride.

Like the army and navy men at Bowdoin, the BNAS men and their families quickly became part of the community and the war effort. Army and navy men worked with Brunswick High School students to help the manpower-strapped post office deliver mail during the Christmas 1943 rush. The station and college loaned trucks, drivers and gas rations to the effort.[176]

Accidents and near-misses were part of station life. A forced landing on a farmer's field and a crash landing near the Androscoggin River demonstrated the dangers. Both pilots survived with few injuries.[177] Another two British pilots who crashed into swampland in Pownal were not so lucky. The two planes collided in midair and burst into flames. Both men were killed. On December 1, 1943, a British plane flown by New Zealander Lieutenant John

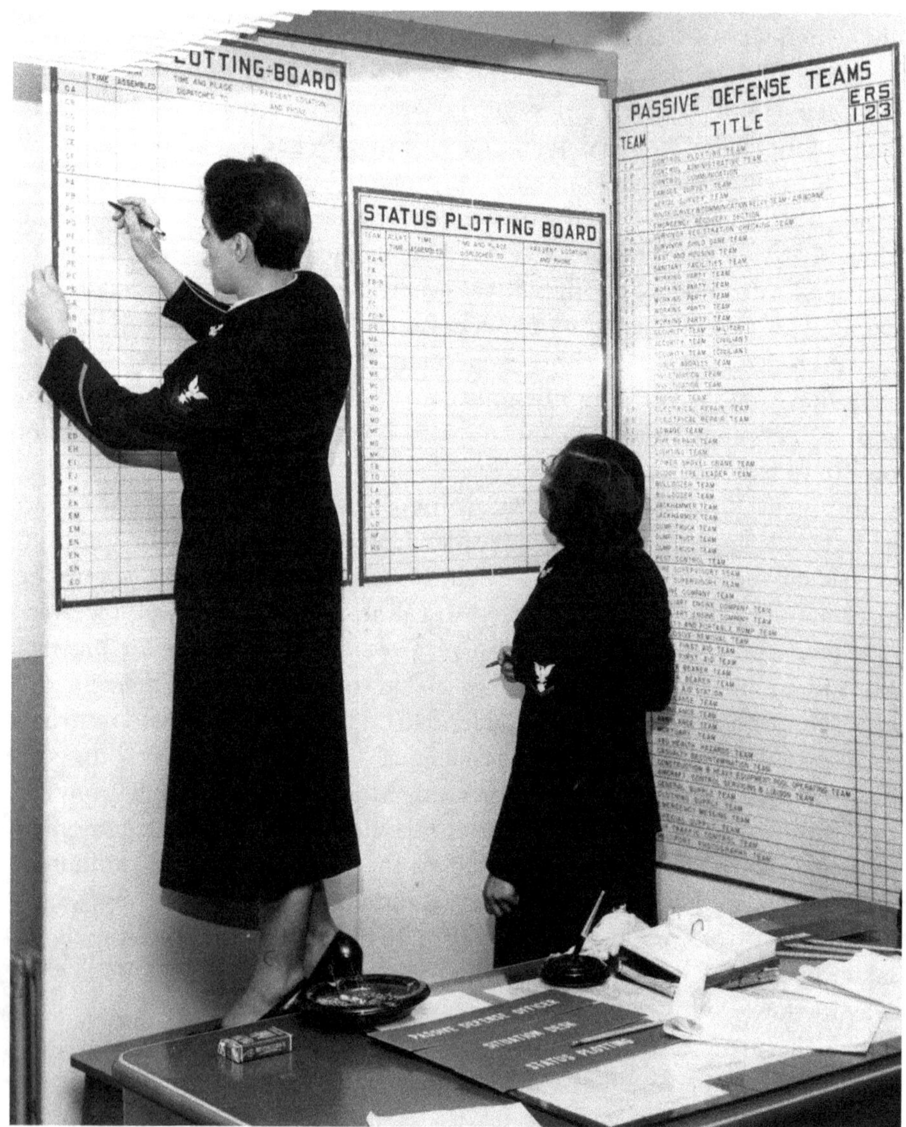

Two WAVES at Brunswick Naval Air Station. *Pejepscot Historical Society*.

D. Wallace had a structural failure, exploded in midair over Brunswick and disintegrated, scattering debris on houses and buildings on Federal Street.[178] Lieutenant Wallace, twenty-one, was killed, but miraculously, no one on the ground was injured. The fuselage and wing landed in the backyard of one house and the other wing in another. The plane's machine gun was found by high school boys near First Parish Church. In an expression of the mood and mindset of the times, Marjorie Libby, whose home was in the path of the plane debris field, wrote to the *Brunswick Record*:

> *Only by an act of God are we here today and I think we should all stop for a moment and give a prayer that we were spared. We must also not forget… that for all we know the boy from across the sea stayed with his plane in hopes he might save a life by giving his own. For that to me is the only way I can think that a greater tragedy was prevented, and I sincerely hope that somehow, some day his family will know how he gave his life over here as our boys are giving theirs over there for those people.*[179]

Chapter 8

AMERICA CALLING

Civilian Defense

Everyone wanted to do their bit, but what was that? In May 1941, FDR created the Office of Civilian Defense (OCD) and put New York City mayor Fiorello La Guardia in charge. The OCD was responsible for managing the homefront war effort. The dean of Harvard Law School, James Landis, was appointed executive director of the national OCD and regional director for New England. In June 1941, La Guardia and Landis held a meeting in Boston with representatives from all the New England states. Since Maine was such a strategic geographic location, they recommended that Maine organize as soon as possible to educate the public on their duties in the event of war.[180] Two months later, La Guardia met with Landis and State Coordinator of Maine Civilian Defense Raymond Adams in Augusta. They decided that Maine civilian defense would be decentralized. This structure allowed Maine to work faster and more effectively than states that opted for state-run organizations.[181]

Each town would have its own civilian defense unit, working through county divisions as necessary. Brunswick, Topsham and Harpswell were defined as their own civilian defense division due to their distance from Portland (the center of Cumberland County activity) and proximity to Bath, with BIW plants and workforce present in each of these three towns.

Municipal officers—"capable men"[182]—were designated to lead the local efforts. They chose the committee chairmen and oversaw the civilian defense efforts of their town or area. Men were chosen to lead air raid defense and the ration board. Each local unit had a women's division charged with organizing and operating the Volunteer Placement Bureau.

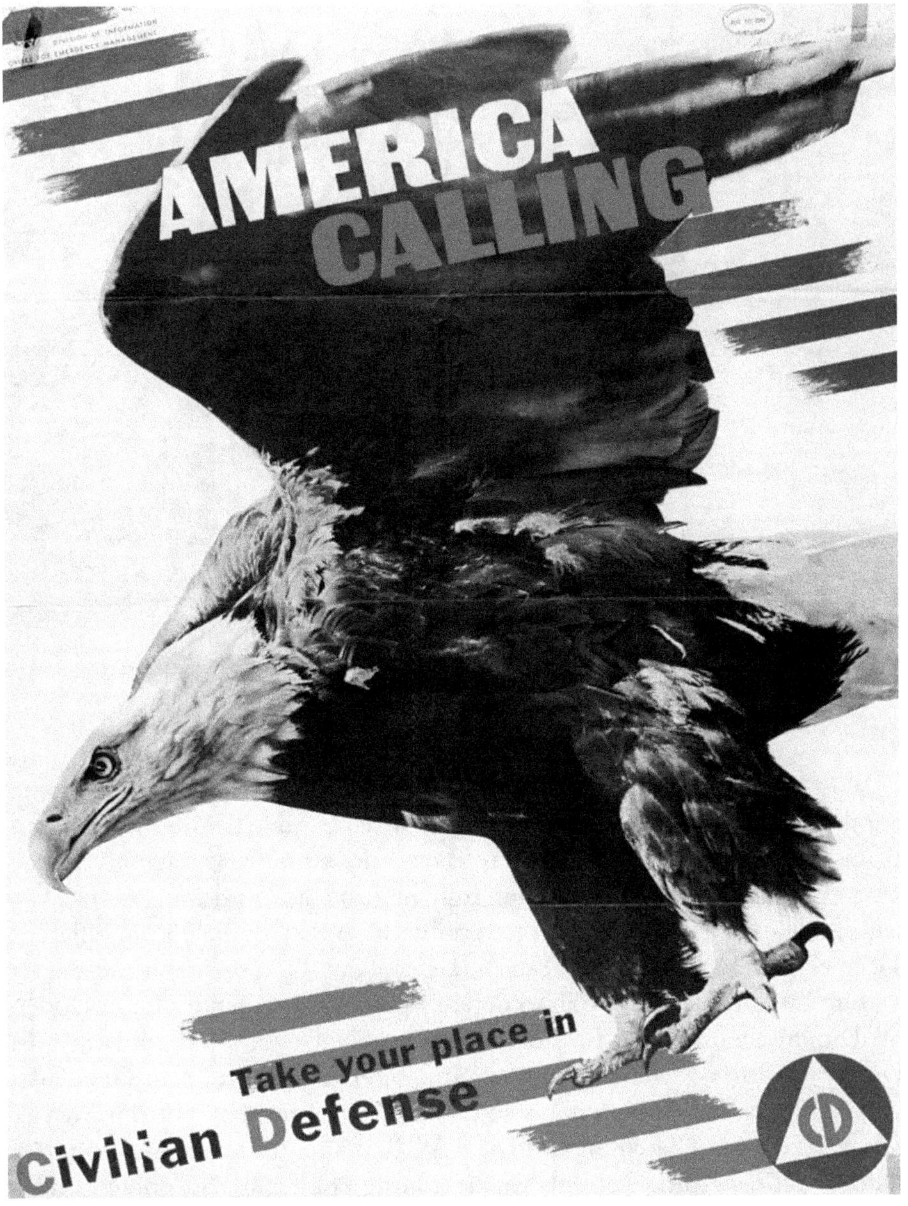

"America Calling—Take Your Place in Civilian Defense" poster, Office for Emergency Management Division of Information, United States Office of Civilian Defense, 1941. *Northwestern University Library, images.northwestern.edu.*

Where to Learn What YOU Can Do

Figures refer to pages in this pamphlet

Accountants, 26
Actors, 33
Advertisers, 32
Architects, 32
Artists, 31

Bankers, 26
Barbers, 27
Bartenders, 27
Beauty parlor operators, 27
Bookkeepers, 26
Boys, 40
Brokers, 26
Builders, 28
Business men, 25
Business Women, 25
Butchers, 27

Canvassers, 28
Carpenters, 24
Cleaners, 28
Clergymen, 30
Clerks, 26

Doctors, 30
Domestic help, 27
Doorkeepers, 28
Dyers, 28

Editors, 32

Electricians, 24
Employees, 25
Employers, 25
Engineers, 33
Entertainers, 33

Factory workers, 23
Farm women, 34, 36
Farmers, 34
Food merchants, 27

Gardeners, 23
Girls, 40
Grocers, 27
Guards, 28

Homemakers, 36

Janitors, 28

Lawyers, 31
Librarians, 30

Machinists, 24
Mechanics, 24
Messengers, 28
Miners, 24
Motion picture theater managers, 27
Musicians, 31

Newspaper men, 17, 32
Nurserymen, 23
Nurses, 30

Painters, 24
Photographers, 33
Plumbers, 24
Press agents, 32
Professional men, 29
Professional women, 29

Radio people, 32
Retail merchants, 25

Sales clerks, 26
Salesmen, 28
Shippers, 27
Social workers, 32
Stenographers, 26

Taxi drivers, 24
Teachers, 29
Truck drivers, 24

Ushers, 28

Waiters, 27
Watchmen, 28
Wholesalers, 27
Writers, 17, 32

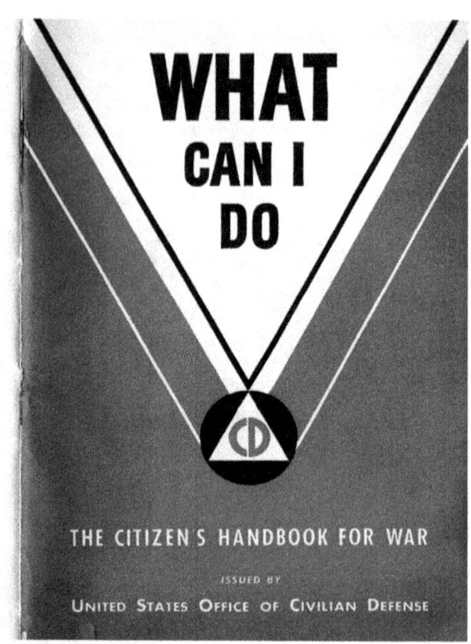

What Can I Do: The Citizen's Handbook for War. United States Office of Civilian Defense, 1941. *Author's collection.*

Most of the people on civilian defense committees knew or knew of one another, but they may never have sat at the same table before. In Bath and Brunswick, the social divisions were economic, ethnic and religious. In the coastal communities, the summer residents did not associate or socialize with the locals. The war effort often brought together people from different social classes, religions and backgrounds, working for a common cause.

The Lincoln County civilian defense unit was headed by Leon Dodge of Damariscotta, fifty, president of First National Bank. Edward B. Denny Jr., forty-seven and general manager of a large local farm, was vice-chairman. Fannie Perkins, sixty, wife of a Boothbay Harbor lawyer, served as county chairman and Dr. R.W. Belknap, fifty, as county medical defense officer. Ruth Robbins was rationing chairman. Seventeen towns and two plantations in Lincoln County had their own civilian defense committees.

Identifying potential volunteers and matching their skill sets to the needs of the community was essential, time-consuming work and required excellent organizational skills. Civilian defense volunteer jobs included air raid warden and observation post staff, auxiliary police and firemen, clerical support,

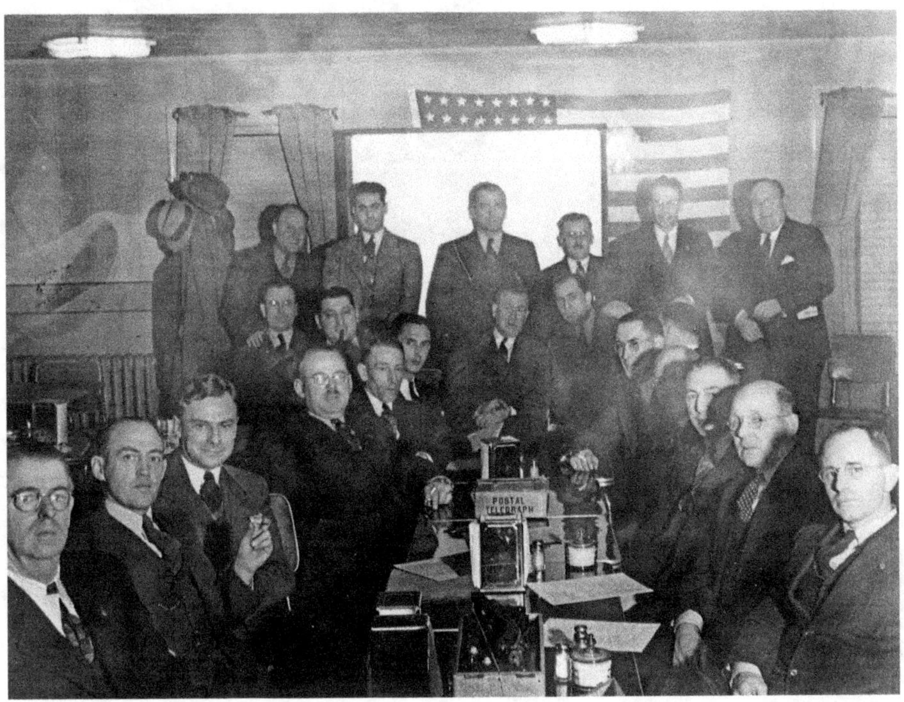

Brunswick Civilian Defense Committee, including Thomas McMahon, Malcolm Morrell, Adam Walsh, Edmond Lachance and Guy Patterson, 1941. *Pejepscot Historical Society.*

drivers, canteen workers, telephone operators, construction workers, road repair crews and more. The Red Cross needed volunteers to train in first aid, nutrition, food conservation and medical services. They were already managing volunteer committees making clothing, rolling bandages and putting together care packages for military and refugees overseas, including the Bundles for Britain campaign.

Jean Bangs, a twenty-six-year-old lawyer, was the registration chairman for Brunswick. She was a remarkable young woman. In addition to her successful law practice, she volunteered for civilian defense, the Red Cross, the United Service Organizations (USO) and the ration board. Her team of volunteers conducted a house-to-house canvass on Friday, December 12, 1941, to register all adults and high school students. Brunswick and Harpswell residents could also register at town hall or at Jean's office at 160 Maine Street. Topsham residents registered at the town office. Within two weeks, two thousand Brunswick residents had registered, with the expectation of another one thousand by month's end.[183] Civilian defense

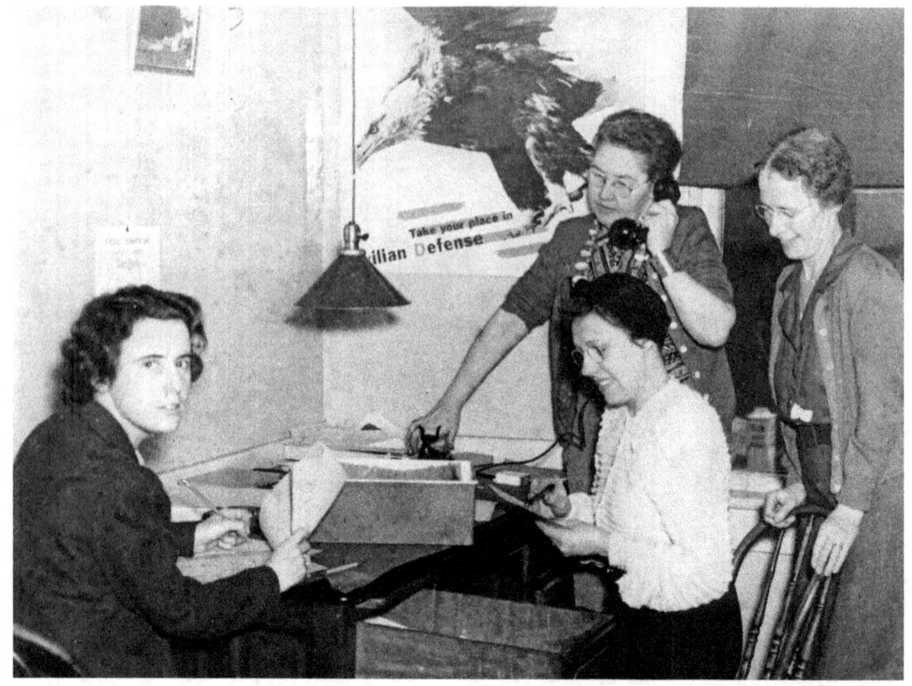

Brunswick Civilian Defense Volunteer Placement volunteers. *Left to right*: Ruth Bangs, Jean Bangs, Susie Sylvester and Helen Campbell, 1941. *Pejepscot Historical Society*.

headquarters and the Volunteer Placement Bureau were set up on January 12 in the downtown office of fire chief Harold Nickerson.

The OCD knew that more women had to take over the jobs of the men who were enlisting, even if it was something women had never pictured themselves doing. The Office of War Information (OWI) launched a national advertising and public relations campaign to recruit women for war work. The center photo on the *Brunswick Record* front page of December 18, 1941, was captioned "Women, Too, Are Needed."[184] The following week, the newspaper reported that seventy-seven women volunteers were staffing the Volunteer Placement office from 9:00 a.m. to 5:00 p.m., six days a week, under the direction of Helen Campbell.[185] Helen, forty-seven, was a writer working for the WPA Maine Writers' Project. She was living with her mother, a retired music teacher, on Mason Street when the war broke out. Helen volunteered her services as a clerk for every major homefront registration throughout the war.[186]

In Bath, the chairman of the Civilian Defense Women's Division was Virginia Parker, thirty-six, wife of the outgoing school superintendent and soon-to-be production manager at Hyde Windlass. Virginia, John and their four children lived on North Street. Virginia Gillies, thirty-five and wife of the president of the Bath Box Company, James Gillies, was director of volunteer registration. She lived with her husband, three small children and their live-in servant Mabel Leach, twenty-eight, on Washington Street. Within days, the Bath Volunteer Placement Bureau reported that four auto mechanics, twenty-nine canteen workers, forty-six first aid workers, four food conservators, sixty-three nurses, five motor corps drivers, ten nurses' aides, forty-five nutritionists, four public relations experts, three wardens and six recreational leaders had registered at town hall.[187]

In the smaller communities, there were fewer people to draw on for all the volunteer jobs. Before the war, Wiscasset, Boothbay, Boothbay Harbor, Southport, South Bristol and Damariscotta had much smaller year-round populations than Bath or Brunswick, but their seasonal populations increased enormously with summer residents and tourists. During World War II, these communities saw their year-round population balloon with servicemen and

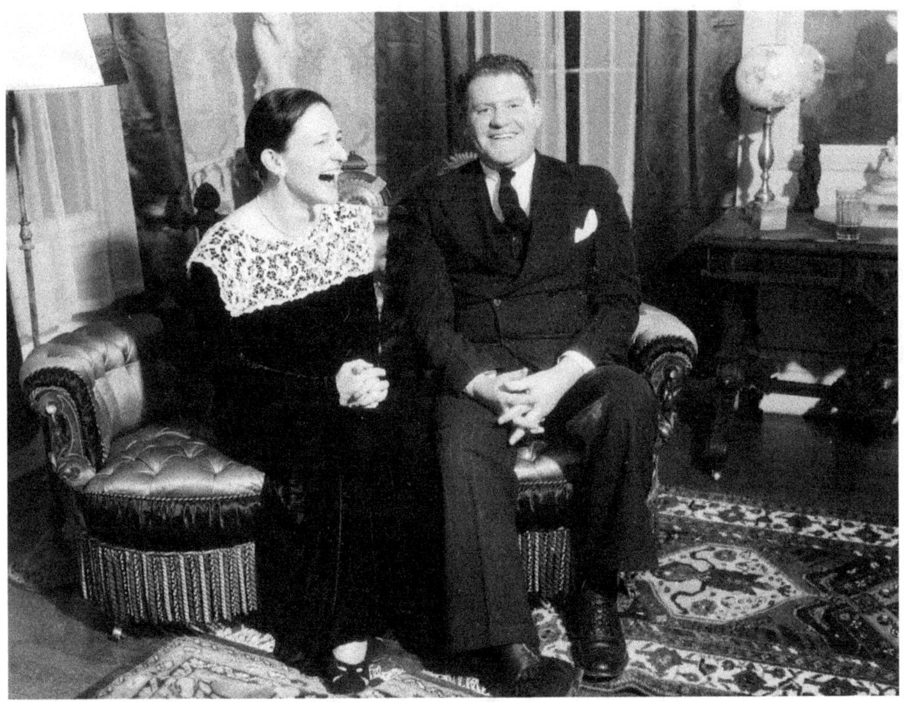

Virginia and James Gillies, circa 1939. *Maine Maritime Museum.*

war workers stationed nearby. BIW workers came farther up the coast to live because they couldn't find houses or apartments closer to Bath. Some seasonal residents from the New York/New Jersey area moved to their summer homes in Boothbay, Boothbay Harbor and Southport because they thought it would be safer for their families. Some put their children in New England boarding schools. Others sent them to local schools.[188]

Angie Dodge was chairman of the Women's Division in Boothbay Harbor. Angie, forty-three, lived with her husband, Harold, a plumber; their two teenage daughters; and Harold's mother on Fullerton Street. The civilian defense office was at the town office, in the "Town Rest Room," which was "a very comfortable post," according to the *Boothbay Register*.[189] The office was open from 4:00 to 8:00 p.m. most days. In May 1942, the office advertised for more volunteers so that everyone could have two-hour shifts.[190] Citizens of these communities had to volunteer for multiple jobs (if the work was going to get done) and still take care of their families and put food on the table.

The East Coast had its first air raid experience on Tuesday, December 9, 1941. A man with confirmed official credentials called the First Army Headquarters on Governor's Island in New York City and asked for confirmation of a radio report, supposedly coming from Washington,

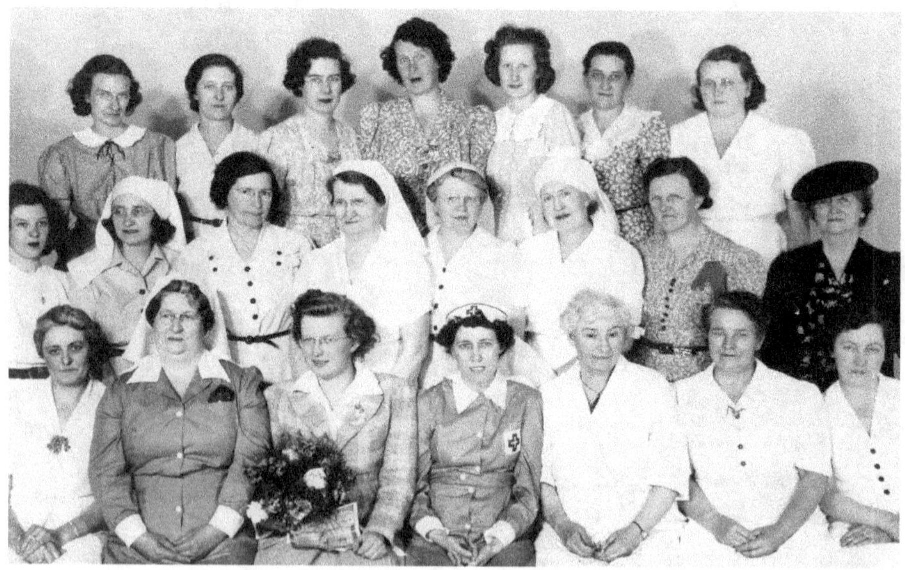

St. Andrews Hospital Auxiliary, with Civilian Defense Women's Division chair Angie Dodge second from the right in the back row. *Boothbay Region Historical Society*.

D.C., that enemy planes had been spotted off the East Coast. The person receiving the message said he hadn't heard that but would ask the officials at First Interceptor Command at Mitchel Field. At that point, it became just like the game of telephone. The Mitchel field man thought the Governor's Island man was telling him that enemy planes *had* been spotted. By the next call, someone had decided that the enemy planes would arrive at 2:00 p.m. Alarms began sounding from New York to New England. At 1:25 p.m., schools were closed and children sent home. All police, including off-duty officers, were summoned to guard highways and key points and stop traffic coming into Boston. Civilians at military bases and defense workers were sent home. Later that afternoon, First Army Command declared that there had been no planes and it had been a dress rehearsal. The climate remained so jittery, however, that the stock market, which had held steady immediately after Pearl Harbor, went into sharp decline at the news of the false alarm.[191]

Brunswick High School held its first air raid drill on Monday, December 15, 1941. All the students went to their lockers and got their coats, and everyone was out of the building in three minutes.[192]

Bowdoin College set up its own air raid organization for the campus, headed by Professor Thomas Curtis Van Cleve, chairman of the faculty military affairs committee. They even published a six-page bulletin explaining what to do in case of an air raid.[193]

In the December 11, 1941 *Bath Independent*, John Newell, assistant manager of BIW and Bath coordinator of civilian defense, warned that they might well become another Coventry, referring to the English city devastated by German bombs in November 1940.[194] People worried that because of BIW and the other shipyards and war production facilities, the midcoast would be a prime target for enemy bombs. Air raid defense plans managed by the Aircraft Warning Service (AWS) went into effect, with chief air raid wardens appointed in every community. The AWS reported to the United States Army Air Force, not the OCD.

Communities began all kinds of civilian defense classes. In addition to air raid warden and plane spotting classes, there were first aid, canteen, motor corps, nutrition, mechanics and machine shop classes. Police departments offered training in chemical warfare defense and how to fight and extinguish incendiary bombs, but it was quickly discovered that the first official directions were developed for the wrong types of bombs. After about a month, the communications regarding such bombs stopped, and people were told to let the civilian defense officers handle the situation.[195]

In January 1942, large public meetings were held to explain the air raid defense system. The AWS needed to manage fears and expectations and reinforce the message that everyone had an important part to play in the war effort. Residents heard from their civilian defense coordinator, chief air raid warden, police and fire chiefs and local officials. Each stressed that every person had a responsibility to follow the rules and obey local air raid wardens. Towns or areas were divided into air defense districts. People learned in what district their house was located and who their air raid wardens were. The *Brunswick Record* published a twenty-three- by eighteen-inch map of the air raid defense zones for Brunswick, Topsham and Harpswell in the April 2, 1942 edition of the paper. Part of the chief air raid warden's job was to ensure that everyone in his district knew what to do and where to go in case of a raid. He personally conveyed that information to every family, assuring them that the alarm would be sounded five minutes before the raiding planes were expected to be over the town, giving them enough time to get to a safe place.[196]

Everyone was supposed to memorize the air raid alarm system, which had several levels, each with different signals. Each level was designated a color to help people remember them. The blue signal meant possible raid, with three five-second blasts on whistles and sirens and slow, measured tolling of church bells. The red signal, continuous two-minute blasts of fire alarms, sirens and whistles, meant planes were overhead. Red signals were always followed by blue signals. The second blue would be followed by the white (or all-clear) signal, which was long blasts on whistles or another tolling of bells for one minute, sounded by police and air warden whistles and radio reports. The "V for Victory" sound would be the opening rhythm of Beethoven's Fifth Symphony: duh-duh-duh-dahhhh.[197] People had trouble remembering that the blue signal followed the red, not the all-clear. There was also a shortage of sirens, so towns had to make do with what they had. In Brunswick, the fire alarm could only do blasts of one length, so the alarm could only be a "continued series of blasts sounding the alarm and continued repetition of the all-clear signal; two blasts indicating the all-clear."[198] Got it? Neither did most people. As with most World War II domestic programs, everything did not run smoothly all the time. Hearing and deciphering the air raid alarm signals remained problematic for over a year.

Programs often went through several iterations before they settled into a successful rhythm. The OCD directed that air raid defense should be managed by the local civilian defense Executive Committee. Brunswick's civilian defense coordinator was electrician and first selectman Thomas

McMahon, fifty-three. McMahon was born in Brunswick, the son of Irish immigrants. He lived on Berry Street with his wife, Margaret, whom he had married when he was forty-two and she was thirty-six years old. McMahon realized that to maximize speed and efficiency of response, there had to be one person in command of air raid defense, not a committee. That person would be supported by deputies, all proven leaders. Adam Walsh, the Bowdoin football coach, was appointed chief air raid warden for the Brunswick area. Walsh came to Bowdoin after coaching at Yale and Harvard.[199] In 1942, he was forty, married and the father of two teenage boys, living with his family on Longfellow Avenue. Walsh's deputies included Malcolm Morrell, forty-seven, athletic director at Bowdoin (who became chief air raid warden the following year) and Edmond Lachance, forty-four, a loom fixer at the cotton mill.[200] Lachance was the leader of a group of men who brought the union to the mill, resulting in improved safety conditions and an increase in employee morale.[201] If an air raid occurred, all activities in Brunswick and Topsham would be directed by the chief air raid warden from the basement of the fire station behind town hall.

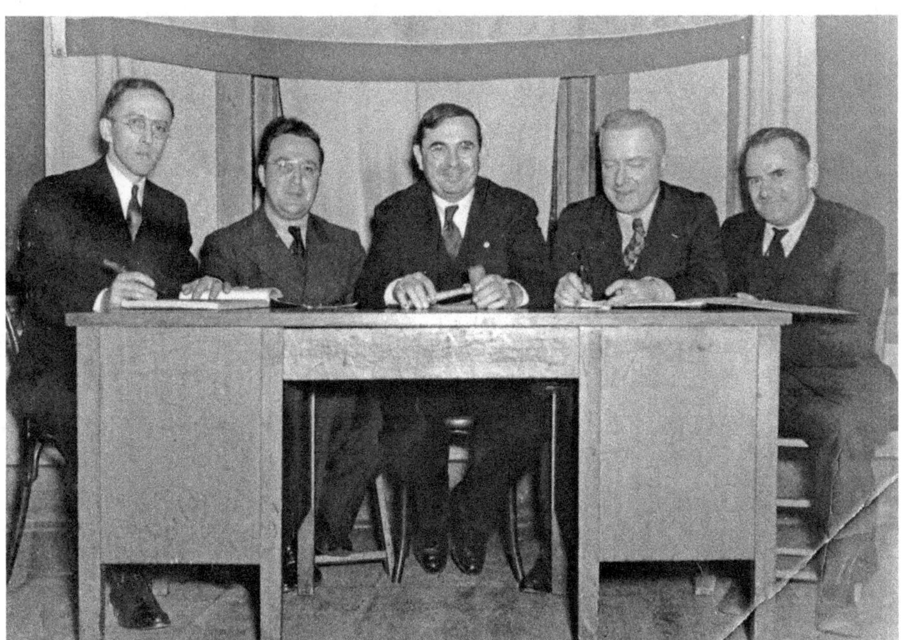

Brunswick Textile Union leaders. *Center*: Edmond Lachance; *second from left*: Emile Bouchard. *Courtesy of Bob Bouchard.*

Brunswick was divided into fifteen AWS zones, eight in town and seven rural. Topsham had fourteen zones, seven in town and seven rural. Harpswell had three zones. Each zone had a leader and team of wardens. Two of Brunswick's air raid wardens were women: Mrs. Harold Nickerson and Mrs. Leon Spinney. Margaret Nickerson was forty-one, married with two grown daughters. Jean Spinney, thirty-three, was a lawyer's wife with three children.

Each town had its own air raid defense corps. Winfield Cooper, Calvin Dodge's future father-in-law, was chief air raid warden for Damariscotta and Newcastle. Cooper's deputy in Newcastle was Ralph Sprague Sr., thirty-nine, a married truck driver with seven children. Calvin remembered Sprague going door to door to make sure residents were obeying the dim-out rules and knew what they were supposed to do in case of an air raid.[202] Nathaniel Grover, forty-three, was chief air raid warden for Boothbay Harbor. He was a married store clerk with one young son. His deputies were Harland West, thirty-nine, a local merchant, and shoemaker W. Maxfield Forbes, fifty-one. In April 1942, eighteen women from Boothbay, Boothbay Harbor and Southport completed air warden classes taught by Women's Division chair Angie Dodge.[203] Nine more completed her classes in South Jefferson and North Whitefield. In Wiscasset, Roy Marston, fifty-two, was chief air raid warden with a corps of twenty-five wardens, men and women.[204] Marston was a married pharmacist and owner of the local drugstore. Wiscasset's AWS classes were held in the Red Brick Schoolhouse in February and March 1942.

The Bath AWS was expertly staffed. Ralph Bragg, fifty-two, chief air raid warden, was a district manager at Central Maine Power with two draft-age sons. Given the presence of BIW, it was essential that the Bath Report Center be manned and open twenty-four hours a day, seven days a week. Ralph's wife, Dorothy, forty-eight, was head of the telephone operators and staff manager. Rupert Irvine, forty-two, a New England Telephone & Telegraph Co. manager, and William Ballou, fifty-two, an engineer at BIW with one son in the navy, mapped and charted any incidents. The fire, police, water and highway departments helped man the center. Air raid shelters were established at Sears, Roebuck & Co. on Center Street, the Central Maine Power office, USO Hall and ration board headquarters. Staffs at all stores and hotels were instructed in air raid procedures, with records kept to ensure all personnel were trained. Reverend Louis Dole, the Swedenborgian minister in town, was an air raid warden. Other immediate defense actions in Bath included closing the Bath city dump at 5:00 p.m. so that the flames

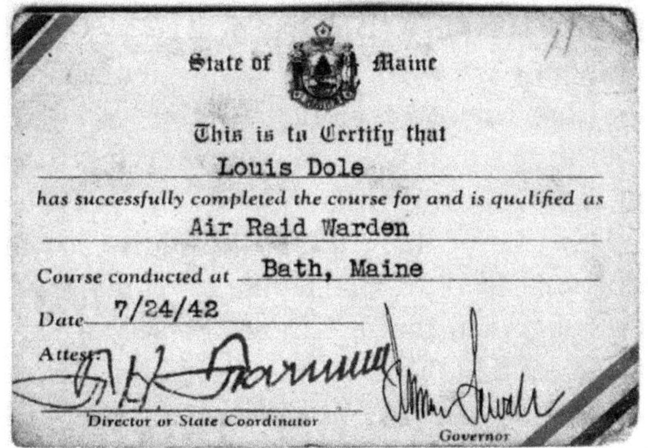

State of Maine

This is to Certify that

Louis Dole

has successfully completed the course for and is qualified as

Air Raid Warden

Course conducted at Bath, Maine

Date 7/24/42

Attest:

Director or State Coordinator

Governor

Left: Reverend Louis Dole's air raid warden card, July 24, 1942. *Courtesy of the Woofenden family.*

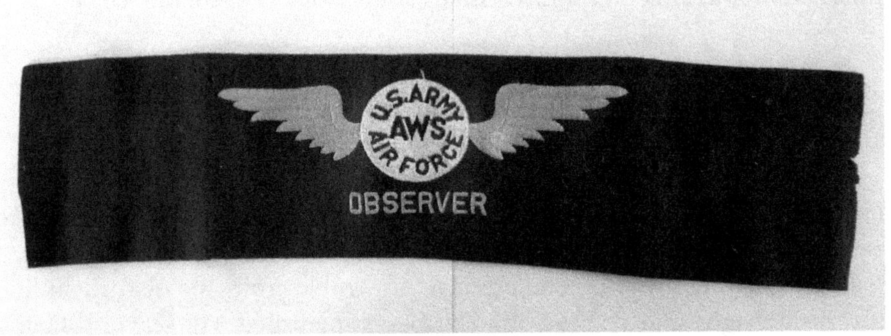

Below: AWS armband belonging to Eleanor Wilson, a sixteen-year-old plane spotter, 1942. *Harpswell Historical Society.*

could not be spotted by enemy planes (an argument staff used to get a better incinerator). The week after Pearl Harbor, New England Telephone & Telegraph installed six phones at Bath City Hall for civilian defense and additional phones at the American Legion Armory for military and civilian defense use.[205]

Southport's chief air raid warden was machine shop owner Cecil Pierce.[206] His deputies included Roscoe Rand, a thirty-four-year-old contractor; Albert Seavey, fifty-one, a married father of two who took care of summer residents' properties; John Swett, sixty-six, a fisherman with seven children ages two to seventeen; Ralph Gray, forty-four, a sea captain with a wife and two daughters; Cliff Buck, forty-one, a married schoolteacher with two children; Douglas Pinkham, thirty-five, a fisherman living with his wife, daughter, in-laws and a lodger; and Edgar Huskins, a fifty-one-year-old lobster dealer. The Huskins were immigrants from Nova Scotia whose son was born in Southport and would soon be draft-eligible.

Despite the Nazi U-boat offensive, the United States government never imposed national blackouts. Cargo ships hugged the coast from

Newfoundland to Florida, going into safe harbors at night whenever possible, but lights from the shore made them easy targets for enemy submarines. Men were dying, but businesses from Maine to Florida fought proposals by the military and federal government to require dim-outs, crying that their businesses would be ruined. For a while, business, money and fears of political backlash won out over the needs of the war effort. Eminent naval historian and witness Samuel Morison called the U.S. failure to require that coastal communities dim out their lights in the first three months of the Nazi U-boat offensive "one of the most reprehensible failures of the war.... Ships were sunk and seamen drowned in order that the citizenry might enjoy business and pleasure as usual."[207] In late April 1942, dim-out regulations finally went into effect for a three-mile radius along the Atlantic coast.

Drills and Dim-outs

The state OCD sent a telegram to local town coordinators with immediate measures to be enforced. All lights on the seaward side of highways had to be extinguished or screened. All lights visible from the sea, including advertising signs and displays, had to be extinguished. All seaward-facing windows had to be blacked out.[208]

The OCD telegram reprinted in newspapers across the country gave the following instructions:

1. Keep cool. Know your air raid warnings and wait for official information before taking action.
2. Stay home. If you're not at home, stay under cover and off the streets. Keep buckets filled with water for the fire department if needed. Choose one family member to be air raid warden, someone who will remember all the rules and what to do—"Mother makes best."
3. Put out lights. Prepare one room in the strongest part of your house, the one with the least window glass. Put food, water, a sturdy table, mattresses, chairs, toilet facilities, paper and a screen there. Put in a few magazines, playing cards and a portable radio if you have one. Don't forget eyeglasses and dentures.
4. If bombs start to fall near you, lie down. A mattress under a strong table combines comfort with safety.

WHAT TO DO IN AN AIR RAID

Official—by the U. S. Office of Civilian Defense

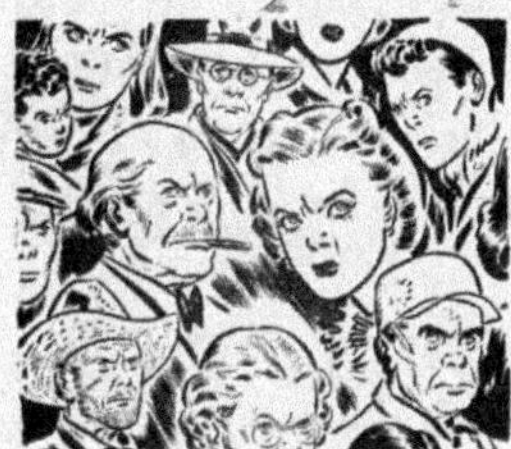

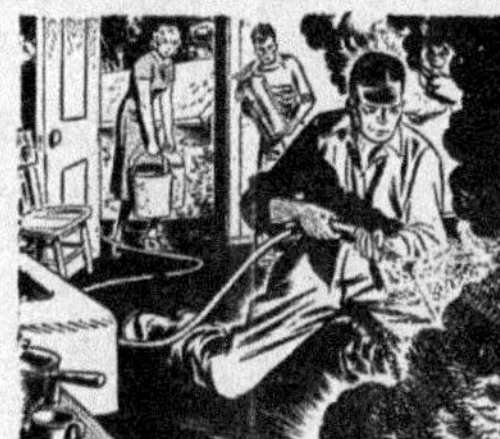

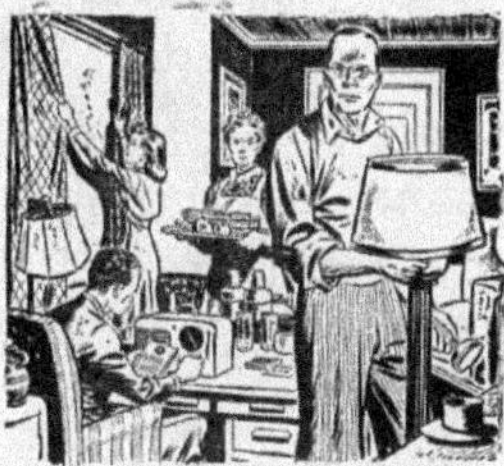

1. KEEP COOL

Above all, keep cool. Don't lose your head.

Do not crowd the streets, avoid chaos, prevent disorder and havoc.

You can fool the enemy. It is easy. If planes come over, stay where you are. Don't phone unnecessarily. The chance you will be hit is small. It is part of the risk we must take to win this war.

Until an alarm, go about your usual business and recreation in the ordinary way.

Think *twice* before you do anything. Don't believe rumors—spreading false rumors is part of the enemy's technique. Don't let him take you in.

Know your air-raid warning. In general, it is short blasts or rising and falling pitch, on whistles or horns. The "all clear" is a steady tone for 2 minutes. *Watch this paper for description of the local signal.* (This is subject to change.)

Await *official* information before taking any action. When the Air Raid Warden comes to your home, do what he tells you. He is for your protection. He is your friend.

He will help you do your part to whip the enemy.

We can do it. We *will* do it, if we stay calm and cool and strong and alert.

2. STAY HOME

The safest place in an air raid is at home.

If you are away from home, get under cover in the nearest shelter. Avoid crowded places. Stay off the streets.

The enemy wants you to run out into the streets, create a mob, start a panic. *Don't do it!*

If incendiary bombs fall, play a *spray* from a garden hose (never a splash or stream) of water on the bomb. Switch to a stream to put out any fire started by the bomb. Switch back to a spray for the bomb. The bomb will burn for about 15 minutes if left alone, only about 2 minutes under a fine water spray. *A jet splash, stream or bucket of water will make it explode.*

Under raid conditions, keep a bathtub and buckets full of water for the use of the fire department in case water mains are broken.

If you have a soda-and-acid extinguisher (the kind you turn upside down), use it with your finger over the nozzle to make a spray. Don't use the chemical kind (small cylinders of liquid) on bombs. It is all right for ordinary fires.

But above all, keep cool, stay home.

Choose one member of the family to be the home air-raid warden—who will remember all the rules and what to do. Mother makes the best.

3. PUT OUT LIGHTS

Whether or not black-out is ordered, don't show more light than is necessary. If planes come over, put out or cover all lights at once—don't wait for the black-out order. The light that can't be seen will never guide a Jap. Remember a candle light may be seen for miles from the air.

If you have portieres, overdrapes, or curtains, arrange a double thickness over your windows. Blankets will do. If you have heavy black paper, paste it on your windows. Don't crowd or stampede stores to get it, however. You probably have everything you need at home. Be ingenious—improvise.

Should you get an air-raid warning, remember to shut off gas stoves, gas furnaces, and gas pilot lights on both. Bomb explosions may blow them out from blast effect. Gas that collects may be explosive later.

Prepare one room, the one with the least window glass, in the strongest part of your house, for a refuge room. Put food and drinking water in it. Put a sturdy table in it. Put mattresses and chairs in it. Take a magazine or two and a deck of cards into it. Take things like eyeglasses and dentures with you when you go into it. Take toilet facilities, paper, a screen. If you have a portable radio, take that too. Above all, keep calm. *Stay at home. Put out lights.*

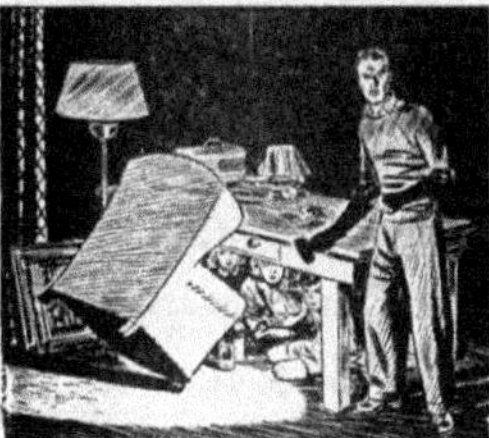

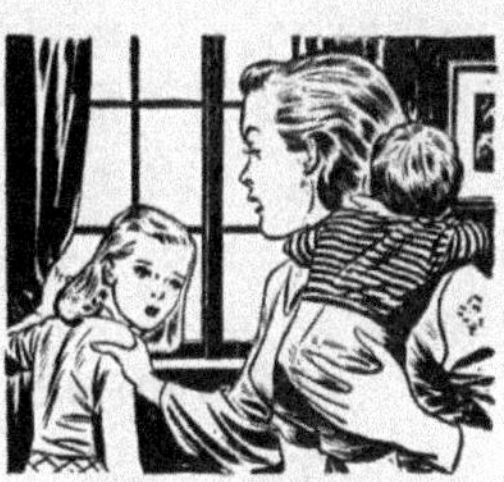

4. LIE DOWN

If bombs start to fall near you, lie down. You will feel the blast least that way, escape fragments or splinters.

The safest place is under a good stout table—the stronger the legs the better.

A mattress under a table combines comfort with safety.

The enemy may use explosive bombs or incendiary bombs, or both. If incendiaries are used, it's more important to deal with them than to be safe from blast. So defeat the incendiary with a *spray* (never a splash or stream) of water, then go back to safety under a table in a refuge room.

Most raids will likely be over *in your immediate neighborhood* in a short time. However, stay under cover till the "all clear" is sounded.

Know your raid alarms. Know the "all clear". Official news of these will come to you from your Air Raid Warden. Don't believe rumors. Watch this paper for air raid alarm description. Ask the warden when he comes.

Should your house be hit, keep cool. Answer tappings from rescue crews if you are trapped. (You most likely won't be either hit or trapped, but if you are, you can depend on rescue squads to go after you). Again—keep cool, and wait. Don't yell after you hear them coming to you, unless they tell you to. *Keep cool!*

Just keeping cool hurts the enemy more than anything else you can do. *Keep calm. Stay at home. Put out lights. Lie down.*

5. STAY AWAY FROM WINDOWS

Glass shatters easily, so stay away from windows.

Don't go to windows and look out, in an air raid. It is a dangerous thing, and helps the enemy. The Air Raid Warden is out there watching for you. Again we say, get off the streets if planes come over.

At night, there is danger of being caught in blast from explosives.

Antiaircraft fire means falling shrapnel. You are safe from it indoors, away from windows. It's more important to shell a plane than it is to see it from a window.

Stay in your refuge room, away from windows. That is the safest place. Go there at the first alarm; stay there until the "all clear".

Above all, *keep calm. Stay home. Put out lights. Lie down. Stay away from windows.* Do not say we are repeating; we would rather repeat until we bore you than have you forget.

You can do all those things without any special equipment other than what you have now in your home.

You can help lick the Japs, with your bare hands, if you will do just those few, simple things.

Be a good fellow and follow instructions and keep well. Do not be a wise guy and get hurt.

6. YOU CAN HELP

Strong, capable, calm people are needed to man the volunteer services. If you want to help, there are lots of opportunities.

If you know first aid, and have a certificate, there is an immediate job for you. If you are a veteran, or a former volunteer or regular fireman, or policeman, there is work for you. If you have no special skills but are strong and husky, there is a job for you in rescue squads, road-repair units, or demolition and clearance squads. If you have and can drive a car, you may be needed for drivers' corps. Older Boy and Girl Scouts over 15 can help as messengers. Both men and women are needed.

Here's how to get started:

If there's a Civilian Defense Volunteer Office in your community, call there and ask where to report. If not, call your local Defense Council or Committee, or the Chamber of Commerce. Phone and ask where to report, rather than going in person.

There are people needed for—

Air Raid Wardens (men and women).
Auxiliary Firemen (men).
Auxiliary Police (men and women).
Fire Watchers (men and women).
Nurses' Aides (trained women).
Emergency Medical Forces (men and women with Red Cross First Aid Certificates).
Rescue Squads (men).
Road Repair Units (strong, husky men).
Demolition and Clearance Squads (strong, husky men).
Electrical Repair units (trained electricians).
Decontamination Squads (strong men and women).
Emergency Food and Housing Units (women who can cook and serve).

Above all, *keep cool. Stay home. Put out lights. Lie down. Stay away from windows. You can help!*

U. S. OFFICE OF CIVILIAN DEFENSE, Fiorello H. LaGuardia, Director. Washington, D. C.

"What to Do in an Air Raid" poster, U.S. Office of Civilian Defense, Washington, D.C., 1941. *Northwestern University Library, images.northwestern.edu.*

5. Stay away from windows.
6. You can help. Volunteer for the war effort, however you can.[209]

Cars had to be driven slowly with the absolute minimum light required. Headlights had to be covered, leaving only a one- by three-inch light. They could be painted, covered with black tape or covered with black cloth, whatever worked.[210] When an emergency blackout signal was sounded, drivers were supposed to pull over to the side of the road, turn off their car lights and distinguish any cigarettes. Street and highway signs were removed entirely.

The first blackout test in Boothbay, Boothbay Harbor and Southport was held on April 27, 1942. All wardens and auxiliary police were present and ready when the yellow "get ready" signal came through. The blue signal followed fifteen minutes later and then the red signal, when the whole area immediately blacked out. At 9:30 p.m., the white signal confirmed the all-clear. Boothbay's test was deemed successful, with all lights out in one minute, but there were a few issues with cars not stopping.

Storekeepers were told that they had to be ready to black out their shops even if they were full of customers. Customers could not be turned out onto the street. They must remain in the store during the blackout. Merchants were warned that they shouldn't be surprised if some merchandise disappeared into the dark.[211]

Brunswick got a bit of excitement the first week in May 1942. A Venture bomber of the Royal Canadian Air Force Atlantic Ferry Command landed with a crew of five at the municipal airport after circling low just after the height of a dramatic spring thunderstorm. A crowd of about one hundred people quickly gathered to see what was going on. The pilot had lost his way in the electrical storm on a trip from Presque Isle, Maine, to Montreal. When the crew climbed out of the plane, their first question was, "Where are we?" Their second question, after being told they were in Brunswick, was, "Where's that?" The plane batteries were low, and they only had an hour's worth of fuel left. The captain asked the airport's chief pilot, Richard Norcross, if they had any gasoline available. When he replied, "Eighty-octane gas," the captain said wryly, "We could put that in our cigarette lighters." Airport staff ran around town collecting storage batteries to get the required twenty-four volts to start the motors again. After much difficulty, the pilot got the motors started just as another storm came through. The plane was finally able to take off around 6:30 p.m., headed back to Bangor for more gas before they could set out for Montreal again.[212]

There were several pre-announced defense mobilizations, as they were called, during May and June 1942. Mobilizations were simulations that required citizens to act as if an invasion or attack was underway. They included school evacuations, business closings and civilian defense workers reporting to their assigned emergency stations.

Surprise blackout tests began in July, including one throughout coastal Maine on July 23. Lincoln County coordinator Leon Dodge congratulated everyone after the test found all units ready.[213] Brunswick also passed, with only two lights spotted on Maine Street.[214]

It was important that everyone know how to identify a civilian defense volunteer so they would know whose directions to follow in case of emergency. Since creating an array of uniforms for all the different areas of responsibility would have used up valuable resources needed elsewhere, the OCD created a family of red, white and blue symbols, one for each of the twenty-six homefront civilian defense corps.[215] The symbols were used on armbands and badges and appeared on posters placed in prominent locations and reprinted in local newspapers.[216] There were glitches in the production and delivery of the armbands to midcoast Maine, but eventually all air raid wardens received one. In July, all civilian defense workers were fingerprinted, a new security measure to guard against enemy infiltration and assist in identifying people in case of emergency. It was also another step toward making homefront volunteers feel they had "enlisted."

Dim-out regulations tightened in the fall of 1942. The area was expanded to fifteen miles inland to reduce any sky glow on the coast. Stores, hotels, restaurants and theaters were allowed no more than a fifteen-watt light for each linear foot of show or display window. All exterior lights had to be shut off or dimmed so they couldn't be seen from the air or the sea. Violators were warned once and, if a second violation occurred, prosecuted. All window shades had to be pulled down at least three-quarters of the length of the window thirty minutes before sundown every night. Each week, newspapers published what that time would be for the upcoming week.

The last pre-announced region-wide mobilization took place on December 21, 1942, the second time that month that local temperatures dropped to twenty degrees below zero. Army "umpires" from Boston, on hand to assess the accuracy, effectiveness and efficiency of responses, planned over twenty "incidents."[217] Local businesses, including Senter's and Brunswick Savings Institution, tested their own emergency drills as part of the exercise. The

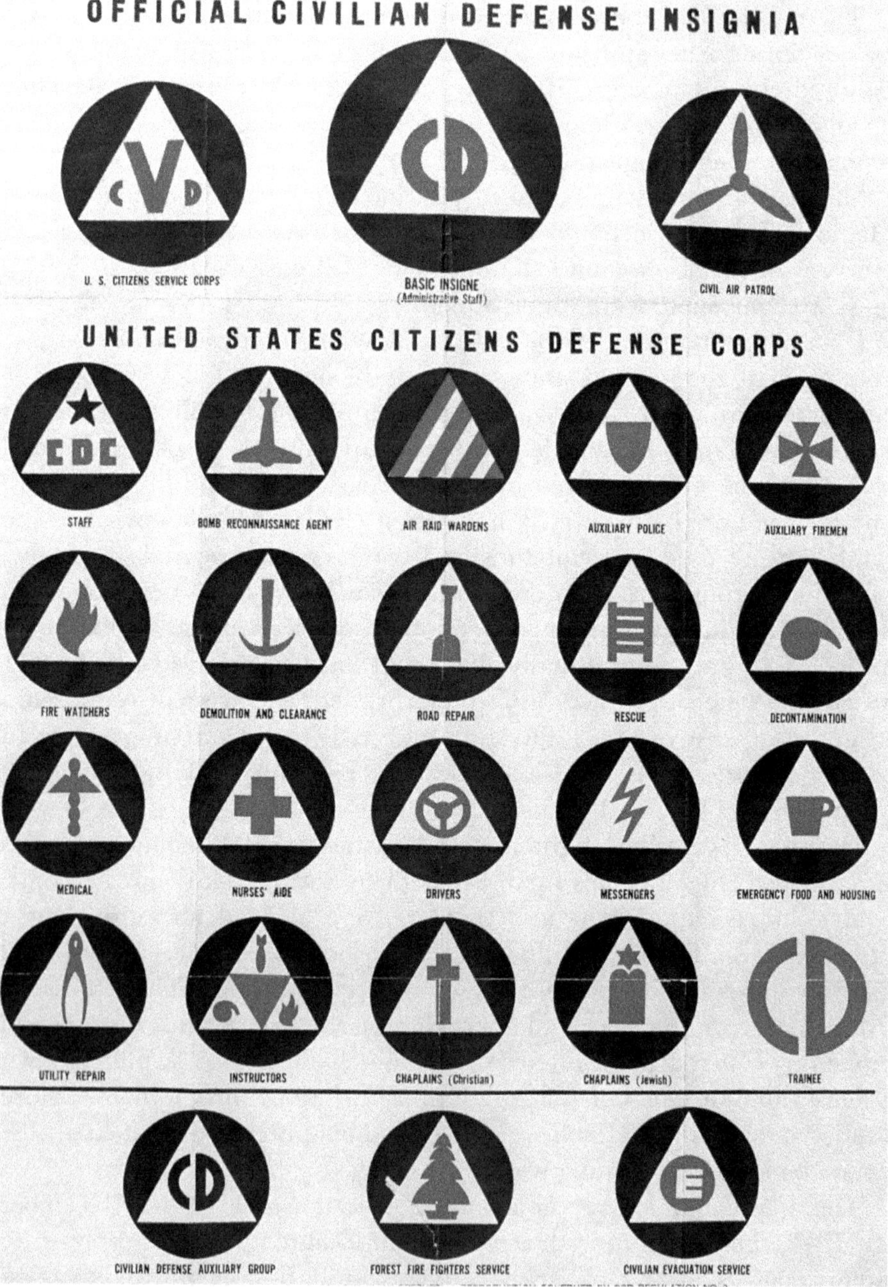

"Official Civilian Defense Insignia" poster, Office of Civilian Defense, Washington, D.C., 1941. *Northwestern University Library, images.northwestern.edu.*

bank was proud that all books, records and securities were stored in pre-assigned safe places within one minute and fifty seconds after the alarm. Senter's left doors open so people on the street could come in and take refuge in the store basement with employees. The test was a success, and the umpires gave high marks.[218]

Dim-outs affected all parts of community life. School dances had to be held in the afternoon or somewhere that could be completely blacked out. High school graduations were changed to an earlier time of day so as not to conflict with dim-out requirements. Fall school bonfires were banned. Stores couldn't light their windows in winter, even though it was dark by 4:00 p.m. There were no outdoor Christmas lights on trees or in windows from 1942 through 1944.

Not everyone was overwhelmed with patriotism and the desire to do their duty. There were robberies and break-ins. Police warned stores to be on guard and especially guard cash registers during dim-out periods. Blackouts and dim-outs were nerve-wracking for everyone.

There were rumors everywhere about suspected spy activity. Newspapers and posters warned against giving information to strangers. After Pearl Harbor, a rumor went around Bath that glass had been found in Japanese packed crabmeat containers with false Russian labels saying, "Product of Kamchatken, USSR."[219] The police proved it to be a hoax. As Geraldine Coombs of Bath remembered, "It was an exciting time, but not in a good way."[220]

On July 21, 1942, a stranger came into the Brunswick selectmen's office and began asking questions about the town's water supply. Chief air raid warden Thomas McMahon said the man claimed to be an army representative but couldn't produce any credentials. McMahon didn't give him any information. At the Brunswick & Topsham Water District, Theodore E. Stimpson was questioned by the same man but also found him suspicious, so he denied the stranger's request to take photographs of the waterworks. McMahon reported the incident to the state intelligence office, but the man disappeared before he could be questioned further.[221] In Southport, a foreign-born district nurse was reported because she refused to obey the dim-out rules, and wardens reported shades pulled up or down in varying degrees at various times. The nurse was suspected of signaling someone. At the same time, a rumor of a submarine in the Sheepscot River was going around. The latter proved to be false, and shortly thereafter, the nurse was reassigned away from the coast.[222] In December 1942, the OCD notified Mainers on how to report suspicious activity. People were told to notify their chief air raid warden, the police or the sheriff. Newspapers published notices that said, "REPORT ESPIONAGE-SABOTAGE-SUBVERSIVE ACTIVITIES AT ONCE to F.B.I. Augusta 280 (collect)."

THE AIR RAID WARNING SERVICE

The AWS built official observation posts on the highest point in each area with an unobstructed view. Where the view was over water, as it was in many places on the midcoast, the observation post could be just a small shed. Elsewhere, they were small buildings on very tall legs. Maine's observation posts were under the supervision of the U.S. Army First Fighter Command in Boston, which inspected the posts periodically. Wiscasset had an observation tower on Langdon Mountain, staffed by volunteers trained by the Bradford-Sortwell-Wright Post 54 of the American Legion. Boothbay had observation towers on Fisher's Hill, the Crow's Nest on Crest Avenue in Sprucewold and Little River in East Boothbay.[223] Southport had a post in the parking lot of town hall.[224] Damariscotta had its post on School Street.[225] The Brunswick Air Defense region had towers on Maquoit Road, Thomas Point, Harpswell Neck, Bailey Island and Cundy's Harbor.

AWS posts were manned by spotters, usually working in pairs, taking two- to four-hour shifts. Anyone from high school age up could be a spotter. An article recruiting volunteers in Brunswick reassured that women would only be scheduled for daytime duty, and shifts could be scheduled around child care and mealtimes.[226] Finding enough volunteers to staff the posts was an ongoing challenge. When twenty-four-hour staffing became difficult, twelve- and thirteen-year-olds were recruited and trained to do a few shifts after school.

Spotters were given decks of cards with pictures of all Allied and Axis aircraft to study and memorize. Most observation posts also had posters illustrating all the planes. The spotter's job was to record every plane they saw and report it to the nearest army filter center using a designated telephone. The army would verify the identity of the plane and alert the appropriate civilian defense center. After placing the call, the spotter filled out a form with the number, type (single- or multi-engine), altitude (very low, low, etc.) and direction of the plane, its distance from the post and whether it was seen or heard.[227]

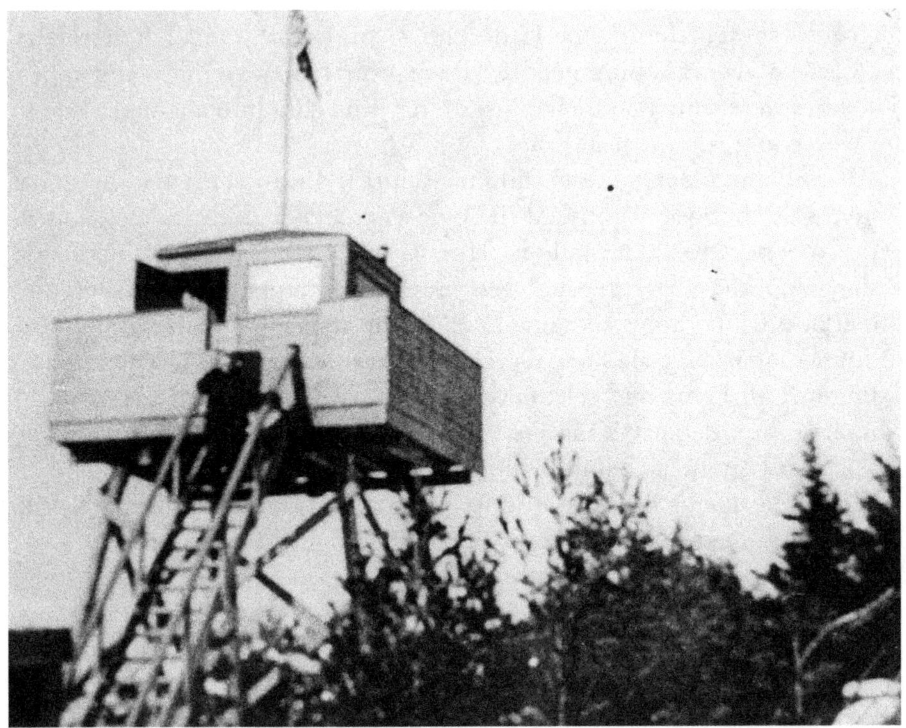

Wiscasset AWS observation tower, 1942. *Courtesy of Phil DeVece from Marion Abbott.*

Everyone kept an eye on the sky. Children found it exciting. Marie DeCosta Spofford, who was ten at the time, remembered that there was an observation post on her family's lawn on Dover Road in Boothbay. Her mother would bring the plane spotters water, newspapers and matches to light their woodstove. Sometimes she found them drinking something other than water and feared they might set the post on fire rather than the woodstove.[228]

In addition to wardens and spotters, each town had a group of boys trained as AWS messengers who would carry messages from the observation post to the nearest civilian defense station. Brunswick had about fifty boys from the Brunswick Junior Police, Boy Scouts and high school. In Boothbay, the Boy Scouts provided the messengers. They included Peter Granger, twelve; John Arsenault Jr., twelve; James Granger, sixteen; Morton Hansen, thirteen; Barry Lewis, ten; and James Murray, sixteen.[229] There were designated stations throughout town where they would bring their messages, including the Littles' house on West Street, Tilton's Dairy on Eastern Avenue, Simmons & Harrington Funeral Home and more. The boys were timed on their runs, so they turned it into a competition to see who could run the fastest.[230]

Air raid and blackout tests continued into 1943. In February, the signal system was changed slightly. At the blue signal, civilian defense personnel were to report to their stations. Homes had to black out immediately. Pedestrians and drivers could continue traveling to their destinations. Street and traffic lights remained on. At the red signal, pedestrians were to immediately take shelter. All vehicular traffic stopped. Drivers had to extinguish all lights and seek cover. The all-clear remained the same. A March test was deemed a success except for radio stations not reporting the all-clear fast enough.[231] Some problems persisted, including the inability to differentiate signals if a fire or ambulance alarm occurred during a drill. People continued to report that they couldn't hear the signals.

A major daylight mobilization held on the evening of May 2, 1943, included jeeps full of armed Maine National Guard and federal troops pretending to be invaders. The purpose was to see if information about enemy ground action could be transmitted fast enough to enable military and civilian defense officers to take effective action. The test was successful. Brunswick received commendations from the area civilian defense coordinator. The drill also went well in Boothbay and Boothbay Harbor. People reported seeing jeeps filled with "enemy troops" every step of their journey, which was exactly what organizers wanted to see.[232] They still had not solved the problem of an effective audible all-clear signal, so it was changed yet again. Instead of relying on whistles and radio stations to communicate the all-clear, it would now be one continuous blast for up to ten seconds sounded by the fire alarm, whistles and sirens.

New warnings about the threat of Nazi bombings appeared in local newspapers the week of April 8, along with requests for more spotters. The state OCD sent Brunswick chief air raid warden Malcolm Morrell a message that senior army officials were convinced that the Nazis were going to bomb the East Coast.[233]

The OCD held rallies at local theaters throughout the war to inspire continued commitment to the work ahead. Movies and film clips of American military action overseas and sometimes a captured Nazi propaganda film were shown. Newsreels and films like these showed the reality of the war in a way no newspaper or magazine photograph could convey. More than 1,100 people came to the rally at the Strand

Theater in Boothbay after the May 2, 1943 mobilization, but the speaker, Lieutenant Roger B. Withington, USAAF, Portland Fifth Area AWS, criticized the audience, pointing out that Boothbay-area observation posts were often only staffed for a few hours a week, demonstrating "increasing indifference to the protection of our coastline." He warned that the newly opened BNAS was the number-one target on the coast and urged people to man the observation posts, saying that "indifference is Hitler's best friend."[234]

The 115 soldiers in the meteorology unit at Bowdoin held combat maneuvers in late August 1943. They staged a commando attack in an area ranging from the campus down Harpswell Road to Mere Point using blank ammunition, tear gas and smoke bombs. Neighbors were notified in advance and reassured that the "attack" would not trespass on private property.[235] It must have been thrilling and frightening to watch.

By fall 1943, many volunteer plane spotters had enlisted; gone to work at a shipyard or the base; or left to spend more time taking care of their families. During the year and a half that the observation posts were open, there had not been any attacks or even near-attacks. Fewer air raid drills were held. Posts began to close. On October 7, Emerson Zeitler, forty-four, chief air raid observer in Brunswick, got a call from the regional director to close the post immediately and only open it on Wednesday afternoons. Zeitler padlocked the door for the first time since the post was opened in April 1942. It had operated twenty-four hours a day every day since then, with all 6:00 a.m. to 3:00 p.m. shifts filled by women.[236] Over the next two weeks, the army held ceremonies to award plane spotters with wings. Seventy-nine men and forty-nine women had worked as observers in Brunswick.[237] On November 1, 1942, the War Department officially ended the dim-out regulations but kept in place rules mandating blackout curtains, headlight covers and emergency supplies, just in case.[238] One *Brunswick Record* writer expressed popular feeling, saying, "Once again store display windows are gay with lights in the evening and the Town Hall clock understudies for the moon."[239] Blackout drills were finally discontinued in August 1944.[240]

Chapter 9

KEEP THE HOME FIRES BURNING

Police and fire departments were hit extremely hard by the draft. Older men and women took up the jobs left behind by men who joined the military. Volunteers were trained in first aid, incendiary bomb defense, emergency response and evacuation procedures. In case of an emergency like a bombing, these auxiliaries would be essential to manage the situation, help save lives and hold off panic. Boothbay Harbor, Southport, Damariscotta and Brunswick all had significant fires that tested their emergency response capabilities and created strong memories for those present.

Boothbay Harbor had two major fires during the war. The first started early Monday morning, April 27, 1942, in a back section of the Porter block on Commercial Street. Boothbay Harbor, East Boothbay and Southport fire departments responded, and a large crowd gathered to watch the blaze. Carbone's Fruit Store, Porter's Drugstore and a Pierce & Hartung building supplies store were all destroyed, but firefighters saved adjacent buildings housing a candy store, liquor store and the post office. The second and much larger fire happened on January 7, 1945, in frigid temperatures and eight inches of snow. It started in the bowling alley owned by Charles Rowe and Leslie Marr. The heat ignited an oil storage tank, which then exploded, setting the *Boothbay Register* building ablaze. The fire then jumped to Poole's Market and the Red Dragon Gift Shop across the street. Church bells from Our Lady Queen of Peace Catholic Church across the harbor sounded the alarm when the fire alarm stopped working in the freezing cold. Five fire departments battled the fire for hours, keeping it away from nearby houses.

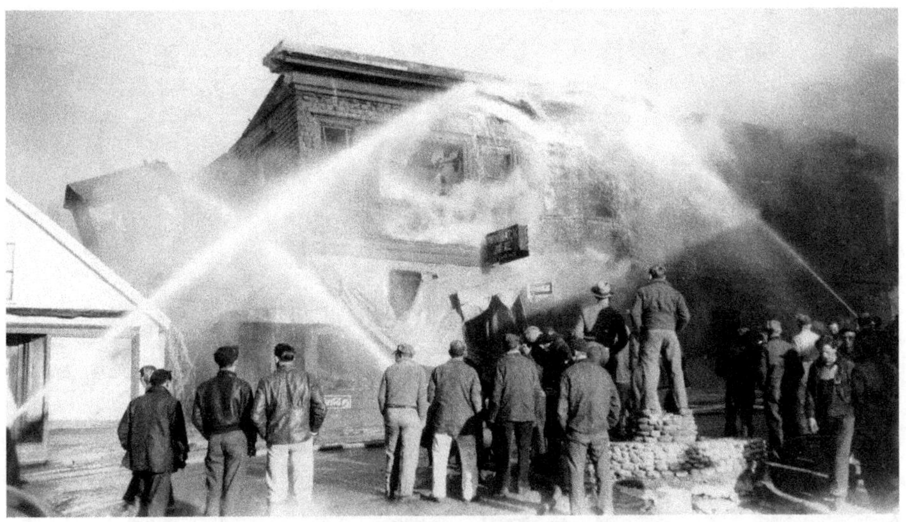

Commercial Street fire, Boothbay, January 1945. *Boothbay Region Historical Society.*

The Campbell Sail Loft, Harris Shop, Scott's boatyard and twenty-seven boats were lost, but the yacht club and a six-family apartment building nearby were saved.[241] No one was injured in either fire.

In Southport, fire was spotted at 3:00 a.m. on April 13, 1943, at the Newagen Inn, a local landmark and popular hotel patronized by the rich and famous. It started in the annex but quickly encompassed the main hotel, built in 1816.[242] By the time firefighters arrived, the four-story building had burned to the ground. Fisherman Leland Snowman's description captures the rumors that surrounded both the fire and its aftermath:

> *The fire had been set, that was obvious, and many rumors started to circulate, even to the extent that the Germans had done it to signal their offshore fleet. The damage was valued at over $250,000. It was quite a feat during the war to get anything* [built] *due to the rationing, so when it was announced that the Inn would be rebuilt, the rumors really started to fly around the island. A crew of forty men worked day and night and the Inn was rebuilt in no time.*[243]

The cause of the fire was never determined.[244]

St. John's School, a Catholic elementary school in Brunswick, was targeted twice by arsonists or perhaps just unlucky teenagers. Around 9:00 p.m. on

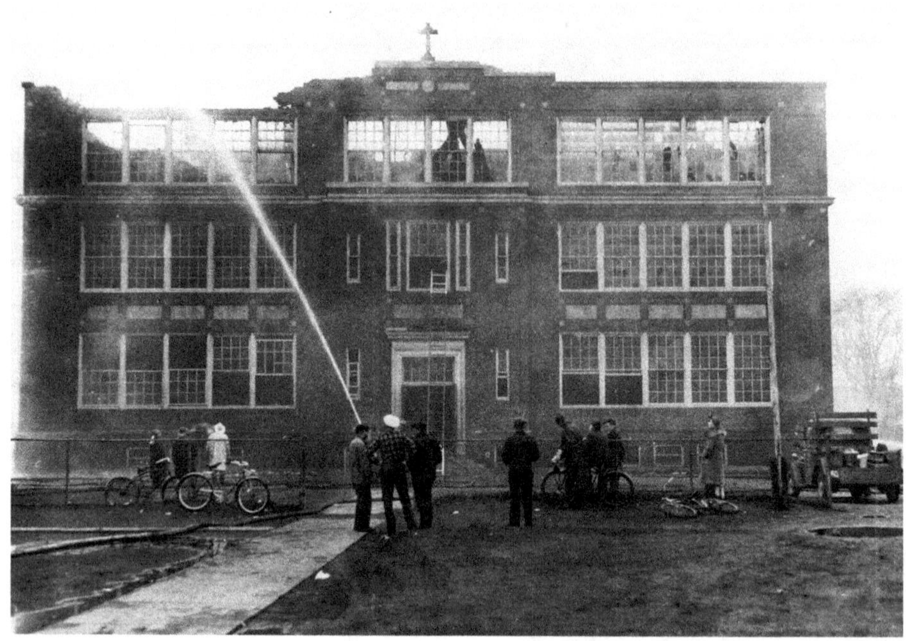

St. John's Catholic School after fire, Brunswick, 1943. *Pejepscot Historical Society*.

Sunday, May 31, 1942, nuns in the nearby convent saw a fire in the school and someone moving about with a flashlight. The church sexton extinguished the fire before any serious damage occurred. A drum of varnish had been poured over crumpled paper on the floor by an arsonist who presumably mistook it for kerosene. Another fire set on the second floor fizzled with the match still stuck in the varnish. The arsonist escaped.[245] At 11:45 p.m. on Thursday, May 6, 1943, another fire started, this time in the school basement. Philippe Gamache, fifty-four, a volunteer firefighter who worked at the convent and lived nearby with his wife and two sons, was returning home from another fire, saw the blaze and raised the alarm. The Brunswick Fire Department and a fire truck from BNAS responded immediately, but the fire quickly raged through the ventilation system in the central part of the building on all three floors. The intense heat kept firefighters at bay, and it was early Friday morning before the fire was contained. The building was destroyed, with nothing but four brick walls still standing. The damage was estimated at around $175,000. A fifteen-year-old Brunswick boy was apprehended, admitted his guilt and said he had sneaked into the school basement to smoke. He accidentally dropped a match or cigarette that ignited nearby cans of varnish, disinfectant and oil. The boy was arrested, taken to court by the police chief, convicted and sent to the State School for Boys.[246] Had he set the first fire? We'll never know.

Brunswick was faced with the immediate problem of what to do with the 750 students attending the school. Brunswick schools were already overflowing with children of local families, war workers and servicemen. Donations to help fund repairs started arriving the day after the fire. Reverend William J. Dauphin, the pastor of St. John's, launched a fundraising campaign two days later, intending to solicit only parishioners, but the Brunswick community was generous, and many others contributed as well. Because of wartime shortages of materials and manpower (and without the connections of the Newagen Inn), the new school was built with only two floors.

The fire whistle began to blow in Damariscotta just after noon on July 19, 1943. Behind the large brick building on the corner of Main and Water Streets, Weeks-Waltz Garage was on fire. The blaze quickly spread to the main building, which housed the *Lincoln County News* and local Office of Price Administration (OPA) offices. Army soldiers and volunteers,

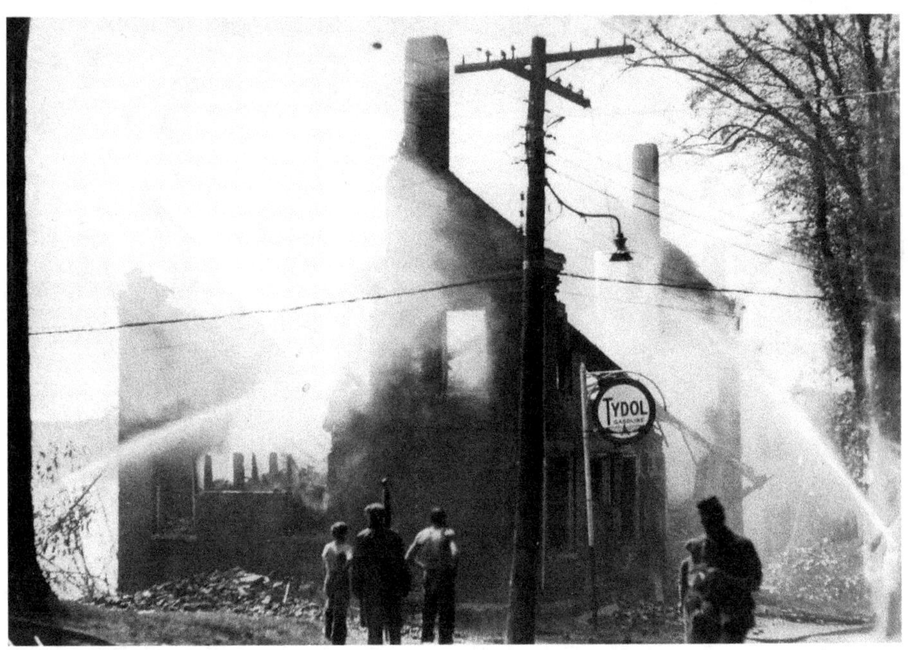

The *Lincoln County News* building burning in Damariscotta, July 1943. *Courtesy of Calvin and Marjorie Dodge.*

including several women, helped man the hoses with the Damariscotta Fire Department. Ten local fire departments came to assist. It was high tide in the Damariscotta River, so there was plenty of water to fight the fire, but not enough pressure to get it up to the steeple of the Baptist church, which had caught fire. A bucket brigade on the church roof managed to contain the fire to the belfry.[247] Six buildings were lost and seven additional buildings seriously damaged, including the Fiske House. Marjorie Dodge, a little girl away at camp in Waldoboro, remembered being frightened when a counselor reported that "Damariscotta was on fire!" She was reassured after her father called to say that everything was OK and that he'd come and pick her up, since her mother was working at BIW. The newspaper went to print in Bath that week and then moved to the *Waldoboro Press* offices, where the staff remained until their new offices were ready in late January 1944.[248]

Chapter 10

ANGELS OF MERCY

The Red Cross and Citizens Service Corps

The Red Cross

The Red Cross was the backbone of non-military civilian defense efforts. It worked closely with the OCD to train volunteers and organize services. Red Cross volunteers produced emergency supplies for war victims, collected scrap and showed people how to plant victory gardens. They rolled bandages, gathered and distributed books and magazines and made clothing for servicemen and refugees overseas. The Red Cross also ran public health programs, including first aid, home nutrition, basic nursing training and vaccination clinics. Hundreds of thousands of American women, in addition to caring for their families and working a war production or civilian defense job, volunteered for the Red Cross. Over 7.9 million American women joined the Red Cross during World War II, 30,000 of them paid employees.[249]

The Red Cross organized the first blood drives. It wasn't easy to get people comfortable with the idea of giving blood. A national marketing campaign was launched to encourage participation. The first blood drive in Brunswick was held in March 1942 at Brunswick Hospital. Prospective donors were reassured that the process was painless and they would be fine. People who didn't want to give blood were encouraged to donate money to help cover the costs of collecting blood for the new blood bank.[250] Part of the supply collected would remain in the area for local emergencies; the rest would be sent overseas. Only seven people donated blood the first time, four of whom

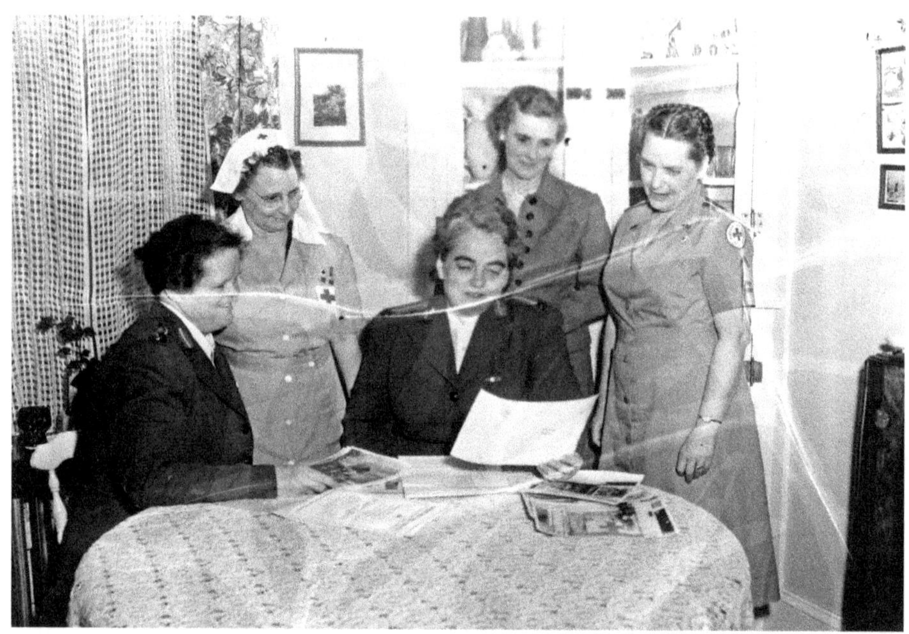

Group of Red Cross volunteers: Margaret Nickerson and Helen Campbell (*left to right, seated*), Susie Sylvester (*in a Red Cross uniform*) and Gertrude Dwyer (*center, standing*), plus one unidentified woman, 1942. *Pejepscot Historical Society.*

were ensigns from Bowdoin. The other three brave pioneers were Viola Tyler and Minnie Given, both military wives, and Donald Pletts, twenty, a doctor's son who would later join the navy. The Boothbay/Wiscasset/Damariscotta area did a little better, with eleven people donating at the September blood drive at Miles Hospital, five of whom were coast guardsmen.[251]

The Brunswick Red Cross was a very Bowdoin affair in December 1941. Morgan Cushing, forty-five, associate professor of economics, was the Brunswick-area Red Cross chairman. His wife, Amelia (called Amy),[252] forty-eight, was chairman of the canteen committee. The Cushings lived at 156 Park Row with their three teenagers. Their son Steven, eighteen, enlisted in the navy in 1942. Charles Burnett, sixty-seven, professor of philosophy and psychology, was the vice-chairman. Helen Varney was secretary. Helen was sixty-eight, single, proprietor of her late brother's jewelry store on Maine Street and a groundbreaking art teacher who had persuaded the superintendent of schools to include art in all grades of education in Brunswick. A teacher for over forty years by 1941, she was also an advisor and honorary member of the Bowdoin Masque and Gown

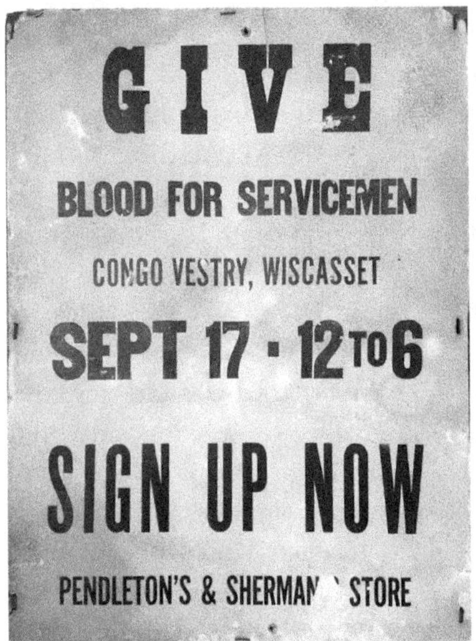

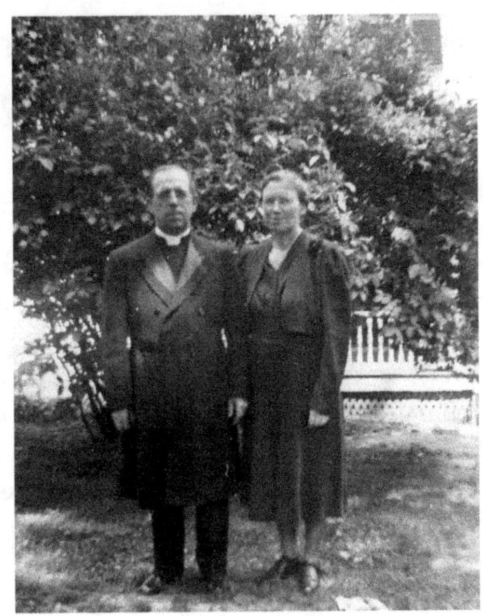

Left: Red Cross blood drive sign, Wiscasset, 1942. *Author's collection, gift of Dan Sortwell.*

Right: Anita and Reverend Louis Dole, 1941. *Courtesy of the Woofenden family.*

Society and taught art and crafts at BNAS.[253] Mary White, forty, mother of six and daughter of Rupert Baxter, Bowdoin class of 1894, was motor corps chairman. Dorothy Niven, forty-three, was vice-chair of the motor corps. Her husband, Paul, was Bowdoin class of 1916 and owner of the local newspaper. Edna Lusher, twenty-six, was head of volunteer services. She lived in the Joshua Chamberlain House with her husband, David, thirty, an instructor at the college. The only non-Bowdoin-affiliated members of the Brunswick Red Cross leadership team were Mabel Cummings, treasurer, a thirty-nine-year-old bank clerk, and Mabel Lovell, thirty-two, production chairman, wife of a marble cutter and mother of a two-year-old son.

The Bath Red Cross team drew leaders from across the city. Former Bath mayor Donald Small, thirty-six, was chairman. Small was from a prominent Bath family, a draftsman at BIW and a man committed to civic welfare.[254] Anita Dole, fifty-two, wife of the minister of the Swedenborgian church and mother of three, was production chairman. Anita devoted her life to serving the community through their church, the PTA, Girl Scouts and other civilian defense efforts. She was known for her beautiful soprano singing voice and her ability to help people with a "rare combination of spiritual insight, practical advice and personal interest."[255] In addition to being a church pastor, air raid warden and Red Cross volunteer, her husband, Reverend Louis Dole, was a chaplain in the Maine State Guard known for his "muscular Christianity." A former wrestling champion, he taught his troops the "gentle art of wrestling…[and through it] the finer art of spiritual wrestling."[256] Reverend Dole volunteered in numerous civilian defense efforts and became Red Cross chairman in 1944.[257]

Volunteering was tiring and hard work. Managing volunteers was even more so. The production chairman had to be someone who could manage people, processes and reports. She was responsible for making sure her Red Cross chapter kept pace with increasingly large production quotas for bandages, surgical dressings, socks, sweaters, robes and pajamas for hospital patients and more. The quotas given to each Red Cross district grew exponentially, and volunteers worked long hours to meet them. By April 1942, 127 Brunswick volunteers had worked just under one thousand hours to make 12,800 surgical dressings toward their quota of 20,000.[258] Each chapter bought its own materials with funds raised locally.

Each community had its own surgical dressings unit. The Bath unit worked in a room in the Elks building on Lambard Street. The Brunswick team was run by chairman Ruth Kirkland, forty-six, wife of a Bowdoin economics professor and mother of a near-draft-age son. Alma Drapeau, fifty-three, wife of a local pharmacist and mother of three adult children and two teenagers, was assistant chairman. Her two eldest sons were both officers in the navy reserves. These two women ran the unit from early 1942 until the end of the war. Their volunteers included Girl Scouts, high school students, seventh and eighth graders and Bowdoin students who worked in a room at 212 Maine Street near First National grocery store. In Topsham, the workplace was a second-floor room in the Topsham Library (the Whitten House) on Pleasant Street.[259] Harpswell, Freeport, Cundy's Harbor and Orr's Island all had their own surgical dressings units.

Marion Sortwell Warland, fifty-four, of Wiscasset, was production chairman for Lincoln County. Marion's family had deep roots in Wiscasset and were quietly generous philanthropists. She had a brother in the navy reserves, and her only child, Joan, was engaged to a navy officer (they married in 1943). Geneva Strout, fifty-two, a trained nurse and doctor's daughter, was the Lincoln County first aid and home nursing chairman. The Lincoln County Red Cross office was on the second floor of the Rundlett Block in Wiscasset. The lower floor of the Wiscasset Academy Building was used for production of surgical dressings, while the upper floor was used for first aid home nursing classes.[260] Damariscotta held Red Cross nursing classes in the Skidompha Library.[261] In Boothbay, the surgical dressings room was in the Congregational church vestry.[262]

The 1941 annual holiday fundraising campaign had just ended when Pearl Harbor was attacked. Fundraising immediately geared up again for the war effort. In two weeks, half the first Brunswick quota of $8,000 had been raised. Businesses, including F.W. Woolworth's and the Pejepscot Paper Company, contributed generously. BIW encouraged employees to donate, and their donations went to the town they lived in.[263] Dances, bridge and whist parties, collections at movie theaters and in schools, art sales, theater benefits, Rotary and other local club activities all helped raise the necessary funds. The March 1943 Boothbay fundraising campaign raised $4,600, double its quota.[264] Red Cross fundraising drives continued throughout the war.

THE MOTOR CORPS

The Red Cross Motor Corps was organized at the request of the OCD. With gas and tire rationing, transportation became extremely difficult for many people. The motor corps offered free transportation for "any worthy purpose," e.g., doctor appointments, hospital or volunteer work or travel to or from war work.[265] The enlistment of women in Red Cross Motor Corps training and the performance of the women who took over men's driving jobs during World War II helped dispel the notion held by many men at the time that women could not be good drivers. In Boothbay, Phyllis Sample, thirty-four, wife of Frank Jr., was chairman of the motor corps.

Mary White began giving motor corps training classes in Brunswick in September 1941. Twelve women with cars enrolled. One of the services they performed was helping servicemen get where they needed to be. In 1942, some young men from Brunswick, Topsham and Harpswell were having trouble getting to their reporting station in Portland. Despite the bravado and humor that were certainly shown by the inductees, there must have been some comfort in being driven to the reporting station by a woman from town whom they knew.

HOME SERVICES

Families across the country were suffering from the dislocations of war. If a serviceman was concerned about a family situation back home, he could tell a Red Cross representative. That information was communicated back to hometown Red Cross Home Services volunteers, who would visit and provide help to the person or family—not always with the expected results. An article in the July 15, 1943 *Brunswick Record* was titled "Red Cross Workers Doing Crack Job in War Effort." The Brunswick chapter was lauded as one of the most efficient in the state, receiving multiple telegrams a day from field directors on behalf of worried men in service overseas asking for a home services visit. Volunteers worked from early morning to late at night handling seventy-five or more cases a month. When one serviceman requested permission to go home because his grandmother was sick, the Brunswick Red Cross received a telegram from the other town saying, "Grandmother's condition unchanged in eight years. Soldier's presence not needed."[266]

VICTORY BOOKS

The Victory Books campaign was a joint effort of the Red Cross, the American Library Association and the USO. Books helped servicemen escape the war for a brief time no matter where they were. Appeals went out for book donations as soon as war was declared. Books satisfied a real need and made a powerful statement—a stark contrast between Nazi book burning and American freedom. Millions of books were collected across the country by Girl Scouts and church-affiliated organizations, including the Girls Sodality of St. John's Church in Brunswick.

At first, the campaign collected only hardcover books. The problem was distribution. Books were a low priority amid all the vital supplies being sent to the troops overseas. Even if they could be delivered, infantrymen couldn't carry a bulky book into battle or when traveling long distances. American publishers got together and created Armed Services Editions (ASEs), which launched the paperback book market in the United States. Publishing houses could inexpensively print millions of current and backlisted titles. *A Tree Grows in Brooklyn* and *The Great Gatsby* became national bestsellers as ASEs due to word-of-mouth recommendations among the military and to

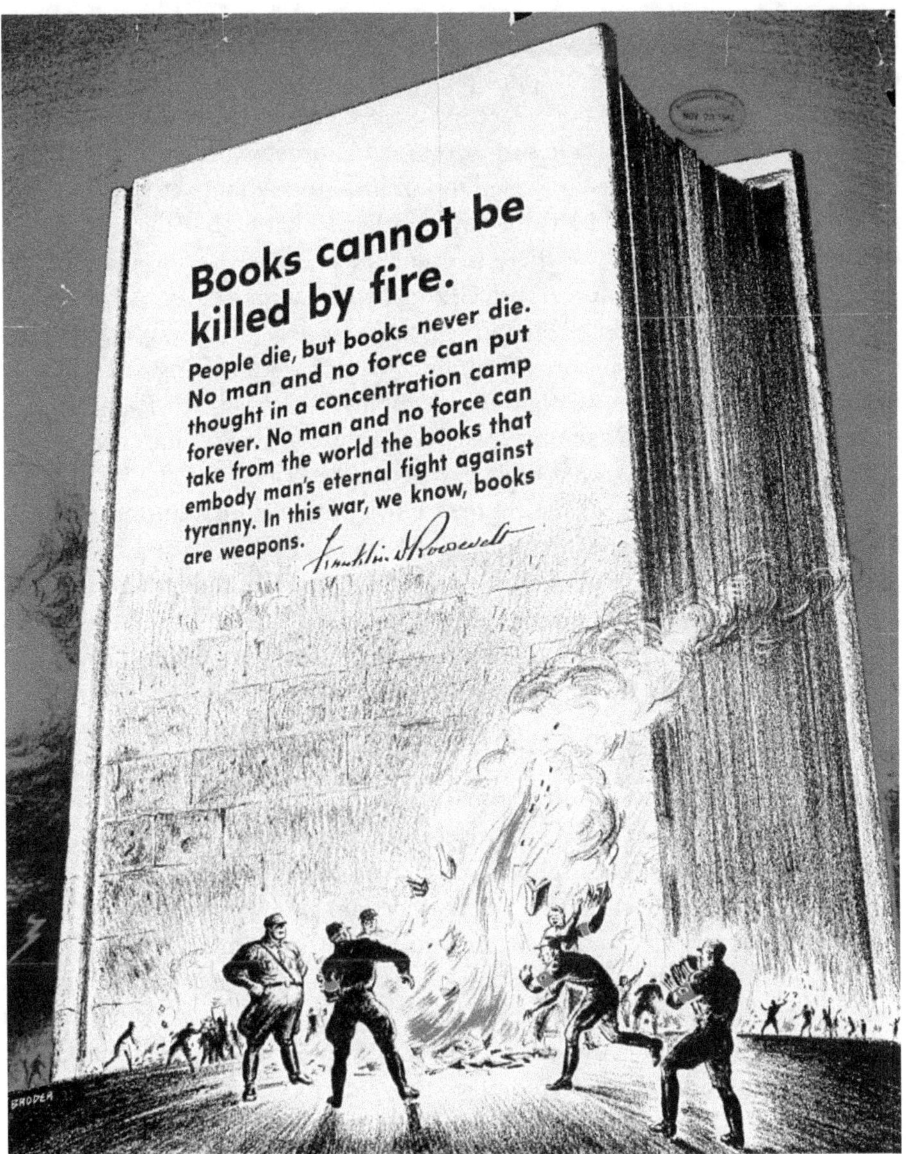

"Books Are Weapons in the War of Ideas: Books cannot be killed by fire" poster, Office of War Information, Washington, D.C., 1942. *Northwestern University Library, images.northwestern.edu.*

folks back home.[267] One servicemen told a *Saturday Evening Post* reporter that the books were "as popular as pin-up girls."[268]

Magazines and newspapers were also collected for distribution overseas. Local newspapers offered free subscriptions to hometown men and women in the service. The editors appealed to families throughout the war to send in addresses so they could let the boys (and girls) know that they were not forgotten and that home was there to come back to.

In November 1942, Reverend George Chiera, pastor of St. Philip's Episcopal Church in Wiscasset, and two parishioners and volunteers in the church office, May Sherman and Frances Somes, began writing a newsletter called the *Wiscasset Gazette* that they sent to Wiscasset servicemen and women overseas. Like Reverend Dole in Bath, Reverend Chiera was also a chaplain for the Maine State Guard. He was described as "the life of the chaplains' corps" in an official report of the Maine state adjutant general for 1942–44. The attorney general said Reverend Chiera used humor to diffuse difficult situations, which promoted a common understanding and tolerance of religious differences among his men. The report continued, "Great-hearted, generous and easy of approach, sympathetic to every human frailty and ill, he commands both the respect and the affection of the personnel of his command who regard him as a father and romp with him as an elder brother."[269]

The *Gazette*'s tone was light and casual, with all the news from home—who enlisted, came home on leave, got married, had a baby, died or was sick and updates on businesses, schools, churches, Boy and Girl Scouts, USO, Red Cross and other war efforts. The servicemen and women were told how much they were missed and how dull things were without them. In 1945, Dana Rines began drawing cartoon sketches of local scenes for each issue. One cartoon in July 1945 was captioned, "Of course most of you guys are too young to remember the old fort as of a moonlit night…." Who knew Fort Edgecomb was the preferred place to watch the submarine races!

Citizens Service Corps

By November 1942, the need for civilian defense in the military sense of the term had diminished. The Civilian Defense Corps Women's Division was renamed the Citizens Service Corps (CSC). Focus shifted from defending against enemy attack to making the American homefront as productive as possible while maintaining the way of life we were fighting for. The reorganization also recognized the critical roles being performed by women and their potential to help solve some growing homefront problems.

The CSC strategy was to address community needs through an initiative called the Neighborhood Plan, creating a network of volunteers to identify and develop solutions to local problems. Committees for nutrition, social protection, family security and recreation were formed in each town or area. Family security meant intervening in cases where a family was in jeopardy because of homelessness, extreme poverty, lack of child care or spousal or child abuse. Social protection meant intervening in cases of economic deprivation—due to the loss of a parent to death or military service—or hunger and poor nutrition that could lead to illness or inability to work. The CSC worked closely with the Red Cross to ensure that families were vaccinated, healthy and cared for—needs exacerbated by the shortage of doctors and nurses.

Towns were broken up into small areas, which were then assigned to volunteers living in or familiar with that neighborhood. Plan volunteers communicated information about rationing, food conservation, nutrition, housing and volunteer opportunities to the families in their area and looked for any problems that existed or might develop. The local CSC leadership developed and conducted surveys to collect information that clarified problems and helped identify potential solutions. The women who were chairmen of the Women's Divisions now became chairmen of their local CSCs: Fannie Perkins for Lincoln County, Angie Dodge for Boothbay Harbor, Virginia Parker for Bath and Amy Cushing for Brunswick.

THE HOUSING SHORTAGE

The midcoast was experiencing an extreme housing shortage. Bath's problem began in the late 1930s as the shipyard geared up for war. BIW's payroll quadrupled between 1940 and 1943, and those workers needed a place to live.[270] By the spring of 1942, there were no rooms, houses or apartments available in Bath. Workers and their families were living in trailers parked outside the shipyard and in rough shacks with no running water or sanitary facilities on the outskirts of the city. Hyde Park, fifty-six brick buildings built in 1941 near Center Street and U.S. 1, was designed as permanent affordable housing for two hundred families. Prefabricated housing was built in town by

January 1942, but more housing was still needed.[271] Lambert Park was built in Bath's North End in 1942; the new complex included two-family houses and dormitories for 1,235 men, 2 to a room.[272] Pete Newell, the president of BIW, wrote personal appeals to the owners of large houses to make room for naval personnel and their wives who tried to spend a few weeks together before the husband's ship was sent overseas.

The housing shortage in the rest of the midcoast began in 1941. Thousands of people moved here to work at shipyards, BNAS and war-related industries, plus the hundreds of military men assigned to Bowdoin College training classes. Despite the number of homeowners who offered up rooms in their houses, the problem remained critical throughout the war.

The tight supply of available housing led to extreme upward pressure on rents. A Fair Rent Committee was formed in Brunswick in February 1942 to manage local rents, and the chamber of commerce established a rent office to help people find housing.[273] Grocery store owner George St. Onge, fifty-six; car dealer Guy Patterson, forty-five; Edmond Lachance (also still working at the mill, as deputy air raid warden and on the War Fund

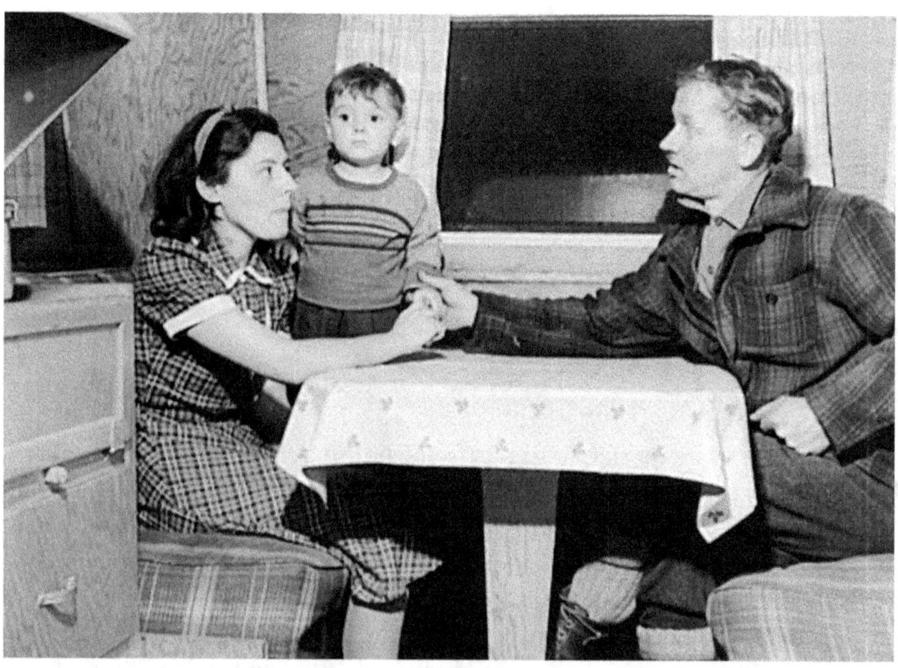

Clyde and Lucilia Burton and son living in a trailer with no electricity or bathroom on the outskirts of Bath, 1940. *Farm Security Administration, Washington, D.C. Jack Delano, photographer. Library of Congress.*

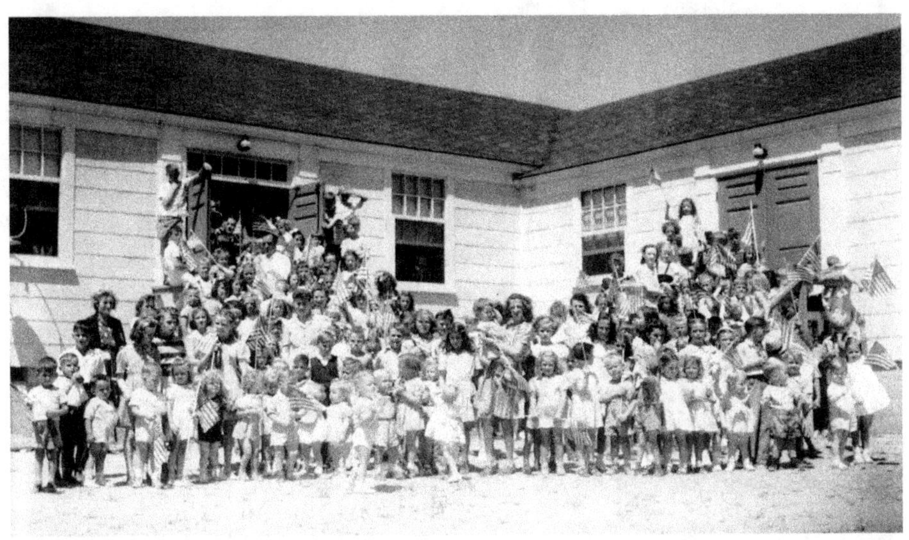

Children at Lambert Park celebration, July 2, 1944. *Photographer Otis. N.E. Card, Richard Card Collection, Sagadahoc History & Genealogy Room, Patten Free Library.*

committee); Glenn McIntyre, twenty-one, bursar of Bowdoin College; and Lloyd Benner, forty-five, a supervisor at Central Maine Power, made up the committee. By December 1942, there were no apartments available. Strong appeals appeared in newspapers weekly asking anyone with rooms to rent to please contact the rent office in the A.B. Holmes Insurance Agency, 129 Maine Street. The agency had curtailed its operating hours, closing Saturday and Monday due to fuel shortages, but volunteer rent office manager Archie Holmes decided that there were too many people in need, so he continued to open the rent office and come to work despite freezing temperatures and burst pipes.

Another problem was finding temporary rooms for families and girlfriends visiting servicemen at Bowdoin, BIW or BNAS. Appeals to residents to house the visitors appeared regularly in local newspapers throughout the war. The army units stationed at Bowdoin College and the USO held a dance on the weekend of October 30, 1943. An article in the October 14 *Brunswick Record* said, "Soldiers Ask Homes to Put Up Their Girls on Night of Dance....Rooms in private houses for guests of the soldiers will be badly needed. Guests will expect to pay rent....The Army men are under a heavy training schedule and are looking forward to having girls from their home towns [visit]....They will be very grateful to those who will help them in accommodating their guests."[274]

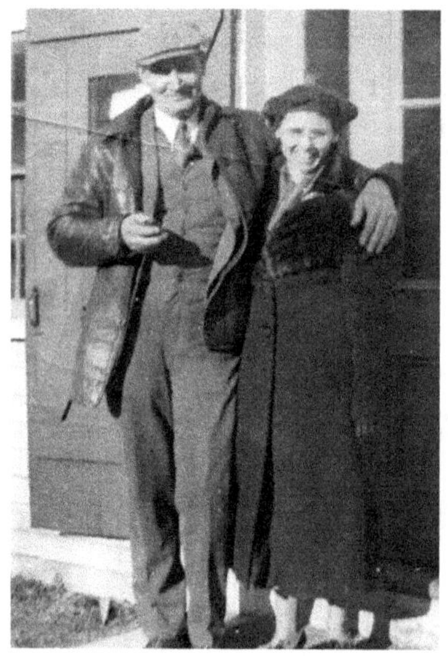
Susie and Howard Sylvester, circa 1940. *Courtesy of the Sylvester family.*

Susie Sylvester was one of Brunswick's most indefatigable homefront volunteers. Raised in Wenham, Massachusetts, daughter of a shoemaker, Susie graduated from Salem Normal School and taught in Lisbon Falls and Topsham before moving in 1923 to Brunswick, where she married Howard Sylvester. She taught in the Growstown and Bunganuc one-room schoolhouses and other public schools until 1940. The Sylvesters lived at 1 Stetson Street in Brunswick. Susie was a tiny dynamo and a perfect example of the can-do attitude of the American homefront. She volunteered with the Red Cross and at her church, served on the ration board and ran the projects of the Neighborhood Plan addressing food conservation and nutrition education needs. She organized first aid training, opened and helped run a new canning center and much more.

In March 1943, Susie was named head of the Brunswick Neighborhood Plan. She recruited volunteers to manage each zone and organized training for them. She and Amy Cushing created a questionnaire, divided the area into six sectors and organized a house-to-house survey of available and potentially available rooms. The survey found seventy-eight additional rooms and six apartments. The August 19, 1943 *Brunswick Record* had a front-page article: "Mrs. Sylvester Is Brunswick's Number One Room Finder—Patriotic Lady Constantly Facing Difficult Problems, Does a Grand Job and Enjoys the Friends She Makes." The article stated that the Sylvesters' phone was constantly ringing with pleas from strangers for somewhere to stay. Susie "solved the problem by stuffing the bell with newspapers so just the faintest tinkle is heard." Among those she helped were a troupe of actors doing a USO show at BNAS, military men at Bowdoin and stranded visitors with nowhere to go. "She was convinced that if people were offered rooms with a bathtub and nothing else, they would take it. 'I never saw people so bath conscious in my life. One naval officer couldn't quite reconcile the idea of taking his baths in the ocean…and women, they are my pet peeve!' What made her 'see red' were the people who started telling how the town should be run, and that in every other town where they've gone to work they had found a room without any trouble etc. etc." The article pointed out that as number-one room-finder, she also "got the kicks" when things didn't work out, which didn't happen very often. The positive side was that many of those who came were "such nice young people!" Susie charged one fee. If the visitors were grateful for having been provided a room, she asked that they volunteer time at the Red Cross, canning center or ration board. "A neighbor and friend of Mrs. Sylvester commented upon the latter's civic activities with the remark, 'Yes, I sit at the window and watch the sailors go by and see Suzy [*sic*].'"

With the opening of Brunswick Naval Air Station in April 1943, the navy needed at least 620 new family units for military and civilian personnel. They also needed permanent housing for the approximately 250 families who were living in trailers. Homeowners were told it was their patriotic duty to rent rooms to base workers.[275] In July 1943, Brunswick began building new temporary and permanent housing. The new construction included 150 three- and four-room prefabricated housing units built in Walker Field off Jordan Avenue, a 90-apartment complex called the Brunswick Apartments built at the corner of Maine Street and Longfellow Avenue and a 12-apartment building called the Mayflower Apartments on Belmont Street.

Men at Bowdoin for army and navy classes were told not to bring their wives and families with them, but since they knew their next posting would almost certainly be Europe or the Pacific, it was understandable that they wanted to share every possible moment with their loved ones, so Brunswick turned a blind eye to the rule.[276] Several families exemplified the generous community spirit of the time. Rupert White remembered that "there was a family in every room" in their large house. He remembered one year when his mother, Mary, cooked Thanksgiving dinner "on a hotplate in one room."[277]

Bowdoin professor Frederic Tillotson and his wife, Marjory, housed and fed sixteen people in their house on Park Row. A February 11, 1943 *Brunswick Record* article said, "Sometimes, with visiting Bowdoin students, there were as many as twenty-two people at one meal at the Tillotsons. Marjory explained that they had simply wanted to help when they saw that families with children who had come to town for their father's job or military service were unable to find a place to live. They never intended the number of people to grow so large, but felt it was the right thing to do to help as many as possible." Frederic Tillotson taught music and theater, and Marjory was a piano teacher. "She quickly realized that the odd arrangements offered a fascinating study of

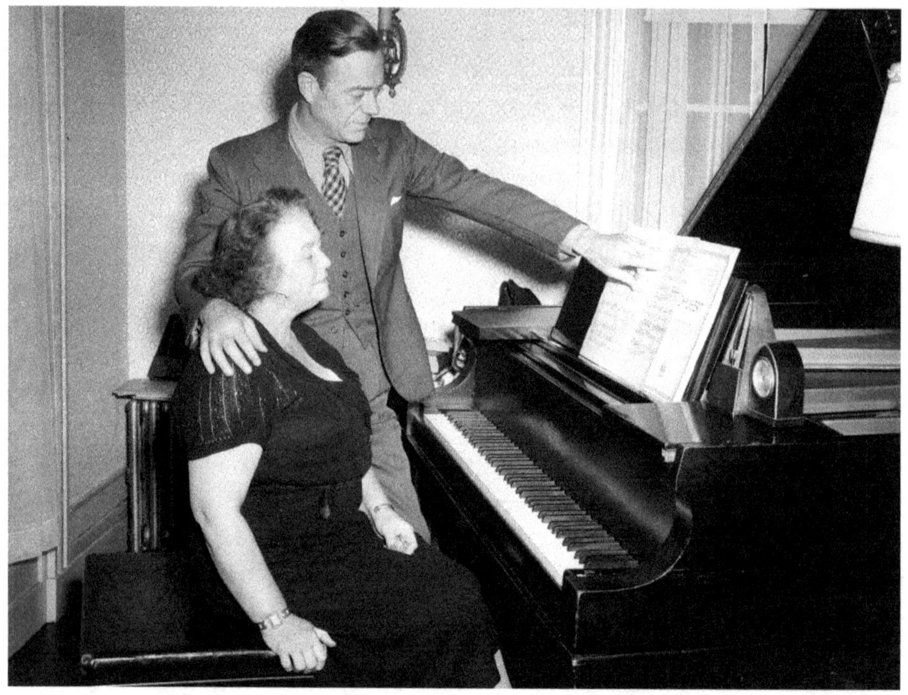

Frederic and Marjory Tillotson at one of their home pianos, 1946. *Courtesy of the George J. Mitchell Department of Special Collections & Archives, Bowdoin College Library, Brunswick, Maine.*

human behavior. People with no apparent common ground found ways to relate to each other by necessity, even when six children from three different families began quarreling. They accepted the fact that children do certain things at certain ages (no matter where they're from) and cannot be blamed." Her clever and sensitive method of feeding so many people at once was to set up a buffet and put small tables in rooms throughout the house where individual families could enjoy their meals together and in relative privacy, thereby allowing some sense of family normality despite the circumstances.

> *Most people made an effort to get along with each other, but she told the story of one married couple from the South who came with a strong feeling of antagonism against the North in general and Harriet Beecher Stowe in particular. Not realizing this, Margery* [sic] *suggested they include the Stowe House in their sightseeing. Despite the strongly negative reaction to her suggestion, she said that they eventually lost their antagonism, and left*

with a much better opinion of the North, having lived under one roof with them under difficult but shared conditions. They even had their pictures taken in front of the Stowe House.

As the war continued, the Red Cross, CSC, ration board and even the Volunteer Placement Bureau all needed more volunteers, but many of the available female workforce had child care responsibilities prohibiting them from helping. Finding child care for working women became a priority. Some companies opened their own nurseries. Brunswick opened a town nursery. The Brunswick Day Nursery School opened on September 20, 1943, in Wheeler Hall at the corner of Federal Street and Jordan Avenue, formerly the Universalist church. The nursery was run by a professional director but staffed and supplied by volunteers.

Juvenile delinquency was perceived as a growing problem exacerbated by the war. Not everyone agreed with that perception, but after a series of break-ins committed by a gang of children led by a twelve-year-old girl and including "a seven-year-old boy whose parents did not know he was out of the house,"[278] Bath residents were ready to acknowledge a problem. The Bath USO stepped in to help. It offered programs for high school students on Tuesdays and Thursdays that included noon entertainment and evening dances.[279] The USO organized bowling at Park Bowling Alley, hillbilly dances (girls wear pigtails; boys wear overalls), scavenger hunts, volleyball games, ping-pong, badminton and checkers.[280]

Volunteers came and went in homefront civilian defense. Some gave just a few hours a week. Others began but couldn't continue. Many more left for war jobs or to enlist. The remaining volunteers worked long hours on top of the everyday work and cares of their lives. They must have been exhausted, yet they kept on giving their time and their energy for years. The strength, dedication and stamina of people like Susie Sylvester, Angie Dodge, Amy Cushing, Jean and Ruth Bangs, Edmond Lachance, Ruth Kirkland, Alma Drapeau, Reverend Louis and Anita Dole, Mary White, Thomas McMahon, Helen Campbell, Helen Varney, Virginia Parker, Virginia Gillies, Reverend Chiera, May Sherman and all the others who continued to work in multiple homefront war efforts year after year were deserving of much more praise and recognition than they ever received. Thomas McMahon died unexpectedly at fifty-five on December 29, 1943, and was mourned by all who knew him.[281]

Chapter 11

SCRIMP, SALVAGE AND SAVE

Another way to do your bit was to save and turn in anything that could be used for the war effort. Paper, tinfoil, cans, string, scrap iron and steel, rubber, rags, rope, burlap bags and toothpaste tubes were all used to make materials needed by the troops overseas. Saving scraps for reuse was already ingrained behavior for most Mainers, but now there was a direct connection between what you could save and a serviceman under fire or injured. One War Production Board (WPB) ad featured a drawing with a Japanese soldier on the ground being bombarded with junk with the tagline "Throw YOUR scrap into the fight."[282]

Tin, rubber and paper drives came first. Iron and steel were next. Whatever historic iron had survived the World War I salvage drives now fell for World War II. In May 1942, the last of the rails of the old A&K Trolley line on mid- to lower Maine Street in Brunswick were torn out to salvage their metal. The WPA paid for the work.[283]

Each town had its own salvage committee. John Parker was chairman in Bath. In April 1942, Brunswick civilian defense chairman Thomas McMahon appointed a committee of civic leaders to manage salvage collection drives. The committee included Harry Schulman, Boy Scout commissioner; George Crimmins, Lions Club; Clyde T. Congdon, Rotary Club; J. Milton Briggs, commander of the American Legion post; George Bamforth, Veterans of Foreign Wars;[284] Napoleon Gagne Sr., Spanish War Veterans; Philip Theberge, Knights of Columbus; Alfred Senter, president of the chamber of commerce; highway commissioner Jesse C. Coffin; and the managers of the three local grain companies.[285]

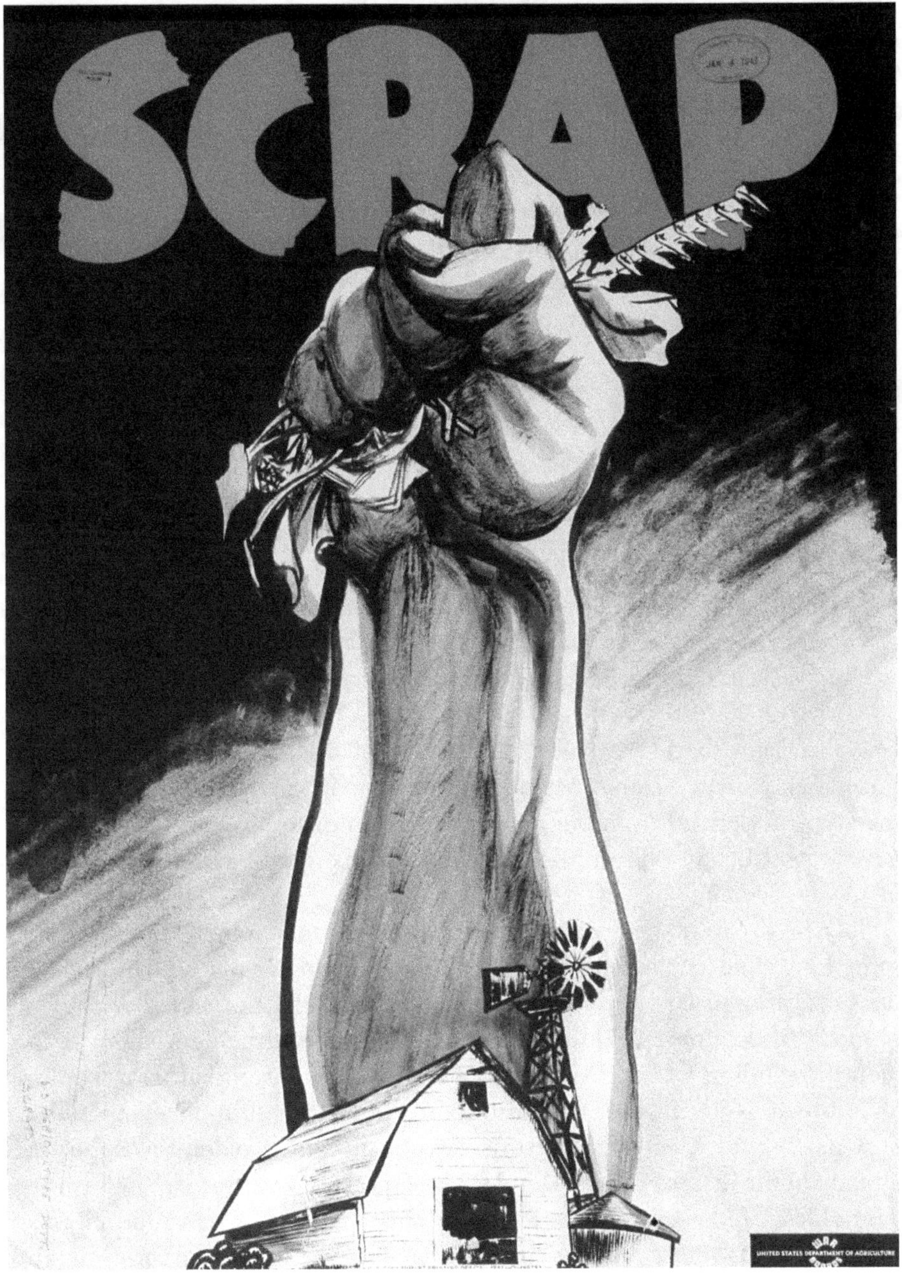

"Scrap" poster, Roy Schatt, artist. U.S. Department of Agriculture, Washington, D.C., 1942. *Northwestern University Library, images.northwestern.edu.*

Nineteen communities in Lincoln County organized their own salvage committees. Lon Jewett, sixty-eight, Alna General Store owner, took charge there. John Sproule, thirty-six, sold furniture and was chairman for Bristol. Real estate salesman John Swett, sixty-two, was chairman in Southport. Larry Haggett, owner of Haggett's Garage, was Wiscasset's chairman. Landscape gardener Alva Bridges, sixty-two, was chairman in South Bristol. Mechanic Wilson Hutchins, thirty-seven, was chairman in Nobleboro. Lloyd Byers, forty-four, was a farmer and chairman for Damariscotta/Newcastle.

Saving kitchen fats was another salvage campaign. Housewives turned in bacon grease and cooking fats at the A&P, First National and other grocery stores with meat counters. One Office of War Information (OWI) ad exhorted women to

> *let your fats flow out of the frying pan and into the fire—the fire of antiaircraft guns protecting your homes, the fire of big guns on battleships and faraway battle fronts, the fire of rifles in the hands of our soldiers and sailors. Kitchen fats make glycerin. Glycerin makes explosives. Housewives, cooks, chefs of America start firing now. Every jar of fat you save…means a bullet in Uncle Sam's cartridge belt.*[286]

Walt Disney made a cartoon called "Out of the Frying Pan and Into the Firing Line" with Minnie Mouse, Pluto and Mickey Mouse showing how the glycerin derived from fats can be turned into explosives.[287] In 1943, the government began offering ration points or tokens in exchange for pounds of salvaged fats.

Salvage drives made everyone feel like they were helping. They were also something children could get excited about. The Boy Scouts held huge paper drives starting in January 1942. The January 22, 1942 *Brunswick Record* had a photo of Scoutmaster Joseph LaBeau Jr., twenty-three, and eight of his scouts, including Gilbert Menard, Carroll Alexander and Robert Paradis, all fourteen. Robert McCarthy, also fourteen, was the fifth of eight children of Charles and Evelyn McCarthy. Two of his three older brothers were already in the army. Francis Mendes and Gerald Tibbetts were both twelve. The oldest of the group was Kenneth Cross, fifteen, who would enlist in 1945. George Malm, twenty-eight, a truck driver for a lumber company, volunteered his time and truck for the effort. Fifty Brunswick-area scouts and ten troop leaders filled a freight car to overflowing with paper.[288]

In June 1942, Brunswick held a weekend salvage scavenger hunt all over town, with all the schools participating. A scrap rubber drive the following month was also very successful. Topsham filling stations alone took in two tons. Harpswell had its own campaign.[289] In 1943, Lincoln County schools collected milkweed floss needed to replace rainforest kapok fiber no longer available. The fiber was a critical material in aviator suits, lifejackets and other lifesaving equipment. Calvin Dodge remembered making big balls of tinfoil and gathering milkweed pods for life preservers.[290] The Damariscotta Town Report of 1944 stated, "The milkweed floss collected by the pupils in this school union was sufficient to make fifteen life jackets."[291]

Big scrap rallies were held. A Labor Day rally on the Mall in Brunswick in 1942 featured old-fashioned oration by schoolteacher and lawyer Bradford C. Redonnett, sixty-five, of Wiscasset.[292] (Redonnett's son Bradford Jr. was in the army air corps.) The accompanying drive collected twenty-five tons of scrap. In September, Boothbay Harbor held a "25-ton Junk Rally."[293] Ben Maddocks, seventy, and Leston Hemore, salvage committee co-chairmen, organized the drive. Leston, fifty-two, was a telephone company lineman and Boy Scout troop leader. Businesses sponsored printed handbills that encouraged people to bring in old wire hangers, steel springs from old furniture, old knives, tools and machines. Schools, churches and civic organizations got involved. A salvage depot was set up behind Kendrick's

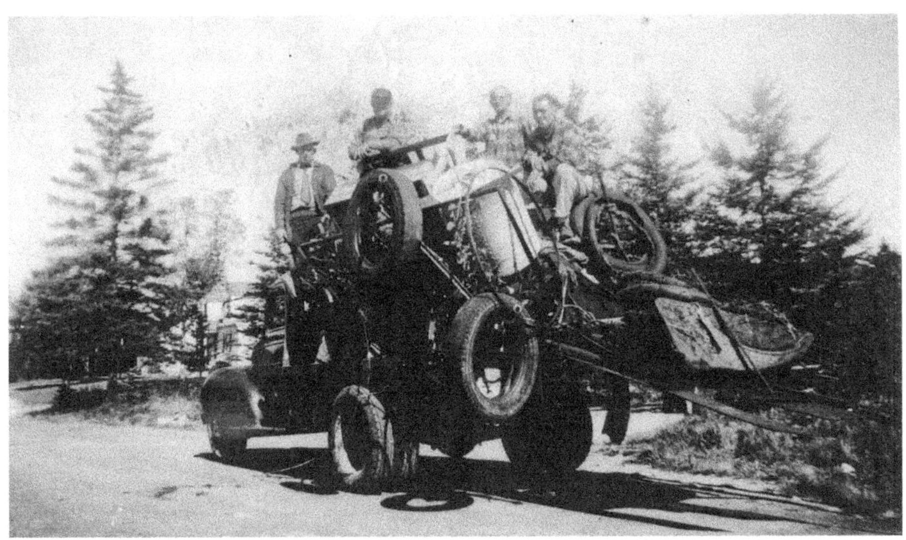

Truck loaded with scrap for iron, steel and rubber drive on Lakeview Road, Boothbay Harbor, September 1942. Pickup crew are Glidden Rines, Donald Giles (owner and driver of the truck), Gardner Williams and Wendell Buster Boyd. *Boothbay Region Historical Society*.

Esso service center at the corner of McKown Street and Todd Avenue. A September 25, 1942 *Boothbay Register* article quoted Ben Maddox:

> *He pointed out a steel safe "There's enough iron in that safe to make a 1,000 lb. aerial bomb....See that old wash bucket? That will make three bayonets."...When asked about an old battery in the heap, Ben said "Isn't that a dandy! There's enough lead in it to go into the alloy for three anti-aircraft guns." An ancient rubber overshoe was a little gem of scrap, supplying half a gas mask.*[294]

Large ugly piles of scrap became a common sight. As the piles grew larger, concern grew when they were not picked up right away. Transporting scrap to where it needed to be processed was a challenge. Finding enough vehicles with the required capacity and the tires and gas rations to travel was also difficult. The army and coast guard helped in the Boothbay area. Navy and BNAS personnel helped in Brunswick. An article in the January 22, 1943 *Boothbay Register* reassured readers that the scrap was vital to the war effort and would not be wasted and urged them to have patience until the scrap could be picked up.

Chapter 12

THE RATION BLUES

The U.S. government had to keep the war machine running at maximum capacity and, at the same time, ensure that everyone—rich or poor—had access to the food, commodities and services they needed at reasonable prices. The Office of Price Administration set ceiling (or maximum) prices and rents and managed the rationing system. Anything needed to feed, clothe, arm, fuel, transport or provide medical care for the troops was rationed.

The OPA and Office of War Administration (OWI) launched a sweeping national marketing campaign to convince Americans that price controls and rationing were necessary and fair. The message was that doing your bit for the war effort required sacrifices, but those were nothing compared to the sacrifices being made by the soldiers and sailors overseas. It was every American's patriotic duty to cheerfully make do and abide by the rules so that everyone got their fair share. That message was repeated everywhere, in advertising, on posters, on the radio and in the movies. Movie studios produced short films with current stars promoting and explaining the new systems. Celebrities endorsed rationing and price controls in magazine articles. Letters and articles appeared in local newspapers, ostensibly written by unnamed servicemen or housewives with a heart-tugging or inspiring story that ended in an appeal to abide by the new rules. The marketing campaign reassured people that food was still plentiful; they were just being asked to cut back on certain things.

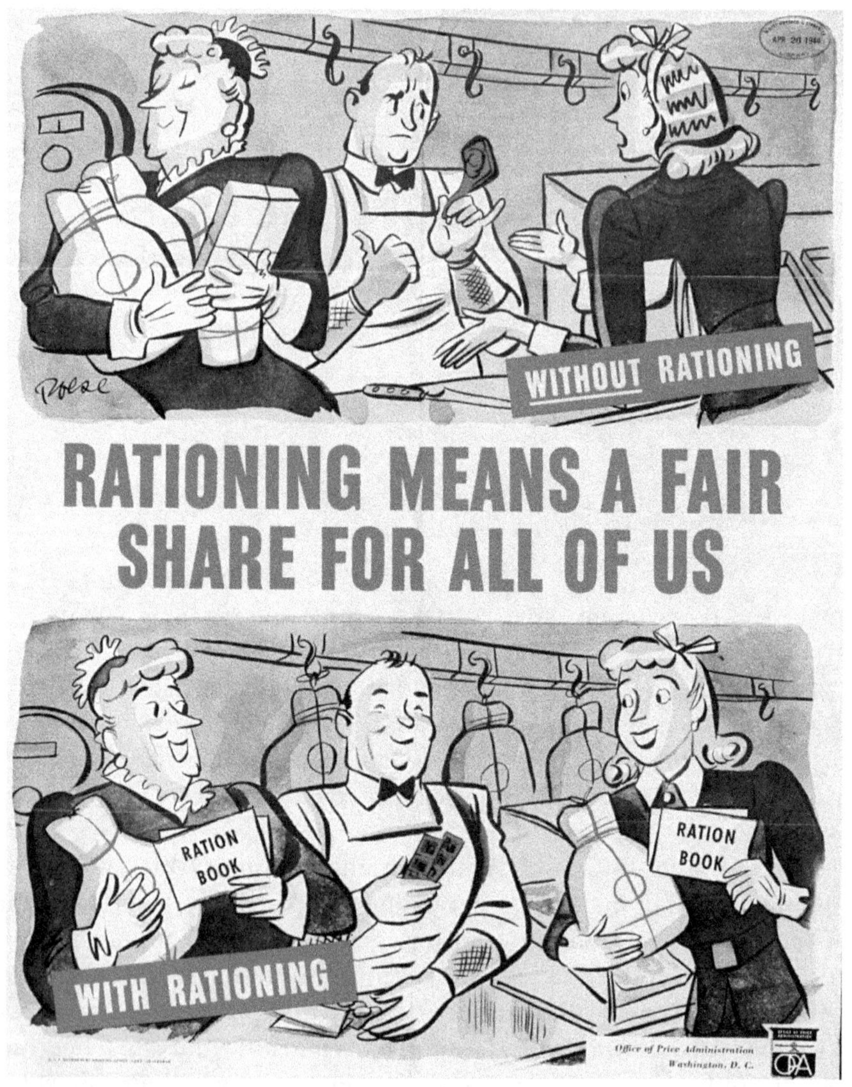

"Rationing Means a Fair Share for All of Us," poster, Herbert Roese, artist. Office of Price Administration, Washington, D.C., 1943. *Northwestern University Library, images.northwestern.edu.*

Fuel shortages started in April 1941, when fifty American oil tankers were diverted from their regular deliveries to deliver fuel to Great Britain.[295] At the same time, national demand was up 25 percent over the previous year because of increased defense needs.[296] Oil for the East Coast came from the Dutch West Indies, Venezuela and Texas.[297] It was carried here on tankers, freighters and barges through shipping lanes under attack from German U-boats.[298] That summer, the federal government asked everyone to observe "Gasless Sundays" to help reduce consumption.[299] The timing was designed to conserve oil in the summer and save it for heating homes in the winter. Voluntary gas rationing began in August 1941, when seventeen eastern states were asked to reduce gasoline sales by 10 percent. But no degree of voluntary rationing could meet the country's need.[300]

The Japanese occupation of Southeast Asia and the Pacific islands cut off the sources of our rubber supply just when we needed it most. Gas rationing helped rubber as well as fuel shortages. If people couldn't drive, they wore out fewer tires. The day after Pearl Harbor, sales of new tires were banned until January 4. The ban gave the government time to set up a system to control existing supplies. After January 4, anyone wanting new tires had to submit a request to their newly created local tire review board. In the spring of 1942, national speed limits were lowered to forty and then thirty-five miles per hour to further conserve gas and tires.

Brunswick's tire review board included George S. Brown, fifty-nine, retired after thirty-plus years in cotton mill management and living on Bath Road with his wife and three teenagers, including a seventeen-year-old son about to enlist; Wilfred Lapointe, forty-nine, the town tax collector who lived at 3 Pleasant Street with his wife, her nephew, her nephew's wife and two children, plus a lodger; and Nathan Pierce, seventy-three, a retired grocer living with his wife on Lincoln Street. These men voluntarily took on one of the most thankless homefront jobs: listening to hundreds of requests from town residents that had to be rejected, thereby subjecting themselves to criticism from unhappy neighbors.

On May 15, 1942, eight million drivers in seventeen eastern states registered for gas rationing, where they were assigned one of five classifications of need.[301] Most people received an A classification, meaning that their driving was deemed nonessential. As such, they were entitled to four gallons of fuel per week.[302] Preferred occupations, like industrial war workers, received a B classification. Their driving was considered essential to the war effort, so they could purchase eight gallons per week. Physicians, ministers, railroad workers, mail carriers, fishermen and school buses were classified C. Their driving was also deemed essential. Classification T was for truck drivers; X was reserved for VIPs and military. There was no gallon restriction for classifications C, T or X. Drivers received a windshield sticker with their designation letter. To get a gas ration card, you had to show your automobile registration. The registrar wrote your license plate number on the card so

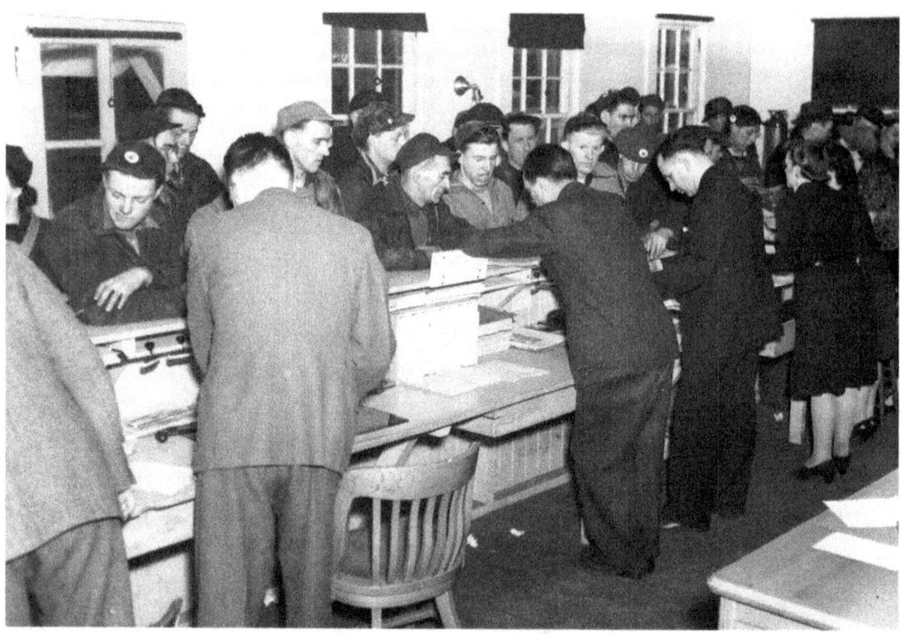

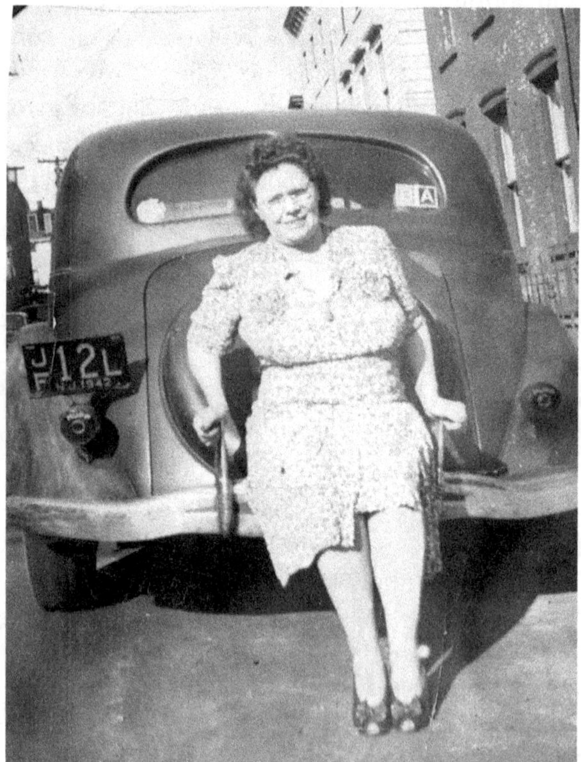

Above: An agitated crowd of workmen signing up for gas and tire rations at BIW Transportation Building, 1941. *Maine Maritime Museum, BIW Collection.*

Left: Margaret Besson with her car showing both an A gas ration sticker and then a B sticker indicating that she had been upgraded because she was working in an essential war industry, 1943. *Author's collection.*

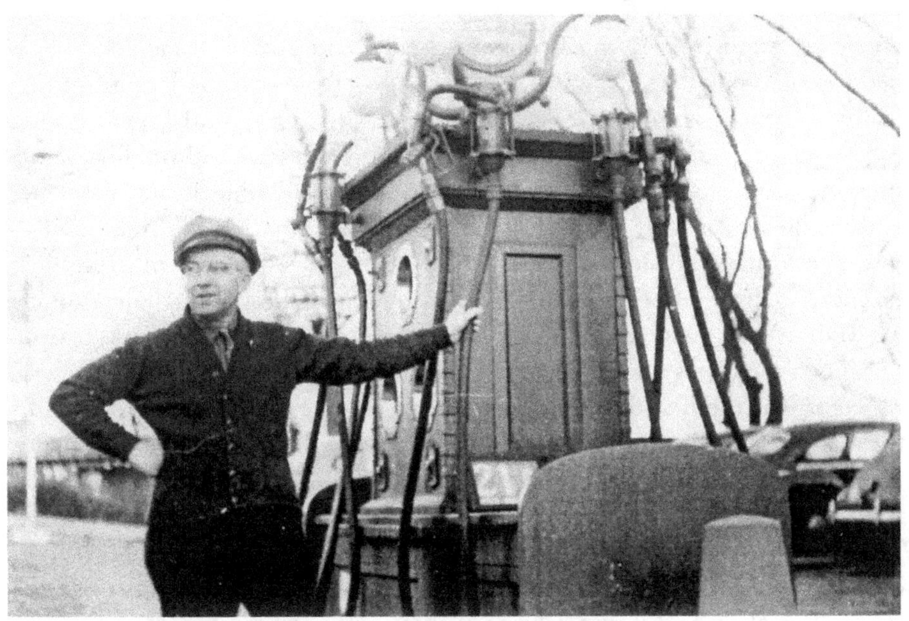

Perleston Pert at the Pert Gas Station, 40 Vine Street, Bath, circa 1942. *Edwin H. Pert Collection, Sagadahoc History & Genealogy Room, Patten Free Library.*

that it couldn't be reissued. As expected, there were many unhappy people who thought they deserved a higher allowance than they received.

When you pulled up to the filling station (as gas stations were then called), you handed the attendant your ration card and money.[303] He—or she, more frequently as the war went on—would punch the square on the card to show it had been used. Criminal ingenuity reared its head almost immediately. Within a month, ration boards were warning against "chiselers": gas station attendants who, for a fee or a favor, would sell someone gas without punching their card. The OPA warned both consumers and gas stations that counterfeit ration books were being sold on the East Coast within weeks after the system started.

In March 1942, rationing was expanded to include cars and typewriters, and tire review boards were told their duties would soon be expanded to include all rationing. Ration boards grew in size as the system became more widespread and complex. The expanded Brunswick ration board moved from a small room in town hall to the showroom of the Lewiston Buick Company on the corner of Maine and School Streets, donated because the owner recognized that he wouldn't need the space until rationing was lifted. By August 1942, the Brunswick board had grown to include twelve people, including three women. The board was divided into subcommittees: commodity rationing (tires, automobiles, bicycles and typewriters), ceiling price controls, gasoline rationing and food rationing. The latter subcommittee was made up entirely of women: Georgia Strout, fifty-one, and Lucille Morin, forty-five, both teachers; and Katherine McMahon, fifty-one. Katherine had been in business for herself as a seamstress in Brunswick for more than twenty-three years and was civilian defense chairman Thomas McMahon's younger sister. In 1943, the board reached its peak size of seventeen members and moved to the Bath Street Schoolhouse.

Sugar was the first food to be rationed. Most of the sugar consumed in the United States came from Cuba and the West Indies in shipping lanes under attack. All sugar sales were halted on Monday, April 27, 1942. Residents of midcoast Maine registered for sugar rations the following week. The *Brunswick Record* predicted that it would be "the biggest registration event ever to hit this section—far bigger than any of the Selective Service registrations."[304] And it was. Over ten thousand people registered for sugar rations in Brunswick alone.[305]

Ration Book One was issued on May 5, 1942. The ration stamps inside (sometimes called coupons) enabled the book-holder to purchase one pound of sugar per stamp within a specified two-week period indicated by the number on the stamp. Each book had twenty-eight stamps that were supposed to last fifty-six weeks. That meant that each person was allowed half a pound per week at a time when rural consumption per person was just under one and a half pounds per week—a 34 percent reduction.[306] You presented the stamp with your money when you made a purchase. Certificates were issued for the purchase of commodities in scarce supply, including tires, automobiles, stoves, washing machines, bicycles and rubber boots. Applicants had to demonstrate need before they would be issued a certificate.

Rationing registration was held in places that everyone knew. Local people in positions of trust, like teachers, school board members and town clerks, handled applications and distribution. Superintendent Leon P. Spinney managed rationing registration for Brunswick and Harpswell at Brunswick High School. Topsham registration was held at Cone and Pejepscot Schools. Bowdoinham registration was held at Coombs High School. Frances Plumstead and other teachers registered their neighbors in the Wiscasset grammar school. Schools were closed for four days because all the teachers were busy registering people for rationing.

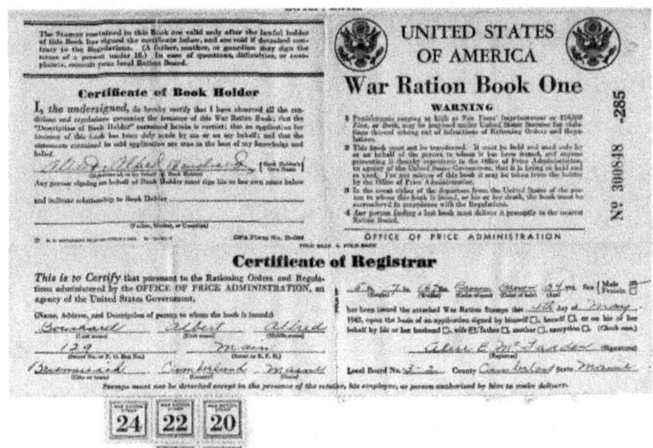

UNITED STATES OF AMERICA

War Ration Book One

WARNING

Nº 300848 -285

OFFICE OF PRICE ADMINISTRATION

Certificate of Book Holder

Certificate of Registrar

This is to Certify that pursuant to the Rationing Orders and Regulations administered by the OFFICE OF PRICE ADMINISTRATION, an agency of the United States Government,

24 22 20

21 19

Ration Book One belonging to Mary Anoncade Bouchard, 1942. *Pejepscot Historical Society*.

The registration process was complicated. Sugar and gas rationing registration were held just thirteen days apart, but the processes were separate, different and held in different places. People had to pay attention to dates, places and instructions published in the newspaper. In the Boothbay region, gas ration registration was held in the high school gym with superintendent H.B. Clifford in charge. Schoolteacher Cliff Buck, forty-two, handled registration at Southport Town Hall. Boothbay's registration was split between central and west residents at the Grange and East Boothbay, Linekin and Back Narrows at the East Boothbay Building. People with boats and non-highway vehicles like lawnmowers, tractors or washing machines applied for supplemental gas rations at the Boothbay Harbor Yacht Club or William Simpson's Garage. Sugar ration registration, which involved everyone, was split between the West Harbor Grammar School, Boothbay Harbor Grammar and all the elementary schools of Boothbay, Southport and Edgecomb. Schoolteacher Lydia Hutchins, thirty-two, registered Back Narrows families at her home.

Everyone was issued their own ration book. One person per family registered for each member of the family.[307] A family was defined as two or more individuals living together in the same household who are related by blood, marriage or adoption. The person designated to register the family needed to know the first, last and middle name of each person, along with their street address, height, weight, color of eyes, color of hair, age in years and sex. He or she needed to be able to state what relation that person was to them and the exact amount (to the pound) of all white and brown sugar currently in their possession. This resulted in some confusion and occasionally humor. Engaged couples were told they couldn't register as a family even if they were getting married the next day. They had to register as individuals and then turn right around and register again once they were married. One man found that when he returned home with the family's ration cards, he was listed as his wife's grandson and his grandfather's husband. Another man couldn't remember how tall his grandson was but could show it on his leg. A child approached school nurse Esther Higgins and told her that his mother said to ask Mrs. Higgins the height and weight of her five children. Since she was the school nurse, the mother assumed Esther would know, even though she took care of 250 children. People with brown eyes insisted their eyes were blue. One man got upset because the registrar would not give him a sugar ration card after he said he had fifty pounds of sugar at home.[308] These were just the stories from Brunswick!

Administrators of the system were also battling something called "Depression psychosis."[309] Some people who had lived through the Depression didn't believe that food and other items would always be available, so like the man with fifty pounds of sugar, they tended to hoard things. In January 1942, Brunswick restaurant owners reported seeing people take sugar from the sugar bowls that were on every table, in anticipation of shortages. The owners' response was to remove the sugar bowls. Waitresses (most restaurants had waitresses rather than waiters) asked people how much sugar they wanted with their coffee or tea when they placed their order. After rationing went into effect, restaurant staff told patrons how much sugar they could get.

Students at colleges and boarding schools turned their ration books over to the school administration, which combined them to purchase what they needed to feed the entire student body. Men and women joining the armed services were asked to turn in their ration books since they would be issued new ones, but sometimes it was hard not to try and leave mother a few extra stamps to buy needed food.

Towns were issued monthly quotas for each commodity. Bath, Brunswick and other midcoast communities whose populations surged with military personnel and civilian war workers were constantly struggling with quotas based on outdated census information rather than current population numbers. Retailers and wholesalers had the same problem. For fuel retailers, supply problems were exacerbated by irregular and less frequent deliveries. Most filling stations were displaying "No Gas" signs the week of July 2, 1942. Gas pumps, complete with signage, were in or right at the edge of the main street in most towns. Two weeks later, the *Brunswick Record* reported that oil companies delivering to filling stations had caused major traffic jams on Maine Street when they arrived just as a shift from BIW was getting off and drivers were waiting in lines for gas.[310]

In mid-July 1942, summer residents were told that they could get supplemental gas ration cards to use on their trip home.[311] That didn't sit well with the general public, for obvious reasons, so the ruling was quickly revoked, and by the following week, newspapers were reporting, "No Gas for Driving Home."[312] In September, hopes of additional gas rations so people could travel to be with loved ones during the holidays were dashed when the OPA announced there would be no extra gas available for the holidays, either.

Rationing for heating fuel (oil and kerosene) began in October 1942, first for dealers and suppliers and then for consumers. This was another separate registration process. There were different forms to fill out depending on the number of occupants in a dwelling and how the fuel oil was used, e.g. heating and hot water versus power or farm equipment. Consumers were told to go to their fuel oil provider to obtain the appropriate forms prior to registering. The Bath and Brunswick quotas were again based on outdated population numbers.

Congress delayed nationwide gas rationing for almost a year after Pearl Harbor, arguing that it would be bad for business and bad for their chances of reelection—still their priorities even though their country was at war.[313] On December 1, 1942, gas rationing went into effect nationwide.[314] One

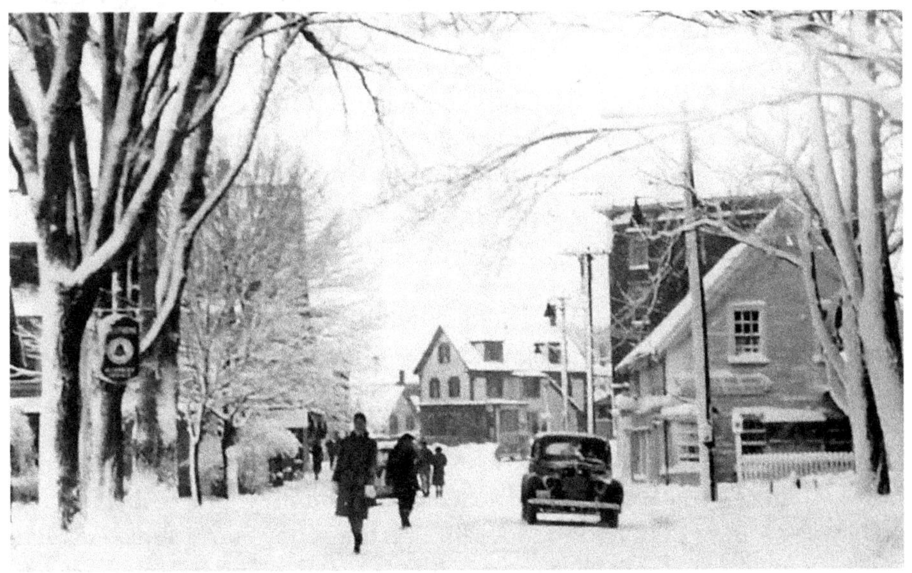

A woman walking home in the snow with her shopping bags in Boothbay Harbor, 1944. *Boothbay Region Historical Society.*

public relations piece appearing in local newspapers told readers that seventy gallons of gas will drive a car one thousand miles but that same amount would only keep a fighter plane in the air for one hour. It exhorted, "This is still a free country. Make your own choice."[315]

Winter fuel woes were exacerbated by Mother Nature. On December 17, 1942, the temperature dropped to twenty below zero in Brunswick. People worried that they wouldn't be able to get enough fuel to heat their homes. Calvin Dodge remembered that the winter of 1942 was so cold that there was thirty-six inches of ice on the Damariscotta River. A twenty-four-year-old local fisherman, Cecil Pryor, was hired to work full time keeping the ice off the ways at Marr's Boatyard while they were building minesweepers.[316] On Christmas Eve 1942, the *Brunswick Record* reported that the ration board had to close the previous Monday because frozen pipes had burst in the office, leaving it too cold to work. Even they had not been able to get enough fuel to heat the office.[317] Twenty-eight downtown stores declared that they would be closed on Saturday, December 26, to save fuel.

Three of the four area oil dealers declared they were out of oil the first week of January 1943. Local fuel committees were formed to help people who didn't have enough to heat their homes. The Brunswick committee included Postmaster George W. Leonard, sixty-one, who lived with his wife, mother and seven children (including three draft-age sons) on Union Street; Don T. Potter, forty-four, the buildings and grounds superintendent at Bowdoin; and Reverend Victor J. Milot, thirty-two, curate at St. John's Church.[318] After researching the problem, the committee found that lack of storage space for large amounts of fuel oil was one of the primary reasons for the shortage. They got permission from companies with large storage tanks to use them for fuel storage for the town. This helped temporarily, but it couldn't solve ongoing problems of shrinking supply and irregular deliveries of oil to dealers.

All local businesses were affected by shortages and the war effort in some way. Many shifted from their usual production to war production. In February 1942, the Bath Pant Company received an order to make seventeen thousand pairs of aviation cadet officers' training pants as soon as possible.[319] Cabot Mill made parachutes. Garages and mechanics' shops suffered from such extreme labor shortages and reductions in business (since people were driving less) that many had to close for the duration. Stores reduced their hours because they didn't have enough fuel for heating or inventory to sell to customers. Libraries were forced to limit their hours and close early because they had no fuel for heating.

FDR created the War Production Board in 1939 to control the supply of materials to all industries and set quotas for war production. Throughout the war, the WPB used advertising to explain and encourage understanding of material shortages. For example, telephone calls used up valuable resources. Nonessential calls used as much equipment, materials and facilities as essential calls, and there wasn't room for both. L-50 was a War Production Order for conservation of telephone materials—copper, aluminum, rubber, steel, etc. New England Telephone & Telegraph Co. ran ads in local newspapers asking people to make fewer and shorter calls. One ad targeted children, saying, "My Mom Says That Even Making One Less Call a Day Will Help," with a little girl holding a chalkboard that read "Telephone Calls Are Needed for War."[320] People with private lines were asked to share party lines instead.[321] New phone installations were limited to those with the greatest need. The WPB also asked all owners of ship-to-shore telephones to make their sets available to the navy and coast guard to help in coastal defense against enemy submarines.[322]

Even fashion was affected by shortages. War Production Order L-85, issued in March 1942 to clothing manufacturers, rationed natural fibers and set limits on the amount of fabric that could be used in clothing.[323] It limited color choices and restricted the length of skirts and the fullness of pants and jackets. Patriotic chic meant shorter skirts, sleeveless tops, zipperless dresses to save metal (buttons instead) and, for men, single-breasted suit jackets with narrow lapels.[324] Vests, cuffs and the second pair of trousers that usually went with the purchase of a man's suit were banned. The most popular colors for 1942 through mid-1945 were neutrals that could be worn year-round—blacks, browns, navy blue and muted shades of red and green. Stripes, polka dots and small prints were good alternatives to solid colors because they didn't need extra fabric to match a pattern. Magazines and catalogues featured articles on how to make one dress or coat into multiple outfits. Cosmetics were also in short supply because most required new packaging using non-rationed materials.

Nylon stocking manufacturers were making parachutes instead. Women reluctantly turned in their stockings for salvage and bought leg makeup. Synthetics like rayon were introduced as substitutes for silk and nylon. New products like NoMend's "Dul-O-TONE" rayon stockings, with "a new elastic twist to prevent runs," were available in three shades at $1.15 to $1.35 per pair.[325] The rubber shortage affected the most essential foundation garment for women: girdles. The April 1, 1943 *Brunswick Record* had a column, "Take Care of Girdle for the Duration." The writer said, "A good girdle gives your dress a better appearance, hence deserves the kindest care." The article then went on to explain how best to preserve and mend elastic fabrics.[326]

Dairies, ice companies and grocers were hit hard by fuel and tire shortages because their customers depended on daily deliveries. Regular customers for bakeries like Nissen, Harris and Cushman's would put a sign in their window to tell the delivery man what they wanted. For those who could afford it, regular laundry deliveries were essential. Citizens Laundry on Maine Street in Brunswick announced in May 1942 that the government would only allow deliveries to a home twice a week or less. Special deliveries were banned. In 1943, laundries had to cease home deliveries entirely. Shortages and lack of staff gradually reduced deliveries further until March 1944, when groceries could no longer be delivered. This increased the burden on already overstressed women with little or no time to shop or wait in line.

Midcoast downtowns were busy and offered a wide range of stores, professional offices, eateries and services. By 1942, Bath's downtown featured six national chain stores: J.J. Newberry & Co., F.W. Woolworth's, W.T. Grant, Sears & Roebuck, First National and A&P. There were two local department stores (Senter's and the Bath Department Store); seven men's and two women's clothing stores; shoe stores; beauty parlors and barbers; banks; realtors; restaurants and lunchrooms; jewelry, hardware and antiques

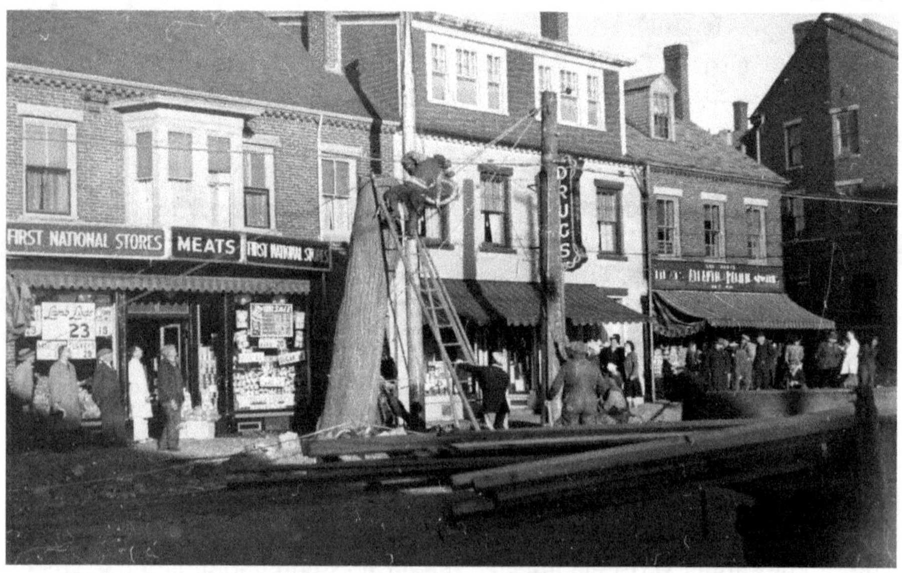

People watching a crew take down the last great elm tree on Main Street in downtown Damariscotta near First National Grocery Store, 1942. *Courtesy of Calvin and Marjorie Dodge.*

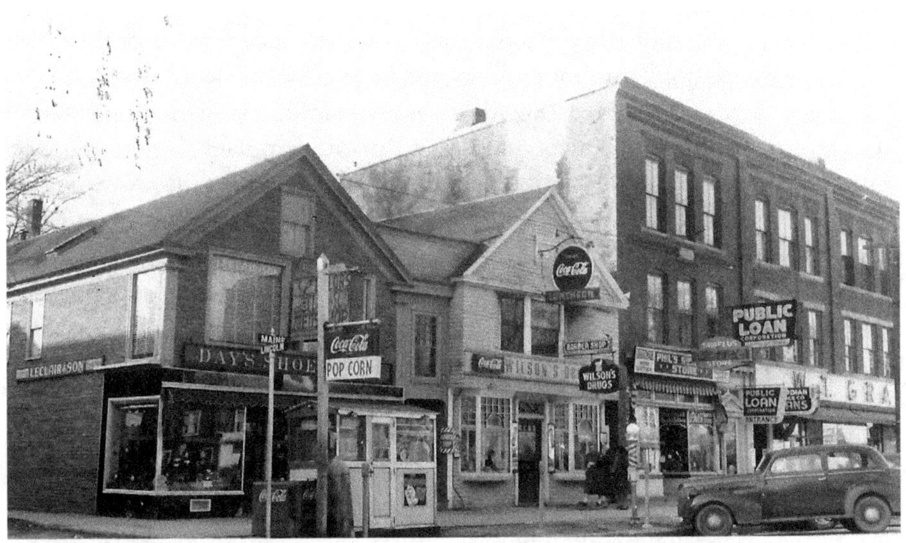

Corner of Maine and Lincoln Streets with popcorn vendor, Brunswick, circa 1941. *Brunswick Downtown Association.*

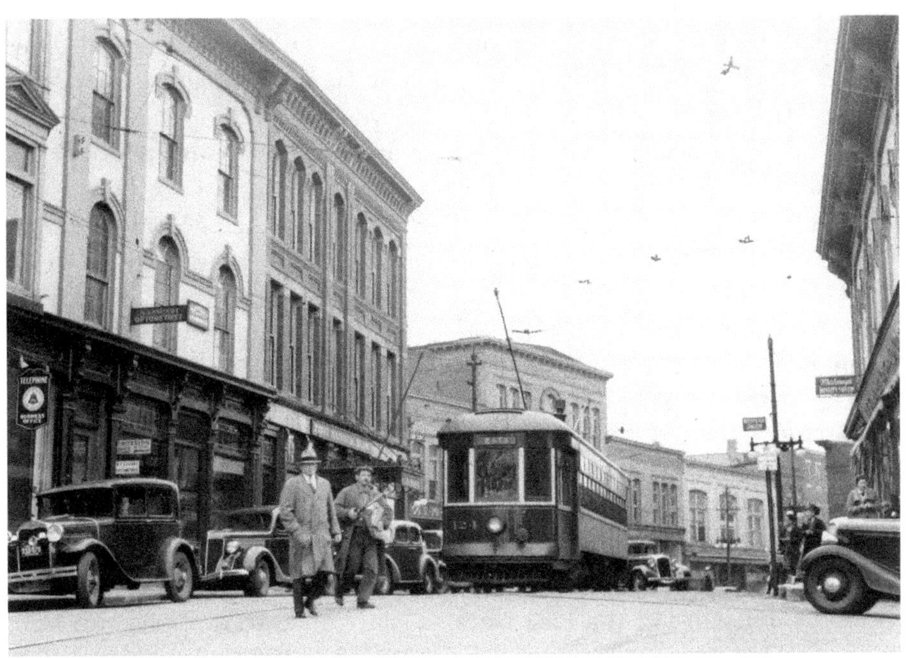

Businessman and worker walking in front of the Center Street Trolley #124 in downtown Bath at First National Bank corner. Woman shopping with children on the right-hand side of the street, circa 1942. *George Sidelinger Collection, Bath Historical Society, Bath, Maine.*

stores; news agents; movie theaters; furniture and wallpaper stores; smoke shops; funeral parlors; and more.[327]

Brunswick also had a busy downtown with a similar assortment of stores, services and eateries, but ones that catered to its population mix of town, gown and mill. There were national chain stores—Woolworth's, Newberry's and Grant's—plus Senter's department store and four grocery stores: A&P, First National, Tondreau's and Curtis IGA markets, which were all on Maine Street. There were six women's clothing stores, a corsetiere, a corset shop, a milliner, four dressmakers, fur remodeling and fur storage shops, five men's clothing stores and a popcorn vendor (until food oil rationing closed it down).[328]

Utility companies had stores in midcoast downtowns from the early days when electricity, telephone and telegraph services were first installed through the 1960s. At Central Maine Power stores, people paid their electric bills and shopped for new appliances (although few were available during the war). New England Telephone & Telegraph Co. had facilities (like the switchboard on the second floor of Senter's department store in Bath) and offices where people paid their phone bills.

Damariscotta was the shopping hub for Wiscasset, Alna, Edgecomb, New Harbor, Nobleboro and Bristol. An old New Harbor saying was that "you went to Damariscotta once a week whether you needed it or not."[329] People often asked their neighbors if they needed anything before they drove down the peninsulas. Downtown Damariscotta had Hall's and Page's shoe stores, Whitcomb & French and Castner's hardware stores, E. Murray Senter's department store, Chapman & Chapman Insurance, Marion Hitchcock's Dry Goods store, two jewelry stores, clothing stores and more. Riverview Restaurant had a bakery. Calvin Dodge remembered, "They always had beautiful homemade rolls, fig squares, baked beans and bread on Saturdays. Mr. Hall owned it. They were always noted for their seafood dinners."[330]

People shopped for food differently in the 1940s than Americans do today. In addition to the grocery stores downtown, there were small, family-owned grocery stores in every neighborhood. Brunswick had twenty-three.[331] Boothbay Harbor had nine grocery stores for a town just under six square miles but with an annual influx of thousands of summer residents and visitors.[332] They included a First National store and an A&P, plus two fruit dealers.[333] Damariscotta, over twice the physical size of Boothbay Harbor but with a smaller population, had a concentrated downtown shopping district where there were four grocery stores: Pierce's, First National, Yellowfront and the A&P.[334] Women bought food several times a week at the nearest

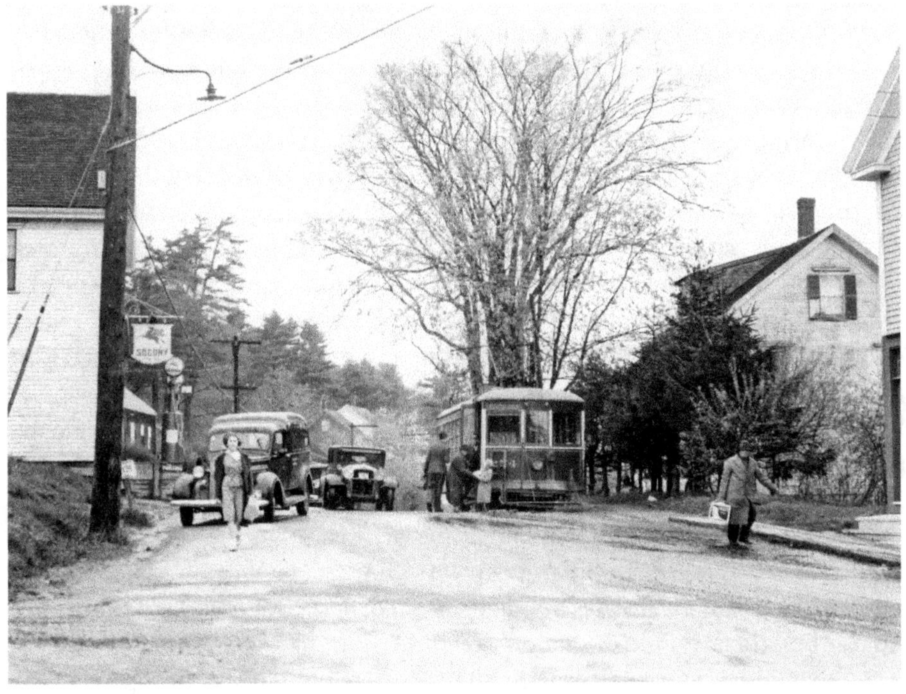

A girl carrying shopping bags near the stopped South End Trolley #254, Bath, near Socony Gas Station and line of cars. Trolley conductor can be seen talking to a man at the front of the trolley car, 1942. *Maine Maritime Museum.*

store. Most didn't drive to the store, so there was only so much they could carry in one trip. Midcoast terrain tended to go from the ocean or rivers, which made carrying purchases any distance difficult, particularly in Bath.[335] This accounts for the four First National Groceries, three A&Ps and forty-one small grocery stores doing business there in 1942.[336]

The number of stores was necessary to feed everyone, since even the chain grocery stores did not have the large quantities and varieties of foods we see today. There were separate fruit companies, like Tito Pecci's and the Sagadahoc Fruit Co. (run by the Pellegrini family) in Bath, Carbone's Fruit Store in Boothbay Harbor and the Kennebec Fruit Co. and Phillips Fruit Store in Brunswick. Most people didn't own freezers or large refrigerators, so they couldn't store perishable food unless it was canned. Customers could call in orders and have their groceries delivered (until rationing prohibited it) or send one of their children to pick them up. Even though more people had more money in their wallets during the war, they still had to stretch it between paychecks. Many mom-and-pop stores allowed regular customers to buy on credit, which was a big draw for customers but a challenge to the small business. Some merchants complained that people bought from them on credit and then went to the A&P or First National when they got their paycheck.[337]

Each grocery store had its own personality. Store staff knew their customers, their families and what each person liked. Nobody thought anything of sending very small children to the grocery store to pick something up for their mothers. Many stores had meat counters where a butcher, often the owner, cut your meat to order. Some had candy counters or sold ice cream that came in paper cups with pictures of movie stars on them with little wooden spoons.[338] Pendleton's in Wiscasset was known for its ribbon candy.[339] Cyr's Market on Front Street in Bath sold S.S. Pierce specialties from the high-end market in Boston favored by summer residents and locals like Jennie Tucker, seventy-five, of Wiscasset.[340] Some stores had lunch counters with take-out sandwiches and hot dogs. Submarine sandwiches were very popular.[341] Powers Market on Washington Street in Bath was famous for Morse's Sauerkraut, corned beef and fish on Fridays (that it bought from a fish market downtown). It also had a molasses barrel with a spigot; customers brought their own containers to fill up.[342] Some stores still had pickle barrels and pot-bellied stoves around which old men could sit and tell stories or put a checkerboard over the pickle barrel and play

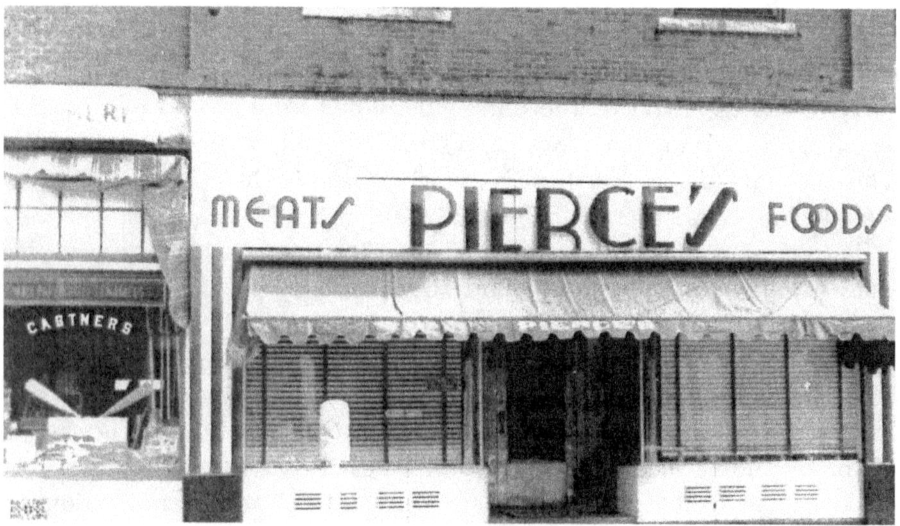

Exterior of Pierce's Grocery Store, Main Street, Damariscotta, 1942. *Courtesy of Calvin and Marjorie Dodge.*

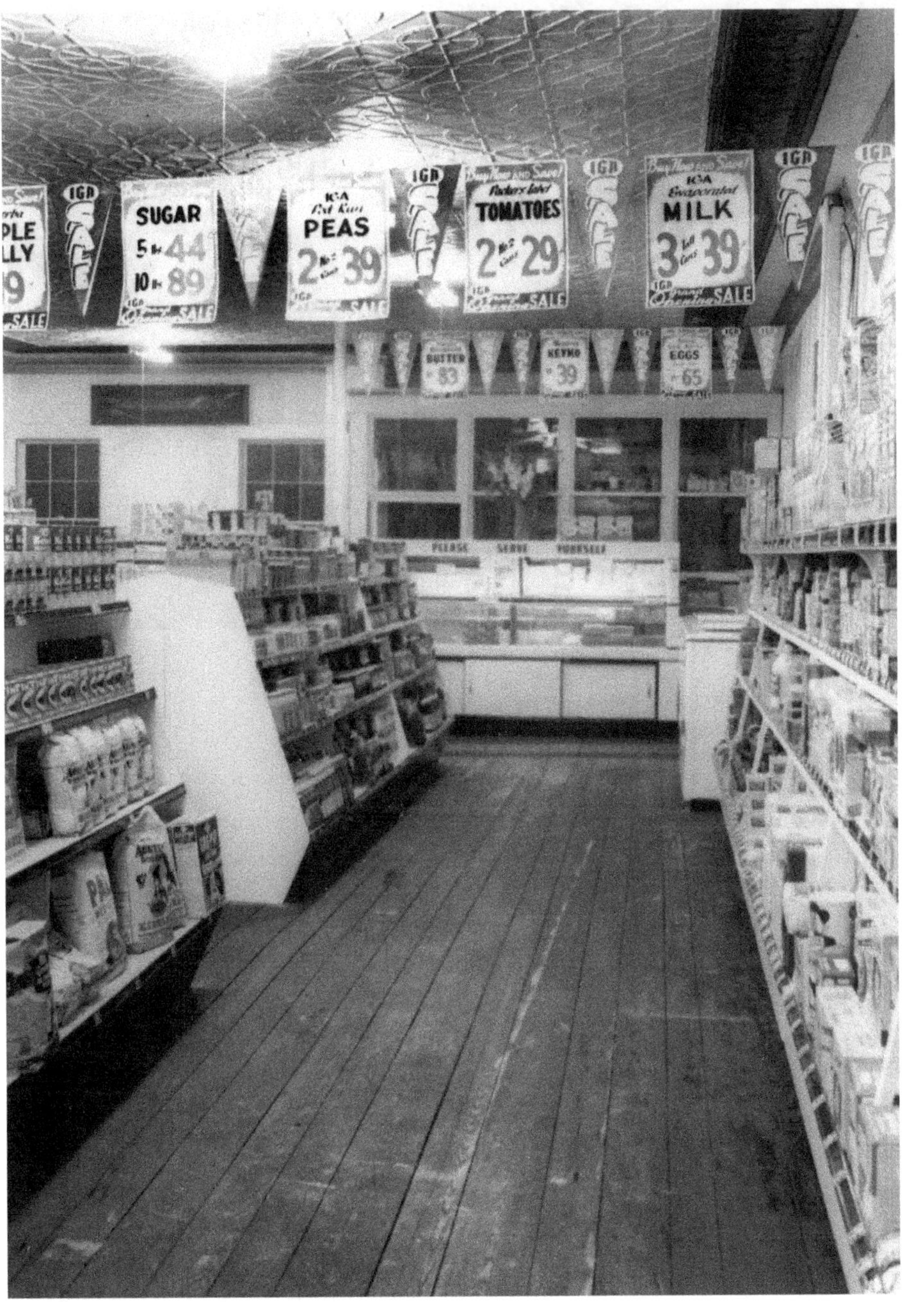

Interior of Pierce's Grocery Store, Main Street, Damariscotta, 1942. *Courtesy of Calvin and Marjorie Dodge.*

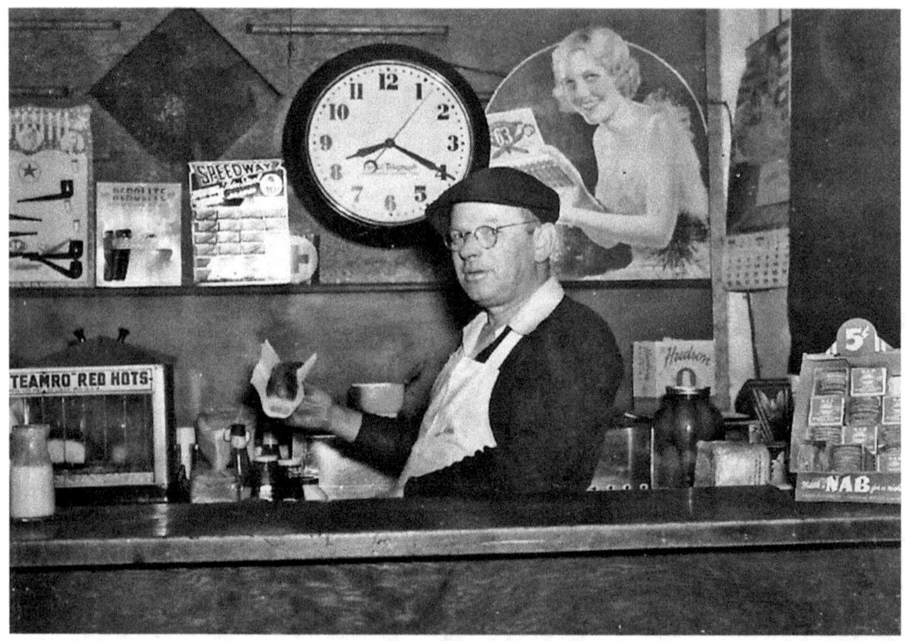

Sam Povich standing behind the counter of his grocery store at 465 Middle Street, Bath, 1943. *Courtesy of Kerry Nelson from Nancy Richter.*

games.[343] Flossie Comeau's market on Floral Street in Bath was known for her homemade donuts.[344] The Damariscotta A&P had a coffee grinder right by the front door, "so it always smelled wonderful as you entered."[345] Pierce's and First National had good butcher counters. "Nothing was pre-cut. You told them what you wanted and it was cut. Meat was delivered in half-side sizes," remembered Calvin Dodge. The First National Store was the first to start selling ready-made ice cream.[346]

Smaller towns and villages had general stores that sold groceries along with other staples. Harpswell had fourteen general stores in 1944.[347] The more rural ones, where there was no home delivery, often had small post offices inside so people had somewhere within walking distance to send and pick up their mail. These stores also functioned as social centers, where you could go hear the latest news and conversations about your neighbors.

Coffee was rationed in November 1942. Each person was allowed one pound of coffee for five weeks. This amounted to less than one cup a day per person, or about half of what most people were accustomed to drinking. People made their rations stretch by reusing grounds and making do with weaker coffee. Substitute drinks like chicory coffee and Postum (made of roasted grains) became popular, but only until coffee rationing was lifted.

Sugar rationing was especially hard for bakeries and restaurants. By January 1943, Nap's Bakery in Brunswick was advertising, "No More Bread or Rolls for the duration."[348] In March, it advertised new rules for Saturday orders and a later opening time.[349] There were to be no more advance orders for Saturday pickup—except for baked beans, which it promised to have available "as long as supply lasts."[350] In April, the OPA ordered substantial curtailment of doughnut production because of cooking oil shortages, so "No Doughnuts for the Duration."[351]

Ration Book Two, effective March 1, 1943, expanded the program to point rationing. Butter; margarine; shortening; salad oil; processed foods; canned, bottled or frozen fruits and vegetables; and juices were added to the list of rationed foods. Margarine was marketed as the substitute for butter.[352] Made primarily from vegetable oils, the margarine came in two parts: the whitish solid and the yellow artificial coloring. Children were often allowed to put the color in and mix it all up. Since children love playing with food, this created another fond memory for many people.[353] Another alternative was to add milk, salt and gelatin to the butter to stretch your rations.[354]

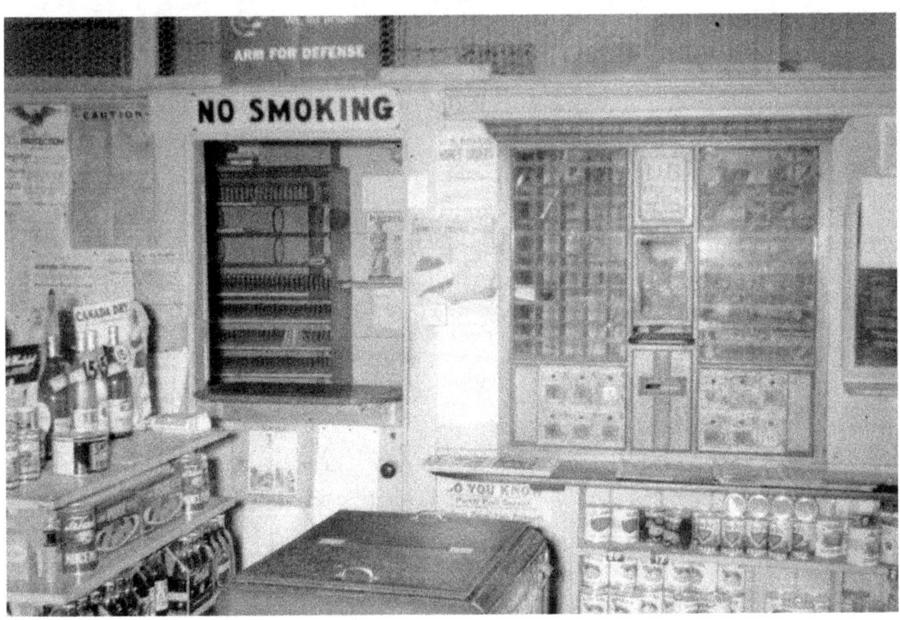

Interior of J.H. Welsh & Son General Store, Boothbay, 1942. *Boothbay Region Historical Society.*

Ration Book Two stamps were each worth a certain number of points that the shopper could spend for any combination of rationed goods. The stamps were blue and red, with different letters and numbers on them. The letter indicated the period during which the stamps would be valid. The number gave the stamp's point value. People had to constantly check the newspapers for the latest schedule of which stamps should be used for which commodities. Merchants and consumers had to be vigilant and stay current with the system to ensure that they obeyed the laws and didn't miss out on getting the food or products they needed. There was a column in every newspaper at least once a week that listed "Important Ration Dates" or "Rationing Reminders."

On March 29, 1943, all meats (including canned meats and fish) and some cheeses were added to the list. Each cut of meat (regardless of type or grade) was assigned a point value per pound based on available supply. Point values and validity timing changed frequently based on supply fluctuations. For the first time under the rationing system, stamps could be given to shoppers for change when they didn't have the exact stamps for their purchases. Retailers could give Red 1-point stamps marked A or B as change, but they would only be valid within their stated time frame.[355]

In Brunswick, Amy Cushing and Susie Sylvester knew people needed help to understand the increasingly complex rationing program. The weekly newspaper columns were helpful but not enough to translate the points, stamps, poundage, values and timing of all the different rationed commodities. Working with the grocers, the CSC Neighborhood Plan posted volunteers in stores to help shoppers. They explained how to plan meals and purchase as many canned goods as possible with the fewest coupons. Volunteers answered shoppers' questions and assuaged fears about shortages and the latest changes in the rationing system. In addition to the weekly OPA columns, Tondreau's and other markets posted large weekly ads telling people what rationed and non-rationed goods were available. Curtis IGA Market, a little farther down Maine Street, called its ad a "Rationing Information Service."[356]

The OWI worked with movie studios to produce films supporting rationing and ceiling prices. *Food and Magic* featured a magician talking to a crowd of people at a fair. After making bread disappear, he told them:

> *Bread is ammunition as valuable as bullets…and every week, two million loaves of bread are wasted that could have gone to feeding our troops. It's like throwing victory in the garbage can.…Food fights for freedom and it's*

> *the weapon in our hands here at home and we can use it to mow down our enemies just as surely as if it were a machine gun and it's easy.*

The movie concludes with the actor exhorting people to follow four simple rules (as "My Country 'Tis of Thee" plays in the background):

> *#1 is Produce. Help however you can whether it's on a farm or with a Victory Garden. #2 is Avoid Waste. Eat the right foods and preserve. #3 Share—with the armed forces, our allies and each other. Accept rationing and shortages cheerfully. And finally #4, Play Square. Make adjustments and play by the rules.*[357]

The OWI also made films to educate audiences about the importance of good nutrition and a varied diet. The message was that you helped the war effort by keeping your body and your family's bodies strong. Good nutrition reduced absenteeism and accidents and helped workers focus and do a better job. The surgeon general appeared in one movie saying that Americans needed to "build an armor of health."[358] The films promoted public nutrition classes and eating balanced meals with milk, meat or other proteins, fresh fruit, leafy salads and cooked vegetables. White bread was recommended as a good source of Vitamin D. The average war worker was said to need twice the amount of green vegetables he or she had been eating before the war. Soldiers needed 25 percent more food than civilians. The narrator of the movie said, "Build a clever, tougher more vigorous nation. Victory depends on better morale and more strength of mind and body than the world's ever known."[359]

A front-page photograph in the January 14, 1943 *Brunswick Record* showed an empty meat counter with the headline "Typical Meat Counter." Meat was an essential part of the American diet, and people got creative about dealing with the shortages. They ate scrapple as a substitute for ham, and lots of Spam.[360] Hamburger meat was the most important ingredient in many recipes of the time, especially for people cooking on a budget. If they couldn't find it in the stores, they looked for substitutes. Women learned when deliveries were coming to their favorite store and would line up hours before the store opened to buy rationed goods. Many grocers usually managed to save at least a few preferred cuts for their favorite customers each time a supply came in—another advantage of shopping at the local market. One meat substitute was made from soy. "It came in powder form, and after you added some water to it, you could make little patties, the size of hamburgers.

We called them 'bean burgers,' and I thought they were really pretty good," remembered Ronald Orchard of Southport.[361] Another surprisingly palatable alternative was horse meat. One Southport man remembered going all the way to Harpswell for meat, even though sometimes all that was available was horse meat.[362] Grace Dodge was a schoolgirl who worked at the First National Store in Boothbay in her spare time. She remembered grinding coffee and putting it in quarter-pound bags to sell. Butter was cut into quarter-pounds as well. Delivery days were always very busy, with people lining up hoping to get what they needed.[363] Once a week, when meat was delivered, the lines were especially long. Sometimes Pinkham's was the only store in the Boothbay region to have meat, so people would "line up all the way around the monument waiting to get some. Customers even came over from Boothbay Harbor for it. One time I sent my children up to the store for stew meat, and they came home with a rack of lamb chops. It was all Charlie [Pinkham] had, so I made a lamb chop stew, and it was real good," remembered Winona Taylor Rand.[364] Liver and kidneys were marketed as good protein-rich substitutes for meat.

Gas, tire and fuel rationing tightened significantly through 1943 and into 1944. On January 6, 1943, the OPA announced an abrupt ban on pleasure and nonessential driving in seventeen eastern states, including Maine. The penalty for disobeying the ban was complete revocation of your gas and tire rationing. Visitors from places not under the ban were told they had to comply with it when in Maine. Anyone who left their motors running, a common practice due to the difficulty of starting some cars in the extreme cold, would have their gas and tire rationing revoked. The publicly stated reason was that "there simply wasn't enough to go around."[365] Heating oil shortages in September 1943 led the OPA to ask that anyone who had converted from oil back to coal heating give their oil coupons back so they could be given to people in need before the coupons expired. The winter of 1943–44 was worse than the year before, beginning with temperatures of twenty below zero on December 21, the first day of winter.[366]

Entertainment and celebrations were also casualties of rationing and shortages. There were no Fourth of July fireworks from 1942 to 1945. The Boothbay Playhouse, a nationally known summer stock theater, had to close in 1943 because so many of its staff were in the military.[367] The annual Lincoln County Fair and Wiscasset's Open House Days were cancelled from 1943 to 1945. The Topsham Fair was cancelled in 1944, the first time in eighty-nine years, due to lack of available manpower.[368] The Brunswick High

School sophomore and junior class prom was scheduled for February 19, 1943, in the high school auditorium. Students, alumni and their guests were all invited, but rationing meant many cars couldn't be used to get people to the dance. The dress code was changed from evening dress to casual since it would be highly impractical to walk to a dance in the winter in a gown or tuxedo.[369]

OPA announcements on pleasure travel sent mixed and confusing messages in the spring of 1943. On April 1, the OPA announced that motorboat owners would be able to get gas that summer for non-occupational purposes, with the amount based on the horsepower of the boat's engines. That didn't seem fair to people restricted from traveling to see loved ones. Then, just two weeks later, the OPA suspended all gas rations for pleasure boats for ten days and warned that further cuts were coming.[370] On April 22, it announced that there would be no extra gas rations for people to travel to and from summer homes and no gas available for pleasure boats. By then, the message was clear: there would be no special deals, even for the tourism industry or the wealthy.

On May 27, 1943, all pleasure and nonessential driving was banned. This created considerable confusion about what constituted "nonessential" driving. Parents could drive children to school only if there was more than one child in the car. Driving to cemeteries for funerals was allowed but not driving to church if other transportation was available, such as a bus. People wondered if driving to go hunting or fishing (which helped with food shortages) or to the market to buy food were considered pleasure driving. If a bowling alley or movie theater was on your direct route to or from work, you could stop there, but only if you did not deviate from your normal route. The recommendation from newspaper writers was to ask yourself if you could convince the ration board that the driving was necessary and make your own decision.[371]

In June, gas rations were cut still further, even for war workers. There was no more extra gas for servicemen home on leave. Town allocations of gas were also cut. The Brunswick Highway Department (including the fire department) had its quota cut by 44 percent over the previous period. Gas rationing continued to tighten through 1944 and into 1945.

VICTORY GARDENS

Victory Gardens were one of the most popular homefront campaigns. Feeding the troops came first, so anything homegrown helped the war effort. Fruits, vegetables, eggs or meat grown or raised for your own consumption added to the food supply and didn't use up valuable war material for transportation, production or packaging, so they were not rationed.

Victory Gardens were also a great way to get children involved in the war effort and teach them good habits and skills. Calvin Dodge remembered helping with his family's Victory Garden. "It was amazing how much you could get out of a small garden by growing all the vegetables in neat lines like they told you to."[372] Newspapers and magazines showed photos of adorable children helping their mothers or older siblings plant these gardens. Schools planted Victory Gardens and used the produce in student lunches. By 1944, 40 percent of all vegetables grown in the United States came from Victory Gardens.[373]

Everyone started a Victory Garden, wherever they lived. Gardens were planted in window boxes and on rooftops. Tenants and boarders helped their landlord or host family work in their garden. The Town of Brunswick offered free Water Street land for people to use for Victory Gardens.[374] Creating and caring for these gardens boosted morale from being outside and near nature and because the gardeners knew they were contributing something to the war effort. It was also a way for families from rural areas who had moved to larger towns for war work to do something that made them feel more connected to home, wherever that home happened to be.

Companies like Central Maine Power (CMP) held Victory Garden contests. CMP's was like an agricultural fair, with employee contestants entering different classes of their produce throughout the growing season. Participants received red, white and blue window stickers, and colored ribbons were awarded to the winners.[375]

Food from Victory Gardens helped stretch ration stamps and provided locally grown fresh produce that added flavor and color to what were often bland ration-constricted meals. Recipes of the period made heavy use of cottage cheese, Jell-O, cabbage and cereal. Agricultural companies published tips on how to make seedlings grow in different climates. The University of Maine sent food and Victory Garden specialists into communities to teach people how to plan flavorful, nutritious meals in wartime. The announcement of their classes in the *Boothbay Register* of March 19, 1943, asked, "Did you know that the Government has taken over for the coming year for the armed

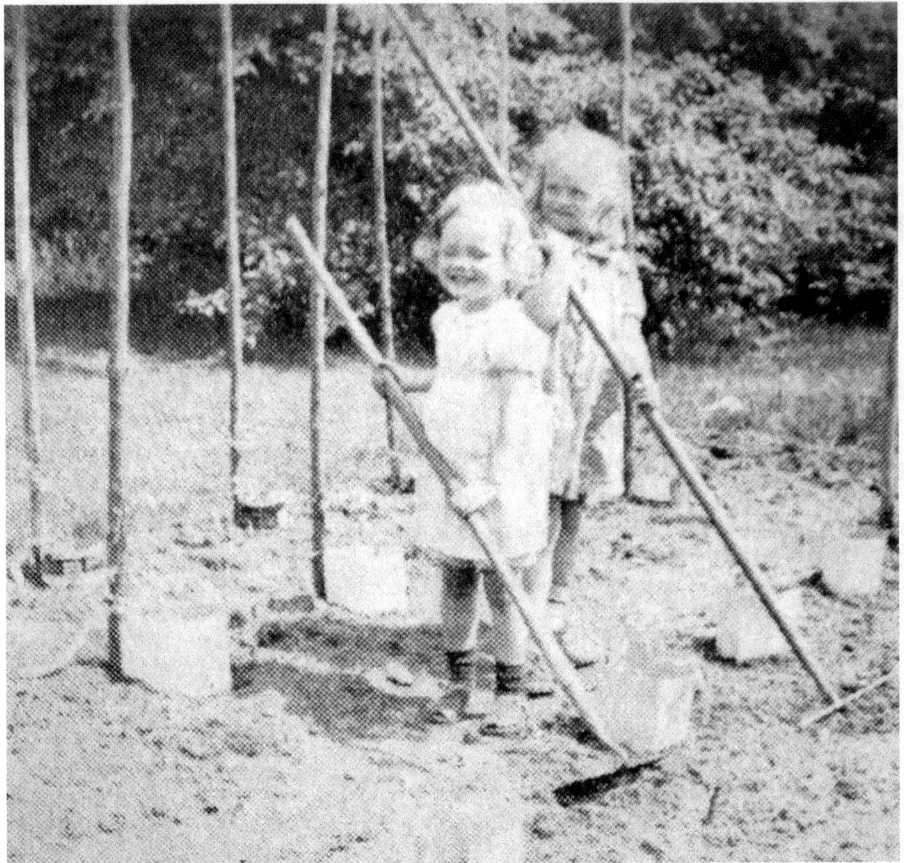

Left to right: Mary Grace Hanks, three, and Nancy Hanks, five, in Mrs. Anthony Lebel's garden on Pleasant Street in Brunswick, near where they lived. Brunswick Record, *June 10, 1943.*

forces and Lend-Lease the following: 100% of the blueberries, 71% of fruit cocktails, 46% of grape juice, 63% of the peaches, 100% of the carrots, 48% of the peas, 81% of the beets. Plan to have a Victory Garden!"[376]

The government published recipe books on how to prepare homegrown vegetables, including some that most people had never tasted before or known they could grow. Tomatoes, carrots, lettuce, beets, peas and potatoes were the most popular vegetables to plant. Victory Gardens helped introduce Swiss chard and kohlrabi into the American diet.

Wartime marketing told Americans how to eat healthy and make everyone feel like they were still eating well despite the shortages. Newspapers and magazines featured articles on food planning, purchasing and presentation.

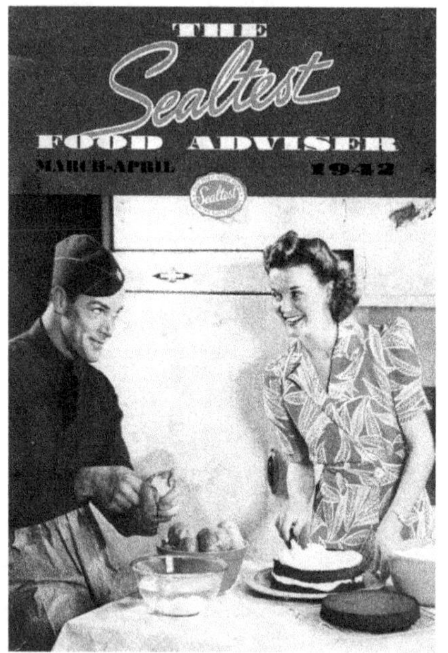

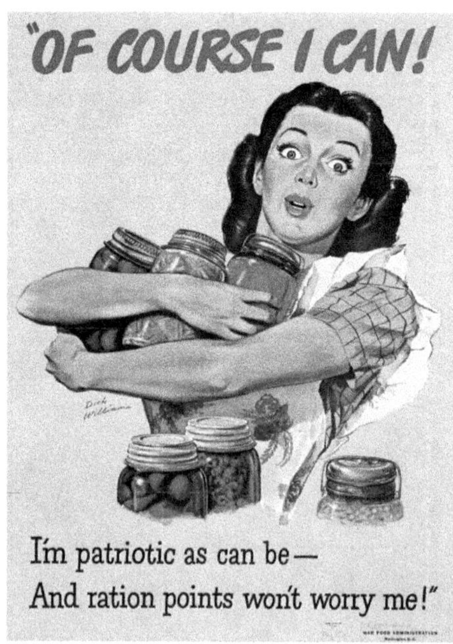

Left: *The Sealtest Food Adviser*, March–April 1942 brochure. *Author's collection.*

Right: "Of Course I Can! I'm patriotic as can be—and ration points won't worry me!" poster, Dick Williams, artist. War Food Administration, Washington, D.C., 1944. *Northwestern University Library, images.northwestern.edu.*

Food companies and grocery chains published cookbooks filled with meal planning guidance, such as General Foods' *Staunch Friends for Today's Kitchen*, filled with recipes using its products, including Grape Nuts cereals, Jell-O products, Bakers Chocolate and Cocoa, Maxwell House and Yuban Coffee, Calumet Baking Powder, Log Cabin Syrup and Birdseye Frosted Foods. Housewives could read Grand Union's *101 Ways to Enjoy Today's Victory Food, Fresh Fruit and Vegetables* or *The Sealtest Food Adviser*, which offered tasty recipes for cream of cabbage and lettuce soup; beet, corn and cottage cheese salad; and cottage cheese vegetable casserole, with a picture of a soldier who looked like Gary Cooper on the cover.[377]

Canning was another good way to stretch the food supply and enable families to have fruit and vegetables all year. As an incentive, home canners were given one additional pound of sugar for every four quarts of finished canned fruit, plus an additional pound of sugar for each family member if they helped pack preserves, jams, jellies and fruit butters.[378] Most towns held canning programs in the summer and fall each year from 1942 to 1944.

In Brunswick, the CSC established a canning center in the home economics room of Brunswick High School and offered a six-week instruction course. Once again managed by Susie Sylvester, the center was staffed by women volunteers, with local farmers contributing the fruit and vegetables. Women were taught "all methods of conserving food in addition to modern canning methods including tin-can canning, drying, salting and krauting."[379] Tin cans were available for four cents a can. Women were told to bring their own foods and their own glass jars, if that was their preferred storage method (plus extra glass jars in case of breakage). One of every four cans went to be used in school lunches at St. John's School and the high school. Beatrice Wells of Boody Street, forty-four, wife of the Bowdoin College baseball coach and mother of two teenage girls, was photographed as she attended the center's opening day.

In 1943, the center was led by two home economics teachers who taught students the fine points of canning. Topsham residents were asked to give one can out of nine for Topsham school lunch programs. Susie Sylvester applied for and received surplus government commodities that were then canned by the Brunswick Teachers' Club for the Longfellow and high school lunch projects.[380] The Brunswick center was very successful, with about six thousand cans put up by September 9. Several men participated that year, including author Harold T. Pulsifer, fifty-nine, and property manager Frank DeWick, sixty, both of Federal Street, and college janitor Billy Frost, fifty-nine, of Boody Street. Susie Sylvester was given a much-needed break in October when Alexine Fortin, fifty-five, took over scheduling for the center, with high school and some eighth grade girls helping.

The harvests of 1943 were very large, and a lot of food would have been wasted without the canning effort. As time went on, people got creative about what they canned, in addition to the expected corn, tomatoes, beans, beets, carrots and apples. Sarah Zeitler, forty-two, wife of an investment broker and mother of three children ages ten to seventeen, brought in chicken to be canned. The newspaper reported that the most unusual foodstuff put up was brought in by Mr. Catlin, the janitor at Brunswick High School.[381] Ernest Catlin, fifty-three, and his wife, Florence, forty-eight (who ran the school's cafeteria), had two sons in the navy, Arnold and Kenneth. Ernest brought in a bushel of quahogs to be canned.

Ration Book Three (for meats and fats) was issued in September 1943 but was replaced in November by Ration Book Four. Shoppers were forced to carry three ration books because stamps from Ration Book Two and Three

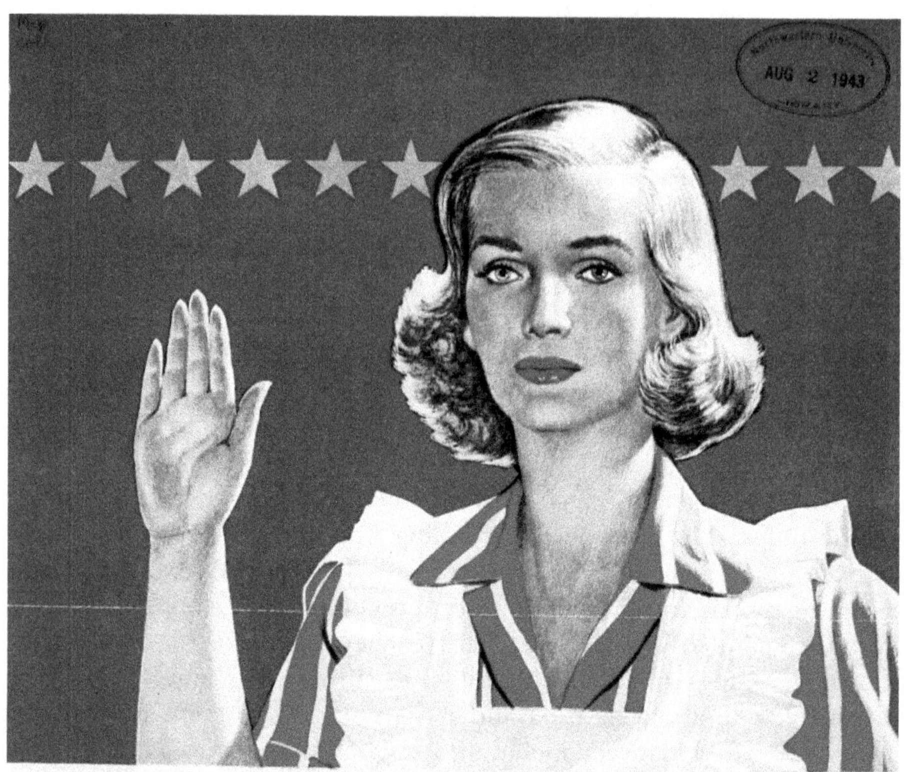

"Make This Pledge: I pay no more than top legal prices," poster. Office of Price Administration, Washington, D.C., 1943. *Northwestern University Library, images.northwestern.edu.*

were still useable when Ration Book Four was introduced. The purpose of Ration Book Four was to simplify a system that had become too complicated for consumers and too cumbersome for retailers. To pay suppliers and service their customers, grocers had to sort multiple coupons and stamps of different sizes and value while also keeping up with stringent OPA accounting and reporting requirements. In January 1944, the OPA made all stamps worth ten points, and plastic tokens were created to be used for change.

Shortages worsened considerably in 1943. Farmers who sold meat and butter had to collect ration stamps from their customers just like retail establishments. Newspapers published more photos of empty meat counters. The Androscoggin and Sagadahoc War Boards published a warning that the black market for meat was a real danger for the midcoast. All farmers who did any butchering were required to get a license and to stamp their meat with an indelible pencil, even if it was only one animal or one part of an animal. A March 25, 1943 *Brunswick Record* article warned that the black market for meat was so strong, it was affecting the supply available to the army and navy.

The OPA launched an intensive marketing campaign to fight the black market. Everyone at home was asked to take the pledge: "I pay no more than top legal prices. I accept no rationed goods without giving up ration stamps." OWI movie shorts hammered home the message that using the black market was unpatriotic. *Prices Unlimited*, made by Universal Picture Company for the OPA and OWI in 1944, showed moviegoers what would happen without price stabilization and rationing. It featured two young women who decide to spend all their ration stamps on an expensive cut of meat. That night, the girl most frustrated by rationing has a nightmare about the ugly behavior that happens when supply is limited and there are no price controls or rationing. When she wakes up, she's an enthusiastic convert to playing by the rules.[382]

Most people accepted rationing as essential for the war effort, but that didn't mean they liked it. One survey suggested that 25 percent of the American public thought using the black market occasionally for a special need was acceptable.[383] But as Geraldine Coombs, who was a student at Colby during the war, said, "Everybody had a responsibility. You didn't feel like you were denying yourself when you couldn't have sugar, etc. You felt like you were doing your bit and the men would get fed."[384]

As the war news improved, American optimism strengthened, and with it the sense that since things were getting better, surely rationing didn't need to be as strict. The OPA had to keep explaining that the reason people felt better about the food supply was *because* of rationing, strict attention to limiting waste and continued diligence in canning and growing food. Given the extreme labor shortage, farmers were hard-pressed to keep producing at the level the country needed. People were urged to help them however they could, whether it be through volunteering to help bring in a crop or continuing to manage their diet and health in strict accordance with the rules of nutrition and rationing. News of the Battle of the Bulge the week before Christmas 1944 was a bitter blow to morale that made everyone realize that hard fighting and sacrifices were still ahead.

The winter of 1944–45 saw the worst meat and fuel shortages of the war. In addition to feeding the troops and the homefront and sending food to Britain and Russia, America was now also helping people in countries liberated by the Allies. Even with military successes and the eventual end of the war in 1945, it took a while for supplies to build back up. Some shortages and price controls continued even after a commodity came off rationing. Coffee rationing was the first to be repealed (in July 1943). Meat rationing was briefly suspended in May 1944 but reinstated that December. Gas rationing ended in August 1945. Meat, canned foods, shoes and then food oils came off the rationing list in November and December 1945. Sugar rationing finally ended in July 1947.[385]

Chapter 13

DON'T SIT UNDER THE APPLE TREE WITH ANYONE ELSE BUT ME

Homefront life wasn't all war work, volunteering and standing in ration lines. There were parties, sports, dances, music, movies and the radio to lighten hearts and add some romance during tough times.

Listening to the radio was an important part of everyday life. People trusted their favorite radio newsmen and found comfort in their voices, even when the news was grim. Gabriel Heatter, born and raised in Brooklyn, New York, by Austrian immigrant parents, had become famous for his reporting of the Lindbergh baby kidnapping trial. With his mellifluous voice, Heatter was as well known to most Americans as his contemporaries Edward R. Murrow and Walter Winchell. Heatter always coupled his news with an uplifting story of life on the American homefront. In 1942, after months of bad news from the Pacific, the United States finally sank a Japanese destroyer. Heatter began his program that night with what became his catchphrase: "Good evening, everyone. There's good news tonight."[386] Calvin Dodge remembered that all the adults in his family in Newcastle and Damariscotta tuned in every night to get their war news from Heatter.[387] Jean Huskins Chenoweth remembered, "My grandmother listened to 'her programs' every morning on an old Philco radio, *The Arthur Godfrey Show* and *The Light of the World*. I think most of what I know about the Bible came from *The Light of the World*."[388] Comedy programs like *Abbott and Costello* and *Amos 'n' Andy* made people laugh during dark times. Children loved programs like *The Lone Ranger*, *The Shadow*, *Captain Midnight* and *Dick Tracy*.

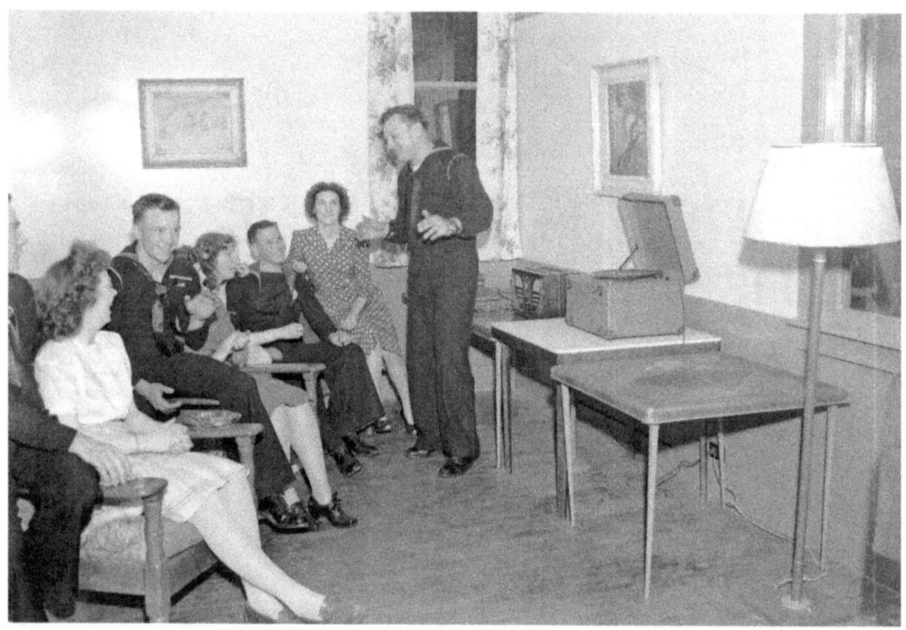

USO music room, 186 Front Street, Bath, April 29, 1944. *Photographer Otis. N.E. Card, Richard Card Collection, Sagadahoc History & Genealogy Room, Patten Free Library.*

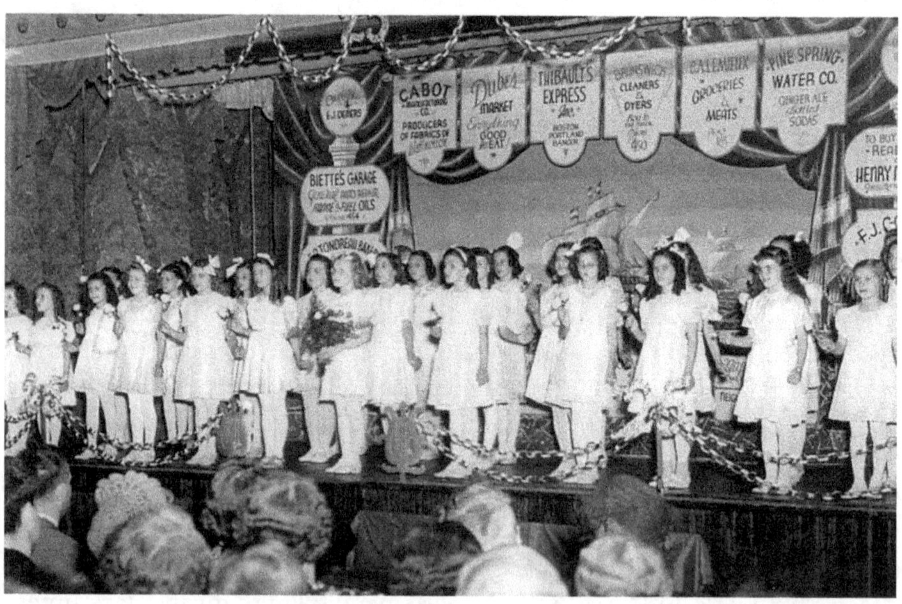

St. John the Baptist Church pageant at the celebration of Reverend William J. Dauphin's twenty-fifth ordination anniversary in the school auditorium, with local business sponsorship banners overhead, 1944. *Courtesy of Bob Bouchard.*

Social life for most people revolved around family, church and school. Churches were important social centers with their own clubs and auxiliary organizations. Catholics, Episcopalians, Baptists, Unitarians, Congregationalists and many other denominations had active congregations throughout the midcoast. Bath had the nearest Jewish temple, Bath Israel Congregation, and a Swedenborgian church, the Church of the New Jerusalem. Brunswick had two Catholic churches: St. John the Baptist, known as the "French" church, and St. Charles Borromeo, known as the "Irish" church.[389]

On the secular side, there were clubs and organizations, many with a mission of service to the community. Local chapters of fraternal organizations like the Knights of Pythias and their women's auxiliaries had active calendars. Granges were important rural social centers. Boothbay, Topsham, West Bath, Freeport, Newcastle, Wiscasset and Woolwich all had active granges. In Boothbay, there was a grange meeting every Thursday night in the town hall with refreshments, music and dancing.[390] Square dancing, country and contra dancing were all popular, the latter two danced to a mix of traditional

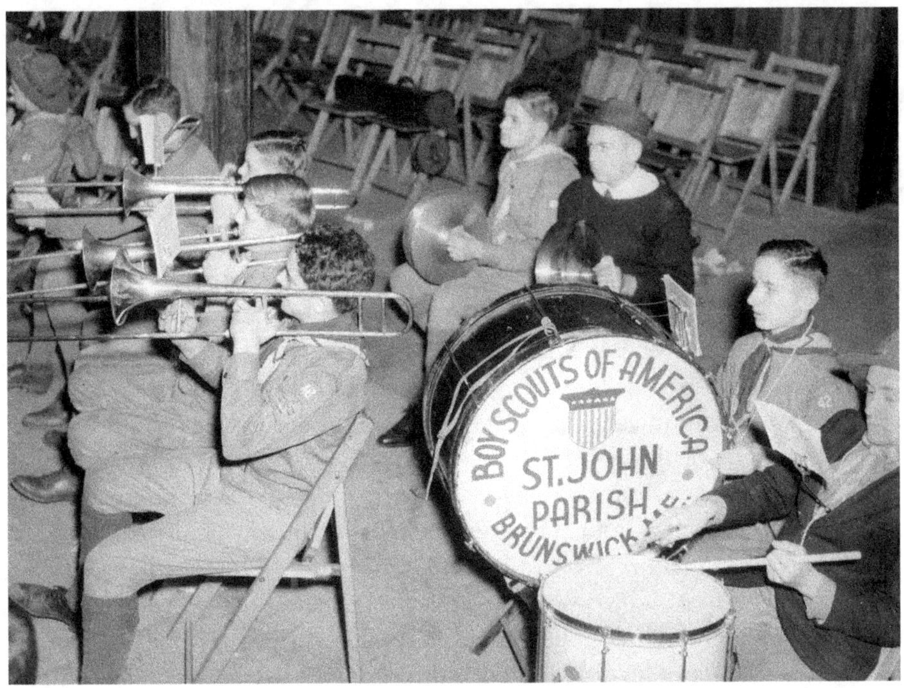

St. John the Baptist Church Boy Scout Band, circa 1943. *Courtesy of Bob Bouchard.*

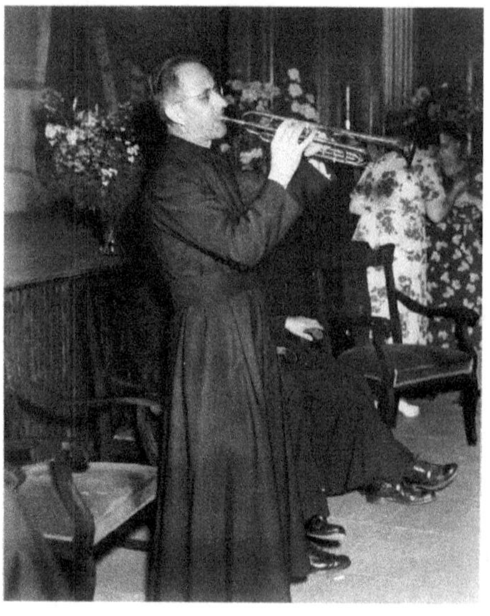

Reverend William J. Dauphin playing the trumpet, circa 1942. *Courtesy of Bob Bouchard.*

folk, bluegrass, Celtic and maritime music. Boy Scouts, Girl Scouts and Campfire Girls were popular organizations for younger people.

Music was an important part of many people's lives. They listened to music on the radio, played records or made their own music. Ethnic heritage was preserved by people playing Irish, French-Canadian, Native American, Italian, Russian or Jewish music taught to them by their elders. Communities, companies, schools and clubs had their own bands that gave well-attended concerts and played at holiday parades and celebrations. Boothbay Harbor, Wiscasset and Damariscotta had municipal bands.[391] St. John's Church in Brunswick had an adult band, a school band and even a harmonica band. The pastor, Reverend William Dauphin, forty-nine, played a mean trumpet and often played with the church bands. Bath had the Dunlap Commandery Band (later the Bath Municipal Band) and BIW's Bath Marine Band. Bailey Island servicemen formed their own band with drums, guitars, an accordion, banjos and a trombone. Choral groups ranged from church choirs to quasi-professional groups like Les Camarades Musicaux (in Bath) to barbershop quartets. Swing music was the soundtrack of the era, with the Glenn Miller, Tommy Dorsey, Harry James and Benny Goodman orchestras selling out performances around the country. The uniquely American music of the 1940s helped raise spirits around the world and left an indelible legacy still enjoyed today.

Brunswick was a hopping place, with downtown restaurants, movies, dances, concerts and theater. There were dances at the town hall on Thursday and Saturday nights organized by Frank Cunha and Horace Atwood, two Verney Mill employees, whose wives collected tickets and checked coats. For the Thursday night dances, the promoter promised, "There will be a snappy eight-piece band to furnish dance music guaranteed to tickle toes right through the toughest G.I. shoes."[392] The dances were free to servicemen and featured bands like Wes Plaisted and His Sensational Orchestra[393] on

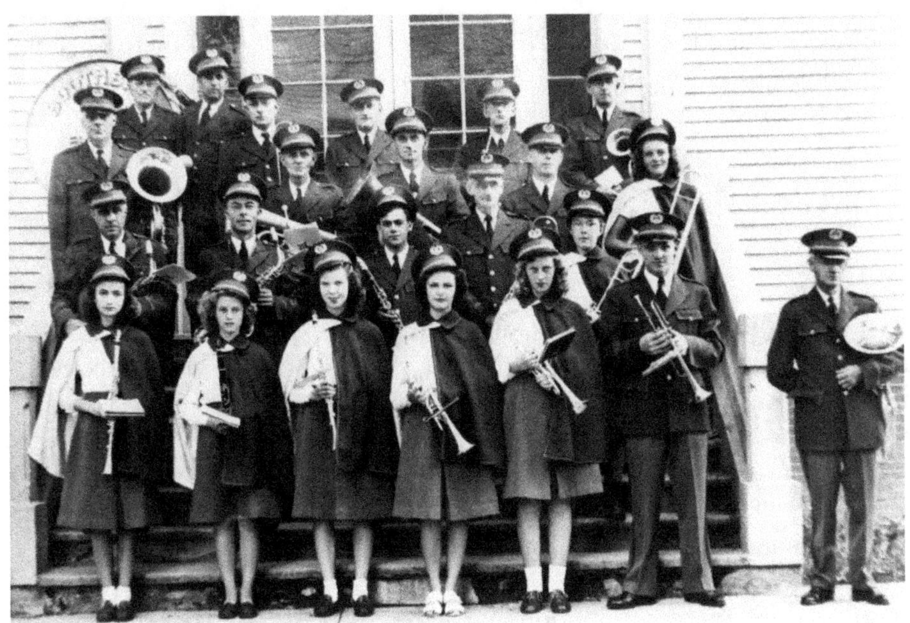

Boothbay Harbor Band, 1940s. *Boothbay Region Historical Society.*

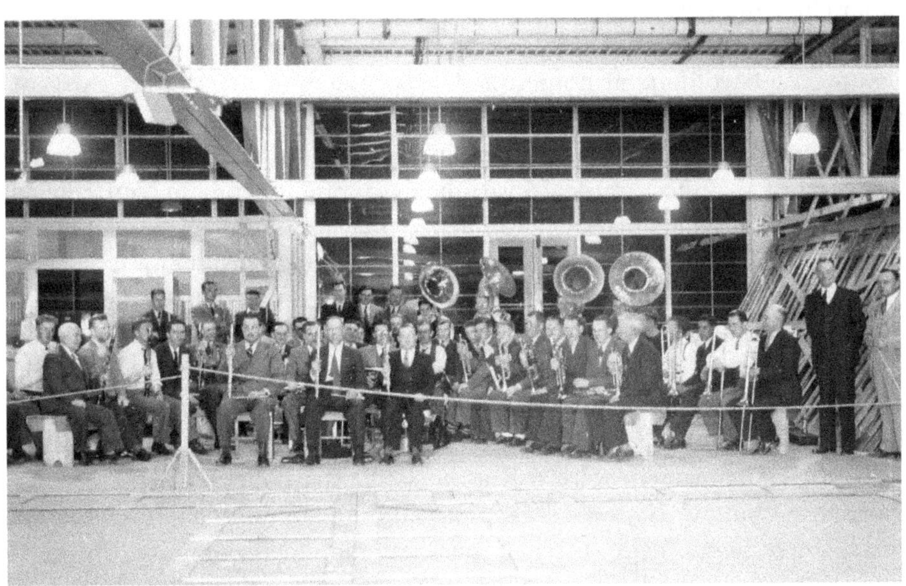

BIW Band, 1943. *Maine Maritime Museum, BIW Collection.*

Saturdays. Attendance ranged from 500 to 850 people, and there were no fights or disturbances reported.[394] Friday nights featured stage shows like the Rustic Radio Revue.[395]

The USO

The USO's mission was to boost morale by helping servicemen and women forget about the war for a little while. It was one of the few organizations that went out of its way to include black soldiers and defense workers. Clubs were established near military posts and defense industries, financed by public donations and organized by volunteers, primarily women. Bath, Brunswick, Damariscotta and Bailey Island had USO clubs. The Bath USO, opened in 1941, was in the Columbian Block that already housed the YMCA and a theater. It offered meals, snacks, programs, a reading room, a game room, a ping-pong table and movies. Holiday programs on Christmas, Easter and New Year's Eve incorporated local talent, vaudeville acts and singers. The facility was also used for meetings and parties for other clubs in town.

What servicemen most wanted to do when they were off-duty was what they would have done at home: read, relax, listen to music, play cards or games, dance and spend time with women. USO clubs gave servicemen and war workers a place to do those things. Communities donated furniture, books, games, radios, musical instruments, sports equipment and cooked food to create home-like environments that were staffed by volunteer hostesses—women ranging in age from high school girls to senior citizens.

The Brunswick USO opened in October 1942 in town hall. Within a year, it was welcoming over 2,400 servicemen a month, with a staff of 65 hostesses ranging in age from fifteen to almost eighty, including Alma Drapeau, Amy Cushing and Ruth Bangs. Two hostesses were always on duty. The youngest hostesses, sixteen-year-old Doris Holbrook and Eleanor Jones and Helen Lacasse, both nineteen, were driven home by the police after their shifts. Doris and "Bunny" Stanwood each played the piano one night a week for two to three hours. Piano teacher, musician and church organist Ernest T. Stanwood, nicknamed "Bunny," played on Tuesday nights, taking requests from the servicemen at the club that night.[396] Eleanor Jones met her husband, Louis F. Emerson, at the USO while he was stationed at BNAS.[397] Another hostess, Juliet Messier, thirty-three, a bank secretary, was the youngest of

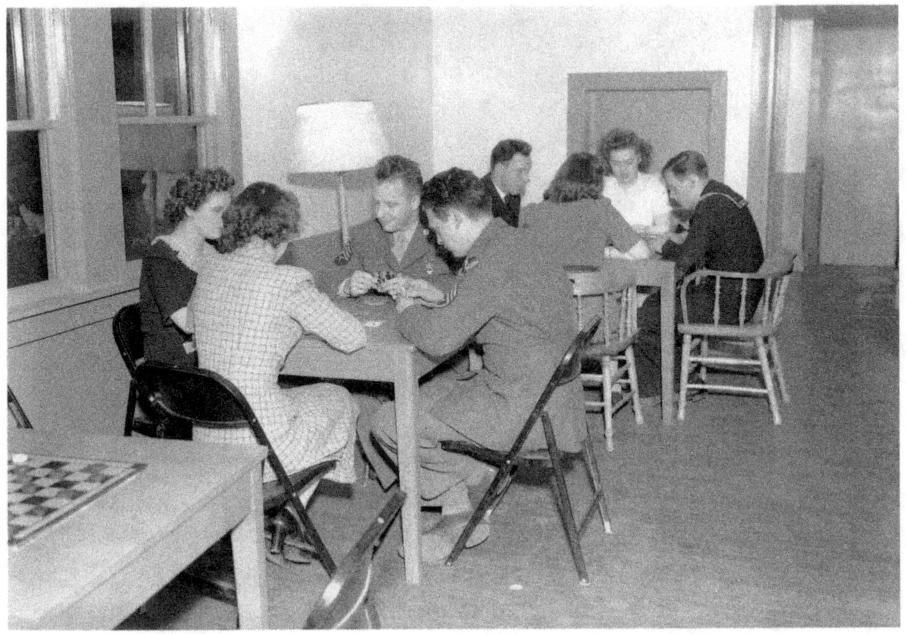

USO game room, 186 Front Street, Bath, April 29, 1944. *Photographer Otis. N.E. Card, Richard Card Collection, Sagadahoc History & Genealogy Room, Patten Free Library.*

ten children and lived with her elderly French-Canadian parents.[398] Pearl Hendricksen, forty-seven, was a widow with four children who worked at the paper mill. Her son Harold Jr., nineteen, was in the army air corps. Ellen Morrell, fifty, wife of the president of Brunswick Coal and Lumber, and Dorothy Niven, forty-four, wife of the *Brunswick Record* owner, both had teenage sons. Dorothy's son Paul Jr. enlisted in 1943 at age eighteen. Alta Reed, sixty-four, was an assistant librarian at the college. Hundreds of other women donated food or money to buy food for the clubs.[399] By December 1943, the Brunswick USO rooms were open ten hours a day, from 1:00 to 11:00 p.m., seven days a week.[400]

The week before Thanksgiving 1942, the USO announced that there were seventeen soldiers in the Bath/Brunswick area with nowhere to go for the holiday. Within days, calls came inviting the men into local homes. The Bluejackets Club in Boothbay also took care of local servicemen, ensuring that everyone had somewhere to go for a holiday meal. Generous citizens made sure that all the clubs were decorated for the holidays. Newspapers encouraged readers to include stationery, billiard chalk, records, books, cigarettes and matches for the servicemen on their Christmas lists.[401]

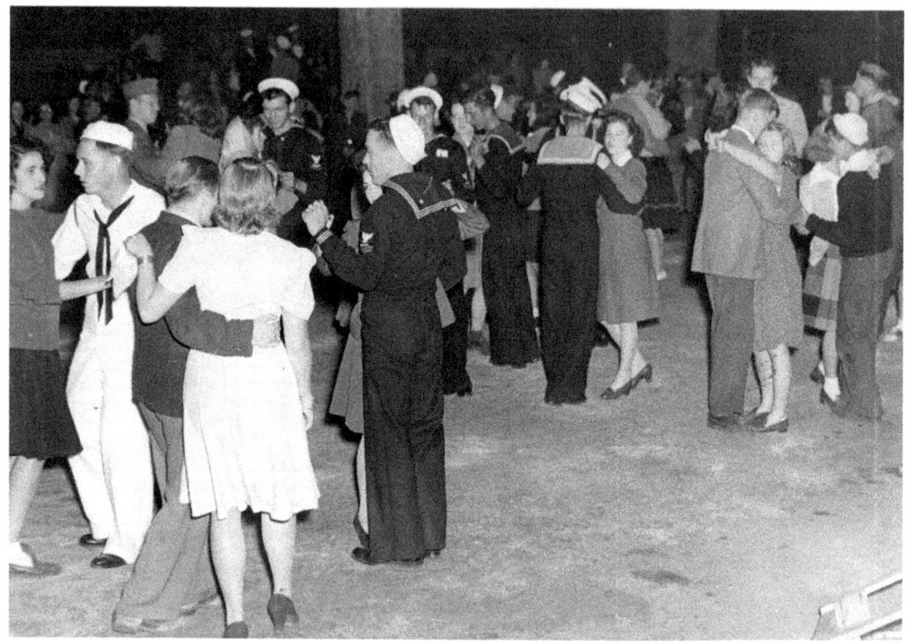

USO army-navy dance at Bowdoin College, 1944. *Pejepscot Historical Society.*

Bailey Island's USO Club was in the Library Building. The June 18, 1942 *Brunswick Record* thanked donors of radios, games, furniture, records, athletic equipment, books and appliances, noting that the men still needed a cornet, horseshoes, spikes, volleyballs, basketballs and a football. The club was open every night and held community singing services on Sunday. The 240th Coast Artillery Band gave a concert on August 30, 1942, to help raise funds to further outfit the club.[402] Orr's Island's Reverend James Herrick, a thirty-seven-year-old married minister with four children, and Nelson McFadden, sixty, a married insurance salesman, helped organize the facility.

Boothbay Harbor's Bluejackets Club was originally planned for navy and coast guard men, but organizers quickly decided that members of any branch of service were welcome. After moving three times in its first six months of existence, the club settled into a home in what had been the Turner Gift Shop on Townsend Avenue. The club was funded entirely by local people and businesses. Visitors walked into a living room–like space with couches, a bookcase built by one of the servicemen, a radio, lots of magazines and a pool table. There was a "bright and clean" kitchen and a ping-pong table on the porch.[403] In November 1942, the *Boothbay Register* printed a letter from Lieutenant Stephen Paine, welfare director for the U.S. Coast Guard, thanking the town for organizing the Bluejackets Club. Local organizers thanked the men building minesweepers at the Samples Shipyard for helping keep the club clean, the coast guardsmen who kept the wood box filled and an unidentified local man who donated repairs and other services to the club, saying, "We wish we could award [them all] a Navy 'E.'"[404]

Like the USO clubs, the Bluejackets Club was staffed by volunteer hostesses. Each worked one day a month and recruited her friends to help, supply food and do whatever needed to be done that day. Unlike at the USOs in Brunswick and Bath, however, almost all the Bluejackets Club hostesses were married women between the ages of thirty-nine and sixty-eight. Most were mothers. Maude Dorr, fifty-five, had a son Paul, eighteen, who enlisted in the marines in 1942. Helen Sprague, sixty-three, was a dentist's wife whose son Edward, twenty-five, had been an army medic since 1940. Fannie Perkins's son James Jr., a twenty-eight-year-old lawyer, enlisted in the army in March 1941. Gladys Clifford, forty-seven, had a son Edwin, twenty, who enlisted in May 1943. Helena Patton, forty-three, was divorced and the mother of three grown children. Her son John, twenty-six, enlisted in the army in 1942. Her son Robert, twenty-four, enlisted in the navy in 1943. Beatrice Marr, forty-two, and Mary Hallett, forty-eight, both had teenage sons about to be draft-eligible. Lucy Hayes, fifty-three, and Marie Simpson, fifty-one, each had two grown children. Ina Hartung, sixty-two, had lost her son at age twelve in an accident. Her daughter and young grandson lived with Ina and her husband during the war. Bertie Thomas, fifty; Dorothy Jackson, forty-three; and Fern Witham, thirty-one, all had young daughters. Ida Leeman, fifty, and Gladys Farnham, forty-five, each had teenage daughters. Frances Marson, fifty-four; Ella Stevens, fifty-two; Irene Blanchette, forty-one; Marie Higgins, thirty-eight; and Mamie Scott were married with no children. At sixty-eight, Mamie was the oldest volunteer hostess at the club.[405]

One of the sailors organized a Flying Aces Club for boys interested in aviation. John Arsenault remembered that the boys were given a book of all military aircraft, friendly and enemy. They had to learn to identify the planes by their silhouettes and to memorize the specifications of each, including speed and cruising range. Other members of the club included Barry Lewis, Jerry Lewis, Marty Hansen and Bill Price.[406]

SPORTS

Where there are boys and men, there will be sports, and the most popular sport in 1940s America was baseball. Damariscotta and Wiscasset had their own teams, as did schools, churches, Cabot Mill and BIW. The Brunswick Cabots were the mill baseball team. They played against the Augusta Loggers, the Wiscasset Athletic Club (the Cabots' "seasonal menace")[407] and the BIW team, among others. Newspapers carried schedules and play-by-play descriptions and commentaries of their games each week. Baseball clubs from BNAS and Bowdoin College played in charity games run by the USO. Basketball and football were also popular. In 1943, the coast guardsmen stationed at Boothbay Harbor formed a basketball team that challenged the BNAS team.[408]

Bowling was another popular team sport. There were church, company, school and club leagues. In Damariscotta, the bowling alley was in what is now Reny's Basement. Brunswick had the "air-cooled" Bowling Bowl, a candlepin bowling alley at 7 Dunlap Street, and the Brunswick Bowling Alleys at 186 Maine Street.[409] Cabot Mill, Pejepscot Paper Co. and BIW all had their own bowling teams.

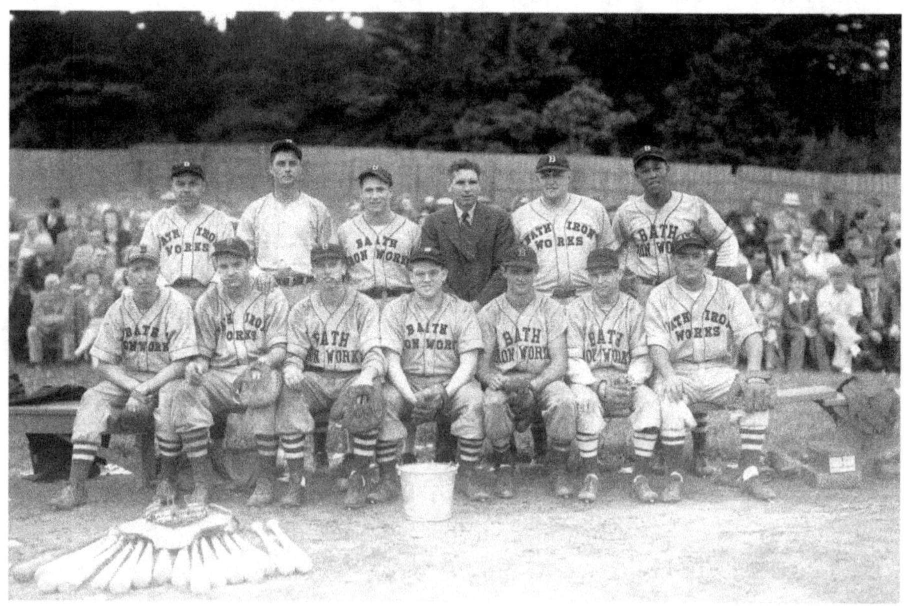

BIW baseball team, September 5, 1943. *Photographer Otis. N.E. Card, Richard Card Collection, Sagadahoc History & Genealogy Room, Patten Free Library.*

THE MOVIES

Movies were the most popular entertainment for people of all ages during the 1940s. Adults and children went to the movies every week. Comedies, musicals, mysteries, adventures and dramas were all popular. Brunswick had the Pastime and Cumberland Theaters. Bath had the Opera House and the Uptown Theater. Boothbay Harbor had the Harborlight and the Strand. Even little New Harbor had the Playland and Surf Casino movie theaters.[410] The movie theater in Damariscotta, the Lincoln Theater on Main Street, was where it is today. They all showed first-run Hollywood features and offered reduced rates for servicemen. Exhausted parents could send their children to the local movie theater on Saturday mornings with money for the double feature and some candy and know they would be safe. Children's admission was ten cents. Westerns with cowboys Roy Rogers, Gene Autry and Tom Mix were favorites.[411] Calvin Dodge remembered that sometimes on Sundays, his mother would go with him to see a musical or some other family-type movie.

After the movies, you could go to the local soda counter for a milkshake or ice cream. Poland's drugstore in Damariscotta had a soda counter that

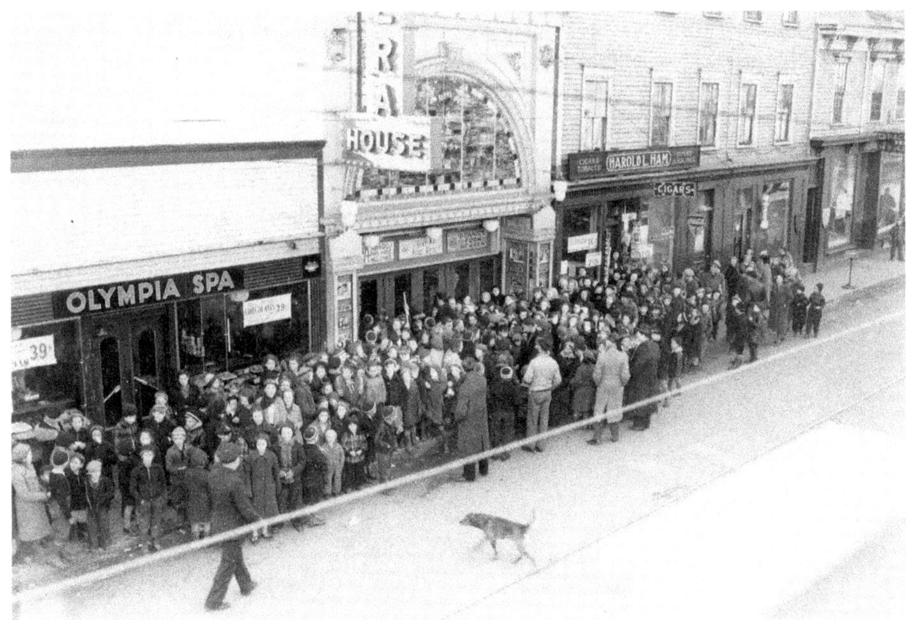

The Opera House movie theater, Center Street in Bath, circa 1945. *Maine Maritime Museum.*

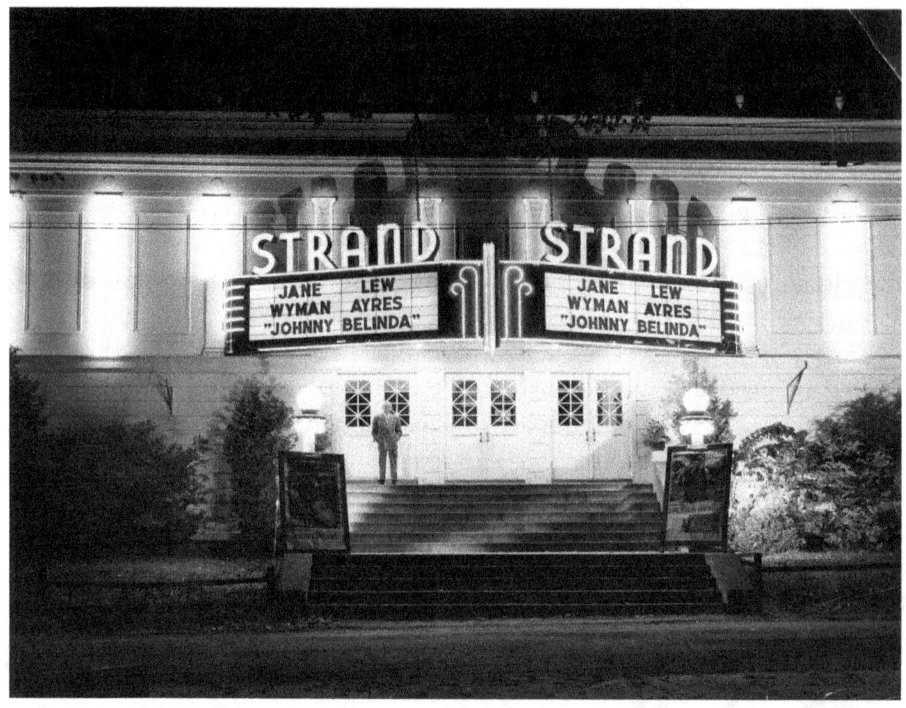

Owner and manager Saul Hayes standing on the steps in front of the Strand Theater in Boothbay Harbor, 1948. *Boothbay Region Historical Society.*

sold ice cream. It had small bentwood tables and chairs where the customers could relax and eat. Dodge remembered going there for sundaes that cost fifteen cents.[412] In Brunswick, you could go to Allen's Drug Store at 148 Main Street and get Deering's Ice Cream or Wilson's Pharmacy Soda Fountain and Luncheonette at 82 Main Street. Wilson's advertising tagline was "Come and see us make our ICE CREAM the Modern Way."[413]

Chapter 14

WHEN JOHNNY COMES MARCHING HOME AGAIN

In 1944 and 1945, many towns dedicated public honor rolls, monuments to local men and women who had served. Boothbay Harbor's honor roll was installed on the Common. In Brunswick, on the Mall, the World War II Honor Roll joined memorials to earlier wars. The Bath Honor Roll was installed in front of the post office on the corner of Front and Lambard Streets. Germany surrendered on May 8, 1945, Victory in Europe (or VE) Day. On September 2, 1945, the Japanese signed the surrender document officially ending World War II.

When the war ended, most people resumed their prewar lives. For the seventy-seven midcoast families who lost a son, a brother or a father, someone would always be missing.[414] The women who had discovered they could work a man's job had a new confidence and improved self-image. Men came back to their jobs, and the women who had replaced them were sent home, many of them unwillingly. BIW laid off thousands but continued to win as many contracts as it could to keep most of its workforce, its business and Bath afloat. Brunswick benefited from the almost immediate military shift into the Korean and Cold Wars, which were the years of peak use of Brunswick Naval Air Station. Bowdoin filled with new students, many taking advantage of the new GI Bill. The tourists returned in droves to Boothbay, Boothbay Harbor and all the coastal communities. Damariscotta and Wiscasset returned to the peaceful rhythm they had enjoyed before the war. The baby boom began.

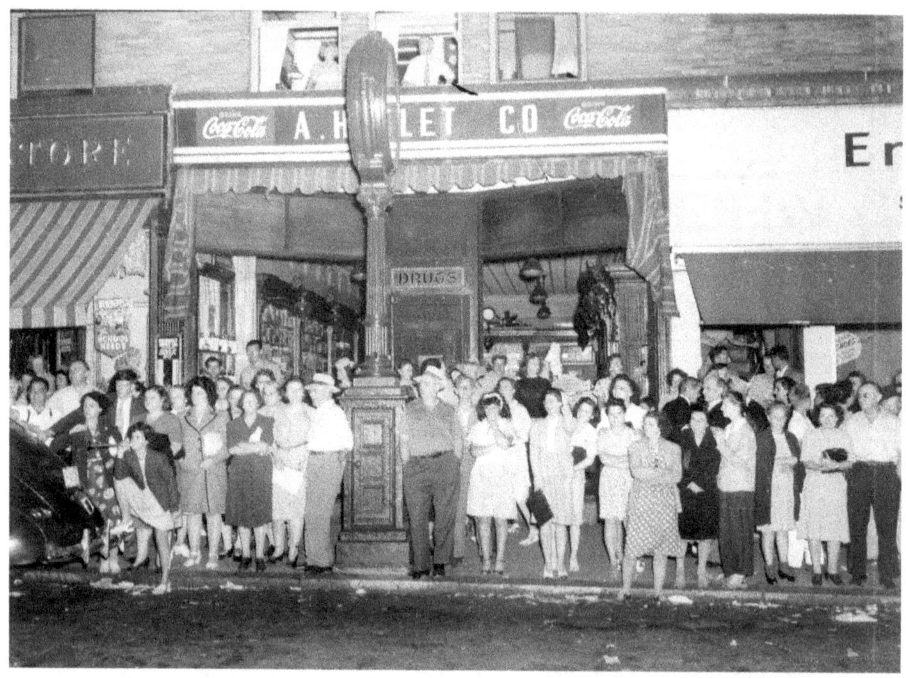

Crowd watching a parade on Front Street in Bath, circa 1945. *Mrs. Frank White Collection. E.L. Stinson Photograph Album and photographer, Sagadahoc History & Genealogy Room, Patten Free Library.*

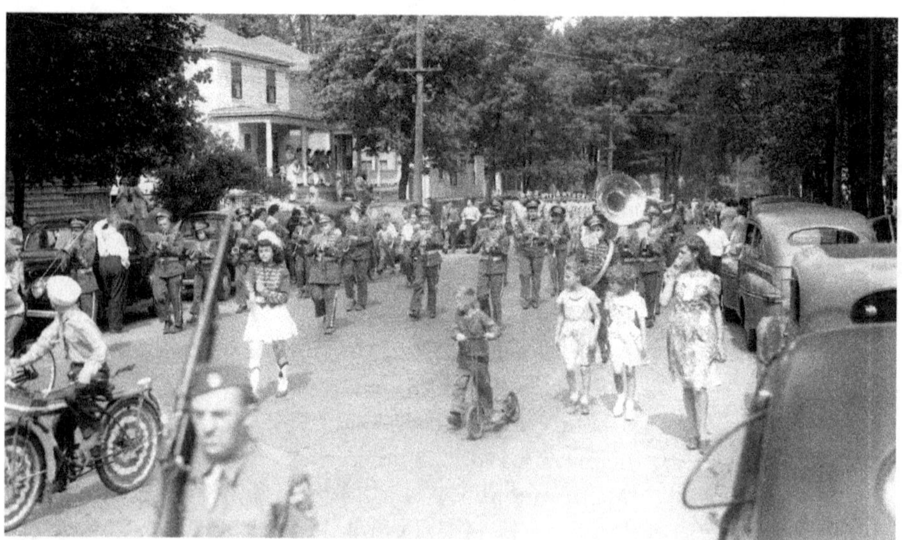

Bath Band in Memorial Day parade, May 28, 1944, on North Street near Fitts Street. *Photographer Otis. N.E. Card, Richard C. Card Collection, Sagadahoc History & Genealogy Room, Patten Free Library.*

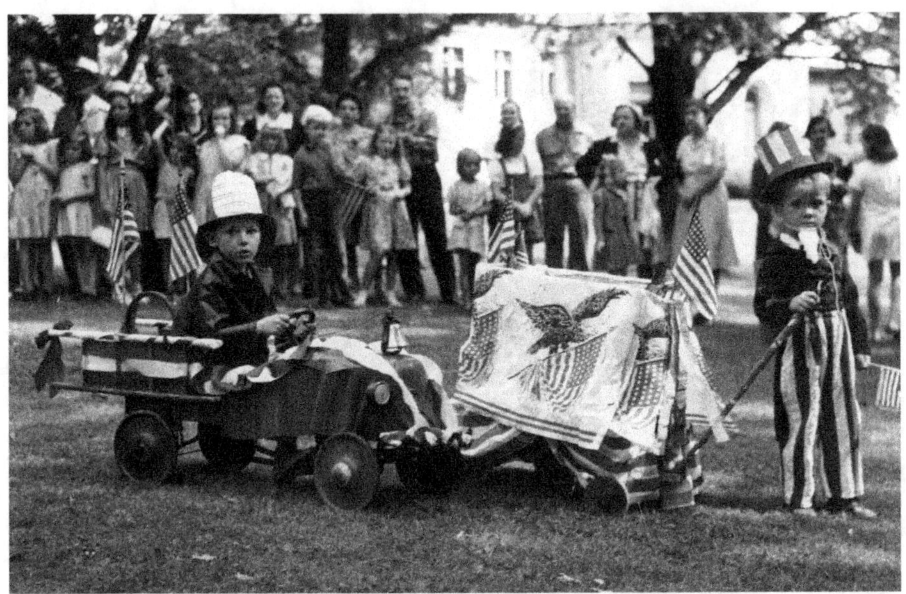

Two little boys, one dressed as Uncle Sam pulling a wagon with flag and eagle ornamentation, the other dressed as a fireman with a pedal-car firetruck, 1945. *Jacqueline McMann Sylvester Collection, Sagadahoc History & Genealogy Room, Patten Free Library.*

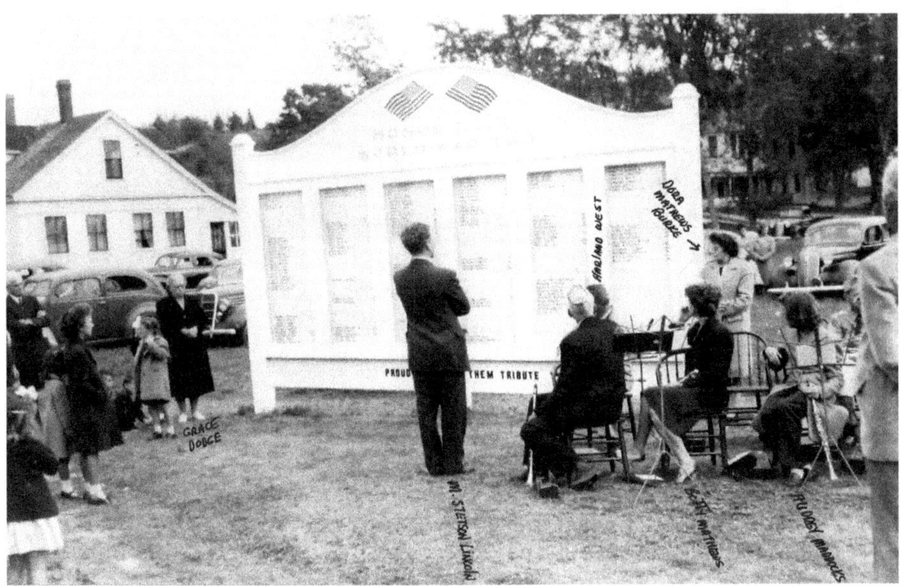

The Boothbay honor roll dedication, September 17, 1944, Mrs. Grace Dodge, Gold Star mother (*standing, left*) and M. Stetson Lincoln looking at memorial. Musicians Harland West, Betty Mathews, Dora Mathews Burke and Audrey Maddocks identified. *Boothbay Region Historical Society.*

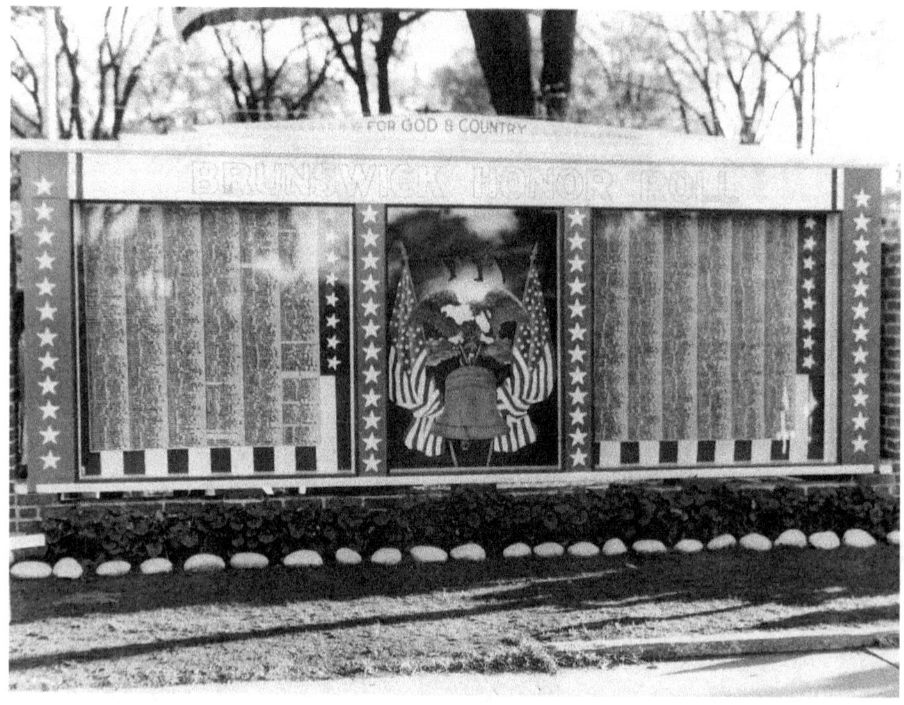

Brunswick World War II honor roll, dedicated in 1944. *Pejepscot Historical Society*.

The hard work, perseverance and sacrifices of the homefront were soon forgotten except by those who lived through them. Many people who were young during the war are just now sharing their memories with those of us eager to hear them. The midcoast Maine World War II honor rolls were eventually removed, replaced by more current monuments or just stored away, forgotten in a basement closet of a town building.

There are no physical monuments to the midcoast Maine homefront volunteers who kept things going until the soldiers and sailors came home, but the National World War II Memorial has established an online memorial to honor servicemen and women and homefront volunteers and war workers. To add a name, visit www.wwiimemorial.com.

Appendix I

WOMEN WORKERS IN CECIL PIERCE MACHINE SHOP

Listed in Cecil Pierce Machine Shop account book, Boothbay Region Historical Society. Ages from Ancestry.com.

Franny Childs, 16
Agnes Lowe Dunton, 25
Bessie Emerson, 44
Grace Gaudette, 25
Peggy Giles, 20
Muriel Greenleaf, 24
Wannneta Greenleaf, 22
Anna Hart, 33
Stella Hodgdon, 23
Rena Holmes, 37
Doris Hutchins, 38
Carolyn Lewis, 28
Lewis Etta Lewis, 60
Lowe Muriel Lowe, 19
Geraldine Williams Mahoney, 20
Madelyn Mudge, 38
Doris Page, 45
Anna Perkins, 23
Aura Perkins, 44
Leona Pinkham, 44

Elsie Poole, 58
Bessie Rust, 44
Rebecca Seavey, age unknown
Violet Smith, 43
Barbara Sturtevant, 20
Lillian Tucker, 33
Carolene Warren, 24
Shirley Williams, 16
Beverley Winslow, 20

Appendix II

BRUNSWICK CIVILIAN DEFENSE OFFICE, CANTEEN AND FIRST AID VOLUNTEERS

From the January 9, 1942 Brunswick Record

Civilian Defense Office Volunteers

Manager: Helen Campbell

Irma Allen
Annie Andrews
Agnes Backman
Doris Baker
Lucien Beauregard
Yvonne Belanger
Marion Benner
Ruth Birch
Ellen Cameron
Susan Chandler
Ruth Coffin
Myrtle Cooper
Janette Cotton
Florence Day
Constance Doore
Prudence Doore
Caroline Dow
Elizabeth Eastman
Sarah Eaton
Edith Emerson
Gertrude Fornier
Gloria Fortin
Justine Hamilton
Cornelia Hartman
Doris Hennessey
Lillian Hoffman
Joan Johnson
Sarah Koucoules
Annie Leathers
Ada Libby
Florence McFadden
Mary Packard
Theresa Paquette
Dorothy Pritham
Marion Racine
Pauline Root
Amelia Skolfield
Constance Thayer
Ruth Thompson
Nancy Tomlinson

Canteen

Instructors: Selma Gregory (Brunswick High School home economics teacher), Theora Stubbert
Elsie Adams
Ada Akeley
Ruth Bangs
Cecilia Barber
Hilda Bartley
Rita Bass
Katherine Belanger
Clara Berry
Dorothy Boggs
Eleanor Boyer
Rowena Brann
Goldie Brawn
Sue Burnett
Florence Catlin
Helen Catlin
Ruth Coffin
Helen Colby
Margaret Coleman
Myrtle Cooper
Eleanor Courson
Marion Curtis
Blanche Dean
Albertine Dow
Caroline Dow
Rhena Foster
Rea Fournier
Marion Heyes
Gertrude Hunt
Jennie Jackson
Grace Jones
Claire Latarte
Mary Leonard
Barbara Leslie
Hilda Lowery
Marguerite MacIntyre
Elizabeth MacVeagh
Emma Marstaller
Alice McFadden
Juliette Messier
Mathilde Nixon
Helen Ormsby
Dorothy Pritham
Clarice Quinlan
Marion Racine
Alta Reed
Esther Roberts
Helen Simard
Amelia Skolfield
Frances Smith
Dorothy Vlahos
Maris Yates
Alice Young

First Aid Course Teachers

Topsham: Mary Baxter White, Dorothy Niven, Hazel Debiasio, Beatrice Adams
Brunswick: Harry Schulman, Loyall K. Barkman, Edward Nickerson, Norman Emerson, Maxwell D. Sawyer, Joseph LaBeau Jr.
New Meadows: Harold Simonds
W.T. Grant Co.: Marjory O'Brien

Appendix III

BRUNSWICK-AREA AIR RAID DEFENSE VOLUNTEERS

/

As listed in the April 2, 1942 Brunswick Record. *Numbers as listed on defense map.*

Chief Air Raid Warden
Adam Walsh
First Deputy Chief Warden
Malcolm E. Morrell
Deputy Wardens
Nathaniel C. Kendrick: Instruction of wardens and messengers
Herbert R. Brown: Personnel of warden and messenger services
Charles H. Livingston: Blackout, refuge rooms, public shelters, household regulations
Henry M. Baribeau: Signals and warnings
E. Randolph Comee: Organization of emergency services
George Crimmins: Public schools
Edmond Lachance: Mills and public buildings

	Address
Brunswick Village Post Warden	
1. Lewis B. Varney	Cabot Mill
Zone 1, Zone Warden Clyde T. Congdon	
2. Edmond Lachance	11 Union Ext.

3. Louis Tondreau	12 Oak St.
4. Clyde T. Congdon	14 Lincoln St.
Zone 2, Zone Warden Mrs. Harold Nickerson	
5. Rev. Sheldon Christian	10 Mason St.
6. Mrs. Harold Nickerson	41 Water St.
7. James T. Black	122 Maine St.
Zone 3, Zone Warden Dr. Wilfred P. Racine	
8. George St. Onge Jr.	45 Union St.
9. Dr. Wilfred P. Racine	111 Pleasant St.
23. Eleanor Black	137 Pleasant St.
Zone 4, Zone Warden Lawrence A. Brown	
10. Rev. George L. Cadigan	27 Pleasant St.
11. Lawrence A. Brown	6 Green St.
12. Herbert E. Mehlhorn	17 Franklin St.
Zone 5, Zone Warden Carleton C. Young	
13. Harold E. Blackman	58 Federal St.
14. William Root	8 Potter St.
18. Carleton C. Young	24 College St.
20. Raymond E. Bonang	3 Bowker St.
Zone 6, Zone Warden William K. Hall	
15. William C. Walker	44 Weymouth St.
16. Rev. John W. Hyssong	2 Oakland St.
17. William K. Hall	6 Whittier St.
Zone 7, Zone Warden Leo Livernois	
21. Leo Livernois	51 Harpswell St.
22. Leo Livernois [*sic*, repeat in newspaper]	51 Harpswell St.
Zone 8, Zone Warden Thomas C. Van Cleve	
19. Thomas Curtis Van Cleve	Bowdoin College

Brunswick Rural Sectors
Mere Point Rd.: Mrs. Leon L. Spinney
Greenwood Rd.: Fred E. Harmon
Hacker Rd.: Hugo Sandelia
River Rd.: Derrill O. Lamb
Hillside: Oakley Irvine
Gurnet: Lloyd Grover
Cundy's Harbor: Harry Jordan

Harpswell Zone, Zone Warden Rev. James E. Herrick
Bailey Island: Edmund F. Black
Orr's and Lower Great Islands: Carlton L. Linscott
Harpswell Neck (Beyond Pierce's Garage): Charles Durgan

Topsham Zone, Zone Warden Walter O. Power
Deputy Zone Warden Thomas White

30. Patrick Raymond	Maine St.
31. J.M. Higgins	Highland St.
32. Loomis E. Dyer	Maine St.
33. Joseph C. Brannigan	31 Elm St.
34. Guy O. Gordon	Middlesex Rd.
35. Walter S. Hall	Winter St.
36. Thomas St. Laurent	18 Prospect St.

Topsham Rural Sectors
Cathance Rd.: Harold Pennell
Pleasant Point: Elmer Tripp
Augusta Rd.: Harold Ward
Meadow Rd.: Robert Strand
Foreside Rd.: Judge A. Hyde
River Rd.: H.A. Russell
Middlesex Rd.: Carl Hanson

Appendix III

Brunswick Plane Spotters
As identified in the October 21, 1943 Brunswick Record

John A. Adams
Alfred Albert
Joseph Aldred
S. Dickinson Allen
Willis Baker
Ruth Bangs
Frank Barker
Jennie Barrett
Streeter Bass
Ruth Birch
Juan T. Bleau
Kenneth Boyer
Goldie Brawn
Herbert Brown
John M. Brown
Lawrence Brown
Ruth Brown
Raymond Caouette
William F. Carnes
Helen M. Catlin
Richard Chittim
Dan E. Christie
Philip Clough
Richard N. Cobb
Eugene K. Colby
Hazel Colby
Roy B. Colby
Myrtle Cooper
Eleanor Coursen
Muriel Cross
Marion N. Curtis
Mamie Dall
John D. Donahue
Ricahrd Dorr
Wilfred Duquette
Gertrude Eaton
Virginia Elliott
R. Hobart Ellis
John R. Elwell
Alexine Fortin
Fred Fortin
Victor Fortin Jr.
Donald Fourier
Priscilla Francis
Stanton Francis
Winifred French
Elizabeth Given
Eveline Hagan
Charles Ham
Mary C. Ham
Velda Harting
Clara D. Hayes
Philip E. Hedges
Ernest C. Helmreich
Clara Henderson
Barbara Hendricksen
Pearl Hendricksen
Charles S. Hendrickson
Archie Holmes
Cecil T. Holmes
Emily Holmes
Richard W. Holmes
Betty C. Hyde
John J. Jaques
Angela Johnson
Harold L. Jordan
Nathaniel E. Kamerling
Robert F. Kingsbury
Lloyd R. Knight
J. Henry Korben
Ruth Koucoulos
Donald Larrabee
Everett C. Lewis
Ethlyn Litchfield

Tristram Little
Eleanor Littlefield
Mary W. MacKinnon
Elizabeth MacVeagh
Hermann N. Martin
Raymond Matharine
Mary McFall
Glenn R. McIntire
Justin McIntire
Nancy McKeen
Bryce A. Minott
Frank Morin
Donald Packard
Mary Packard
Eugene A. Parsons
Helen Peabody
Ernest Prindall
Alta Reed
Marguerite M. Richards
Beatrice Richardson
Thomas A. Riley
Arthur Ross
J. Gerald Russell
Mary Sawyer
Doris L. Scribner
Emma L. Scribner
Willard M. Sewall
Harold M. Simonds
Elizabeth S. Smith
Florence E. Smith
Howard Clifton Smith
Stanley Barney Smith
Walter R. Snyder
Ethel Temple
Albert R. Thayer
Sadie M. Thomas
Frederic Tillotson
Jean Tyler
Mrs. Dorothy Vlahos
Ralph C. Walker
Chester Woodbury
Gerald M. York

Appendix IV

BOOTHBAY HARBOR AIR RAID WARDENS AND MESSENGERS, SOUTHPORT AIR RAID WARDENS, BOOTHBAY-AREA AWS SPOTTERS

From the October 9, 1942 Boothbay Register

Chief Air Raid Warden: Nathaniel A. Grover
Deputy Chief Air Raid Wardens: W. Maxfield Forbes, Harlan West
Director of Messengers: Rev. Kenneth Gray

Report Center Messengers
John Arsenault Jr., Messenger
James Granger, Messenger
Peter Granger, Messenger
Morton Hansen, Messenger
James Murray, Messenger

No. 1 Sector Post: Harold Simmon's basement
Sector Warden: Paul Abbott
Shirley Dickson, Warden
Edward Dunton, Warden
Saul Hayes, Warden
Leston Hemore, Warden
Roy Kelley, Warden

Leon Marston, Warden
Edward Sproul, Warden
Glenn Littlefield, Messenger
James Mclauflin, Messenger
Sonny Simmons, Messenger

No. 2 Sector Post: Pierce and Hartung's office at the Coal Wharf
Sector Warden: Clifton Hartung
Lawrence Bennett, Warden
Richard Brewer, Warden
Norman Hodgdon Jr., Warden
Weston Page, Warden
Walter Witham, Warden
Robert Fish, Messenger
Lewis Gerald Lewis, Messenger

No. 3 Sector Post: Chester Tilton's house
Sector Warden: Chester Tilton
A. Abbott, Warden
Donald Boyd, Warden
Lester Boyd, Warden
Albert Harrold, Warden
Simon McDougall, Warden
Sidney Mudge, Warden
Bert Sherman, Warden
Robert Mudge, Messenger

No. 4 Sector Post: Ralph Scott's office
Sector Warden: Ralph Scott
Alfred Barter, Warden
Archie Campbell, Warden
Maro Hammond, Warden
Oscar Jacobsen, Warden
Harold Jordan, Warden
Margaret Hammond, First Aid
Robert Perkins, Messenger
Richard Tibbetts, Messenger

No. 5 Sector Post: Mrs. Forbes' basement on West Street
Sector Warden: William Forbes
Louis Carbone, Warden
K. Weston Farnham, Warden
Lowell Paine, Warden
Clark Rowe, Warden
Sherb Stevens, Warden
Merlin Abbott, Messenger
William Parmenter Jr., Messenger

No. 6 Sector Post: Chester Swett's house at West Harbor
Sector Warden: Chester Swett
Donald Bowie, Warden
Earl Carleton, Warden
John Dorr, Warden
Thomas Dorr, Warden
Leslie Mello, Warden
Ben Miller, Warden
Norman Nelson, Warden
Ernest Pilman, Warden
Albion Reed, Warden
Walter Scott, Warden
Gladys Smith, Warden
Edward Swett, Warden
Helen Taylor, Warden
Roscoe Pinkham, Messenger
Alton Swett, Messenger

No. 7 Sector Post: Lowell Newcomb's house
Sector Warden: Lowell Newcomb
Maynard Brewer, Warden
Sheridan Brewer, Warden
Fred Curtis, Warden
Alfred Greenleaf, Warden
Fred Higgins Jr., Warden
Eddie Hipps, Warden
Clinton Jones, Warden
Eugene Pinkham, Warden
Levi Tomer, Warden

Robert Boucher, Messenger
Howard Brewer, Messenger
Edmond Brown Jr., Messenger

No. 8 Sector Post: Tom Andrews' house
Sector Warden: Tom Andrews
Carl Brewer, Warden
Elden Hodgdon, Warden
Billy Price, Messenger
Joseph Westcott, Messenger

Southport
Chief Air Raid Warden: Cecil Pierce

Deputy Chief Air Raid Wardens: Rand Roscoe Rand, Albert Seavey, John Swett, Ralph Gray, Douglas Pinkham, Edgar Huskins

Spotters
listed as having completed AWS course in Boothbay Register *of April 17, 1942*

AWS Instructor: Angie Dodge

Boothbay
Ida Barth
Louise Blake
Pearl Brewer
Esther DaCosta
Cecil Davis
Ruby Davis
Dodge Grace Dodge
Virginia Dolan
Lillian Gray
Margaret MacDonald
Pauline Rowe
Birdene Schackleton
Josephine Stover

Boothbay Harbor
Gladys Smith
Helen Taylor

Southport
Frances Gray
Jeanette Gray

North Whitefield and Jefferson
Velma Banks
Harry Blanchard
Margaret Boynton
Maurice Brann
Amos Fish Jr.
Evelyn Hagan
Bryan Hodgkins
Ernes Kennedy
Inez McCurdy
Ned Packard
Harold Pircher
Arthur Turner
Margaret Turner
Morris Weaver

Appendix V

BRUNSWICK USO VOLUNTEER HOSTESSES

As identified in the July 22, 1943 Brunswick Record
Note: The newspaper gave the women's married names only. I have added their first names as found on Ancestry.com and in town directories.

Ruth Bangs
(Mrs. Charles T.) Sue Burnett
(Mrs. Morgan B.) Amelia Cushing
Ethyl F. Davis
(Mrs. George) Alma Drapeau
(Mrs. Gilbert Jr.) Virginia Elliott
(Mrs. Ernest W.) Delia George
(Mrs. E.) Pearl Hendrickson
Doris Holbrook
Eleanor Jones
Helen Lacasse
(Mrs. William) Dorothy Leighton
(Mrs. John) Dorothy Levesque
Juliette Messier
(Mrs. Robert E.) Michaud
(Mrs. Allen E.) Ellen Morrel
(Mrs. Paul) Dorothy Niven
Alta Edith Reed
(Mrs. William) Pauline Root
(Mrs. Maxwell D.) Mary Sawyer
(Mrs. Kenneth) Edith Sills
Ruth Taft
Nancy Webb
(Mrs. Carleton) Alice Young

NOTES

Chapter 1

1. Snow, *Bath Iron Works*, 267–82.
2. Morison, *History of the United States Naval Operations in World War II*, 34.
3. Snow, *Bath Iron Works*, 318.
4. Morison, *History of the United States Naval Operations in World War II*, 64–65.
5. *Bath Independent*, December 11, 1941.
6. Ibid.
7. *Brunswick Record*, December 11, 1941.
8. Ibid.
9. *Brunswick Record*, December 18, 1941.
10. Ibid., "Colored Soldiers Occupy Armory," December 18, 1941.
11. Ibid.
12. Ibid.
13. Ibid., December 25, 1941.
14. *Bath Independent*, January 8, 1942.
15. Ibid.
16. *Brunswick Record*, December 25, 1941.

Chapter 2

17. Calvin and Marjorie Dodge interview, December 7, 2016. Calvin Dodge was born in 1937 in Newcastle, Maine.
18. *Brunswick Record*, December 11, 1941.
19. Ibid., April 30, 1942.
20. Ibid.
21. *Boothbay Register*, October 30, 1942.
22. *Brunswick Record*, June 17, 1943.
23. *Boothbay Register*, November 27, 1942.
24. Brewer, *Heroes Among Us*, 503.
25. Sutter Family letters, author's collection, gift of Judith and Bill Sutter.
26. *Bath Independent*, March 12, 1942
27. Ibid., September 22,1943.
28. Federal Security Agency, "United States Cadet Nurse Corps."
29. Fairchild, "Honoring Our Veteran Mothers' Courage."
30. Yellin, *Our Mother's War*, 114–15.
31. *Kennebunk Star*, July 31, 1942.
32. Bellafaire, *Women's Army Corps.*
33. *Boothbay Register*, November 6, 1942.
34. Brewer, *Southport*, 194–95.
35. *Brunswick Record*, March 25, 1943.
36. Brewer, *Heroes Among Us*, 444–45.
37. Brewer, *Southport*, 140.
38. Naval History and Heritage Command, "Women in the U.S. Navy."
39. Myers, "America's Navy."
40. Ryan et al, "The Designer."
41. U-S-History.com, "WAVES."
42. *Brunswick Record*, May 11, 1944.
43. Ibid., January 21, 1943.
44. Sherman, *Heroes Among Us*, 454.
45. Ibid., 443.
46. Ibid., 449.
47. *Bath Independent*, September 23, 1943.
48. U.S Army Film Misc.-958, "It's Your War, Too." 1944.

Chapter 3

49. Office of War Information poster, "Keep the Home Fires Burning…You are a PRODUCTION SOLDIER," 1942.
50. Snow, *Bath Iron Works*, 328.
51. Martin and Snow, *Maine Odyssey*, 59.
52 Snow, *Bath Iron Works*, 225.
53. Ibid., 319.
54. Ibid., 318.
55. Ibid., 322.
56. Ibid., 323.
57. Snow, *Bath Iron Works*, 323.
58. Ibid., 317.
59. BIW, *Bulletin*, September 9, 1943.
60 Snow, *Bath Iron Works*, 363.
61. Lin Snow interview, February 17, 2017.
62. *Brunswick Record*, April 15, 1943.
63. Duncan, *Coastal Maine*, 490.
64. www.gamageshipyard.com.
65. *Boothbay Register*, July 31, 1942.
66. Brewer, *Heroes Among Us*, 513.
67. *Boothbay Register*, November 27, 1942.
68. Insertion of the ages is mine for purpose of comparison.
69. Brewer, *Heroes Among Us*, 513.
70. Duncan, *Coastal Maine*, 490.
71. Brewer, *Heroes Among Us*, 513.
72. Ibid., 514–15.
73. Duncan, *Coastal Maine*, 490.
74. Brewer, *Heroes Among Us*, 513.

Chapter 4

75. Pejepscot Historical Society, "Brunswick Women's History Trail, Loop B."
76. *Brunswick Record*, April 3, 1942.
77. Ibid., April 8, 1942.
78. Brewer, *Southport*, 240.

79. *Brunswick Record*, May 27, 1943.
80. Ibid., February 25, 1943.
81. Ibid., April 2, 1942.
82. Ibid., July 15, 1943.
83. Brunswick High School 1942 Yearbook, Ancestry.com.
84. *Brunswick Record*, July 8, 1943.
85. Ibid., June 18, 1942.
86. Ibid., April 29, 1943.
87. Ibid., September 23, 1943.
88. Ibid., J.E. Davis Co. advertisement, July 1, 1943.
89. Ibid., February 25, 1943
90. Ibid., July 1, 1943.
91. Ibid.
92. Ibid., January 14, 1943.
93. Ibid., April 29, 1943.
94. Weatherford, *American Women and World War II*, 132.
95. Ibid., 136.
96. Ibid., 135.
97. Snow, *Bath Iron Works*, 320.
98. *Wiscasset Gazette*, Wiscasset Public Library.
99. BIW, *The Bulletin*, June 29, 1945.
100. Brewer, *Heroes Among Us*, 504–5.
101. BIW, *The Bulletin*, September 7, 1945.
102. Brewer, *Heroes Among Us*, 501.
103. Ibid., 501–2.
104. Ibid., 515.
105. Brewer, *Southport*, 239.
106. For a list of the women who worked at Pierce's Machine Shop, see Appendix I.
107. Brewer, *Southport*, 240.
108. List, Table I.
109. Brewer, *Heroes Among Us*, 499.
110. Brewer, *Southport*, 246.
111. Weatherford, *American Women and World War II*, 162–63.

Chapter 5

112. *Brunswick Record*, April 30, 1942.
113. Ibid., July 9, 1942.
114. Ibid.
115. Brewer, *Southport*, 236.
116. *Brunswick Record*, June 11, 1942.
117. Ibid., November 26, 1942.
118. Ibid., January 28, 1943.
119. Ibid., April 22, 1943.
120. Ibid., August 19, 1943.
121. Ibid., April 8, 1943.
122. Sundin, "World War II War Bonds."

Chapter 6

123. *Brunswick Record*, December 11, 1941, 2.
124. Calvin and Marjorie Dodge interview, December 7, 2016.
125. Per the college website, Bowdoin College received its charter in 1794, but the first classes did not begin until 1804. The first mill on the site was a cotton mill, per www.waterfrontmaine.com.
126. *Brunswick Record*, January 8, 1942.
127. Ibid., June 4, 1942.
128. Cross, "Whispering Pines: Eleanor Roosevelt's Day."
129. Brunmier, "Intrepid Idealism."
130. The women taught military classes, so their positions ended when those programs ended.

Chapter 7

131. Morison, *History of the United States Naval Operations in World War II*, 268.
132. Brewer, *Southport*, 267.
133. Morison, *History of the United States Naval Operations in World War II*, 25.
134. Ibid., 198.
135. Ibid., 157.

136. Ibid.
137. Ibid., 269.
138. *Boothbay Register*, July 1, 1942.
139. Ibid.
140. Morison, *History of the United States Naval Operations in World War II*, 270.
141. A&E, *Sea Tales*.
142. Morison, *History of the United States Naval Operations in World War II*, 273.
143. Larson, "Bravo Zero."
144. A&E, *Sea Tales.*
145. Ibid.
146. Brewer, *Southport*, 230.
147. Ibid., 262.
148. Chenoweth, "Out of the Past."
149. Brewer, *Southport*, 263.
150. Ibid., 267.
151. Chenoweth, "Out of the Past."
152. Brewer, *Southport*, 263.
153. Brewer, *Heroes Among Us*, 512.
154. Brewer, *Southport*, 268.
155. Brewer, *Heroes Among Us*, 496.
156. Rumsey, "January 1944 Storm."
157. Duncan, *Coastal Maine*, 484.
158. Morison, *History of the United States Naval Operations in World War II*, 270.
159. Brewer, *Southport*, 265.
160. Ibid., 288.
161. Duncan, *Coastal Maine*, 485.
162. Ibid., 486.
163. Morison, *History of the United States Naval Operations in World War II*, 288, 130.
164. Brewer, *Southport*, 266.
165. Ibid.
166. Brewer, *Heroes Among Us*, 495.
167. Ibid.
168. Ibid.
169. Information on the Civil Air Patrol is from two sources: Morison, *History of the United States Naval Operations in World War II*, 276–80, and Farnum, *History Maine Civil Defense Corps*, 1945.
170. Ibid.

171. *1840 Squadron*, reproduction of a typed article. Author and donor unknown. Pejepscot Historical Society, Brunswick, ME.
172. *Brunswick Record*, June 17, 1943.
173. Ibid., January 21, 1943.
174. Calvin and Marjorie Dodge interview, December 7, 2016.
175. Wilde, *U.S.S. McFarland*.
176. *Brunswick Record*, December 23, 1943.
177. Ibid., September 16, 1943.
178. Noddin, "State of Maine Military Aircraft"; and Ancestry.com, "UK, Army and Navy."
179. *Brunswick Record*, December 4, 1943.

Chapter 8

180. Farnum, *History Maine Civil Defense Corps*, 3.
181. Ibid.
182. Ibid.
183. *Brunswick Record*, December 11, 1941.
184. Ibid.
185. Ibid., January 15, 1942.
186. For a list of volunteers who staffed the Brunswick Civilian Defense office area and those who completed canteen service classes or taught first aid classes, see Appendix II.
187. *Bath Independent*, December 25, 1941.
188. Conversation with Barbara Rumsey, 2016.
189. *Boothbay Register*, May 1, 1942.
190. Ibid.
191. Lingeman, *Don't You Know There's a War On*, 30.
192. *Brunswick Record*, December 18, 1941.
193. Ibid.
194. *Bath Independent*, December 11, 1941.
195. Lingeman, *Don't You Know There's a War On*, 53. The instructions had been developed without consulting the British, who had firsthand experience with German bombs. The British military informed the OCD of the error.
196. *Brunswick Record*, January 8, 1942.
197. Ibid.

198. Ibid.
199. Adam Walsh had been Notre Dame football team captain under Knute Rockne.
200. For a list of Brunswick, Topsham and Harpswell air raid wardens, see Table III.
201. Conversation with Bob Bouchard, January 25, 2017.
202. Dodge and Dodge, "Damariscotta and Newcastle Played an Active Part."
203. For a list of Boothbay Harbor AWS volunteers, Southport air raid wardens and Boothbay-area spotters, see Table IV.
204. *Bath Independent*, March 19, 1942.
205. Ibid., December 18, 1941.
206. Brewer, *Southport*, 242.
207. Morison, *History of the United States Naval Operations in World War II*, 130.
208. OCD telegram, April 10, 1942
209. OCD poster, 1942, Northwestern University Library Collection. Online Digital Archives.
210. Brewer, *Southport*, 243.
211. *Brunswick Record*, May 30, 1942.
212. Ibid., May 5, 1942.
213. *Boothbay Register*, July 29, 1942.
214. *Brunswick Record*, July 30, 1942.
215. OCD, August 1941. These included the emergency medical corps, nurses' aids corps, bomb squad, messenger squad, air raid wardens, chaplains, citizens service corps, utility repair, civil air patrol, decontamination, road repair, emergency food and housing, auxiliary police and auxiliary firemen.
216. OCD poster, 1941.
217. *Brunswick Record*, December 10, 1942.
218. Ibid., December 24, 1942.
219. *Bath Independent*, December 18, 1941.
220. Geraldine Coombs interview, May 2013.
221. *Brunswick Record*, July 23, 1942.
222. Brewer, *Southport*, 265.
223. Brewer, *Heroes Among Us*, 502.
224. Brewer, *Southport*, 242.
225. Calvin and Marjorie Dodge interview, December 7, 2016.
226. *Brunswick Record*, April 9, 1942.
227. Grigg, "Air Spotters of WWII."

228. Brewer, *Heroes Among Us*, 505.
229. For a list of Boothbay air raid wardens in October 1942, see Appendix IV.
230. Brewer, *Heroes Among Us*, 498.
231. *Brunswick Record*, March 18, 1943.
232. Ibid., May 4, 1943.
233. Ibid., April 8, 1943.
234. *Boothbay Register*, May 7, 1943.
235. *Brunswick Record*, August 26, 1943.
236. Ibid., October 7, 1943.
237. For a list of Brunswick plane spotters, see Table III.
238. Farnum, *History Maine Civil Defense Corps*.
239. *Brunswick Record*, November 4, 1943.
240. *Bath Independent*, August 31, 1944.

Chapter 9

241. *Lewiston Daily Sun*, January 8, 1945.
242. Brewer, *Southport*, 260–61.
243. Ibid., 231–32.
244. Ibid., 260–61.
245. Clipping from the *Brunswick Record*, June 1, 1942, courtesy of Bob Bouchard.
246. *Brunswick Record*, May 11, 1943.
247. Calvin and Marjorie Dodge interview, December 7, 2016.
248. *Nobleboro History* notes by George Dow, *Lincoln County News*, May 17, 1982; "A Little History of the Lincoln County News," Damariscotta Historical Society, *Lincoln County News*, November 8, 2007.

Chapter 10

249. American Red Cross, "World War II and the American Red Cross."
250. *Brunswick Record*, March 5, 1942.
251. *Boothbay Register*, September 25, 1942.
252. Conversation with Cushing family friend Rupert White, January 20, 2017.

253. Pejepscot Historical Society, "Women's History Trail."
254. Martin and Snow, *Maine Odyssey*, 23.
255. "Mrs. Anita Sturges Dole, 1889–1973," obituary provided to the author by her grandson Todd Woofenden, January 15, 2017.
256. *Adjutant General Military Records*, 89.
257. *Bath Independent*, May 11, 1944.
258. *Brunswick Record*, April 9, 1942.
259. Ibid.
260. Ibid., December 25, 1941.
261. *Boothbay Register*, May 8, 1942.
262. Ibid., December 24, 1943.
263. Ibid., January 15, 1942.
264. Ibid., April 9, 1943.
265. Ibid., January 30, 1942.
266. *Brunswick Record*, July 14, 1943.
267. Newman, "Armed Services Edition."
268. Ibid.
269. Adjutant Report of the Adjutant General of the State of Maine, 1942–44, California State Library, Sacramento; Ancestry.com. U.S., Adjutant General Military Records, 1631–1976.
270. Snow, *Bath Iron Works*, 319.
271. *Bath Independent*, January 15, 1942.
272. Martin and Snow, *Maine Odyssey*, 65.
273. *Brunswick Record*, January 29, 1942.
274. Ibid., October 14, 1943.
275. Ibid., March 25, 1943.
276. Conversation with Rupert White, January 20, 2017.
277. Ibid.
278. *Bath Independent*, May 11, 1944.
279. Ibid.
280. Ibid., July 13, 1944.
281. *Brunswick Record*, December 30, 1943.

Chapter 11

282. *Brunswick Record*, December 30, 1943.
283. *Brunswick Record*, May 7, 1942.
284. George's son Leon was in the army air corps and was killed in action in July 1944.
285. *Brunswick Record*, April 26, 1942.
286. *Dedham Transcript*, July 17, 1942.
287. Walt Disney Studios, "Out of the Frying Pan."
288. *Brunswick Record*, January 22, 1942.
289. Ibid., June 25, 1942.
290. Calvin and Marjory Dodge interview, December 7, 2016.
291. *Damariscotta Town Report* 1944, 41.
292. *Brunswick Record*, September 3, 1942.
293. Rumsey, "Scrap Drive 1942."
294. Ibid.

Chapter 12

295. Morison, *History of the United States Naval Operations in World War II*, 253.
296. *Brunswick Record*, August 21, 1941.
297. Morison, *History of the United States Naval Operations in World War II*, 253.
298. Ibid., 57, 88. Hitler was not targeting U.S. ships yet, but some of the freight-carrying vessels traveled under European flags. On April 10, 1941, the U.S. destroyer *Niblack* was threatened by a U-boat that had just sank a Dutch freighter. After *Niblack* attacked with depth charges, the U-boat withdrew. On September 4, 1941, the USS *Greer* was torpedoed by a German U-boat twice but managed to evade both bombs and respond with depth charges, chasing the attacker away.
299. Ibid.
300. Bales, "Lawrence County Memoirs."
301. Lingeman, *Don't You Know There's a War On*, 238. The states were Maine, Massachusetts, New Hampshire, Vermont, Rhode Island, Connecticut, New York, New Jersey, Pennsylvania, Ohio, Delaware, Maryland, Virginia, North Carolina, South Carolina, Georgia and Florida.
302. In the 1940s, cars averaged fourteen to fifteen miles per gallon, based on an OWI PR article published June 18, 1942.

303. Bales, "Lawrence County Memoirs."
304. *Brunswick Record*, April 30, 1942.
305. Ibid.
306. U.S. Department of Agriculture, *Family Food Consumption*.
307. Rationing details are taken from the official instructions published in the *Brunswick Record* of April 4, 1942. These were published in newspapers across the country.
308. All these stories are from the *Brunswick Record*, May 7, 1942.
309. Jeffries, *Wartime America*, 20.
310. *Brunswick Record*, July 3, 1942.
311. Ibid., July 17, 1942.
312. *Boothbay Register*, July 24, 1942.
313. Long, "Mandatory Gas Rationing."
314. Ibid.
315. *Brunswick Record*, June 18, 1942.
316. Calvin and Marjorie Dodge interview, December 7, 2016.
317. *Brunswick Record*, December 24, 1942.
318. Ibid., January 14, 1943.
319. *Bath Independent*, February 26, 1942.
320. *Boothbay Register*, February 12, 1943.
321. Wiscasset and other small towns along the coast still had party lines.
322. *Boothbay Register*, July 31, 1942.
323. Winkler, *Home Front U.S.A.*, 42. The goal was to save forty to fifty million pounds of wool a year.
324. Ibid., 32.
325. *Brunswick Record*, J.E. Davis Co. ad, November 12, 1942.
326. Ibid., April 1, 1943.
327. The difference in the number of men's versus women's clothing stores in Bath and Brunswick was due to the different demographics and economies of each community. Also, many middle-class women in Maine made their own clothes, whereas men didn't wear homemade suits or industrial clothing.
328. *Brunswick Town Directory*, 1942.
329. A quote from the author's husband, Gus Konitzky, as told to him by older neighbors in New Harbor when he opened a boatyard there in the 1970s.
330. Calvin and Marjorie Dodge interview, December 7, 2016.
331. *Maine Register 1944–45*.
332. U.S. Census Bureau.

333. *Maine Register 1944–45.*
334. This area was 12.42 square miles, per U.S. Census Bureau.
335. Bath's problematic geography pointed out by Burden in "Memories of Bath."
336. *Maine Register 1942–43.*
337. Burden, "Memories of Bath."
338. Burden, "Bath's North End Grocery Stores."
339. Marion Abbott interview, Wiscasset, 2003.
340. An S.S. Pierce receipt is still on view at Castle Tucker, a historic New England house museum in Wiscasset.
341. Burden, "Bath's North End Grocery Stores."
342. Burden, "Memories of Bath."
343. Ibid.
344. Nelson, "Bath's South End Grocery Stores."
345. Calvin and Marjorie Dodge interview, December 7, 2016.
346. Ibid.
347. *Maine Register 1944–45.*
348. *Brunswick Record,* January 21, 1943.
349. Ibid., March 4, 1943.
350. Ibid.
351. Ibid., April 15, 1943.
352. Trex, "Surprisingly Interesting History of Margarine."
353. Conversation with John M. Shiels, 2014, and subsequently backed up by audience response at every World War II homefront lecture presented by the author.
354. Kearney, "Taste of Wartime Rationing."
355. *Brunswick Record,* March 25, 1943.
356. Ibid., March 11, 1943.
357. OWI and WPB, "Food and Magic."
358. OWI and WPB, "Wartime Nutrition."
359. Ibid.
360. Brewer, *Southport,* 258.
361. Ibid., 259.
362. Ibid., 256.
363. Brewer, *Heroes Among Us,* 505.
364. Brewer, *Southport,* 256.
365. *Brunswick Record,* January 7, 1943.
366. Ibid., December 23, 1943.
367. *Boothbay Register,* June 18, 1943.

368. *Brunswick Record*, September 23, 1943.
369. Ibid., February 4, 1943.
370. *Boothbay Register*, May 7, 1943.
371. *Brunswick Record*, June 3, 1943.
372. Calvin and Marjorie Dodge interview, December 7, 2016.
373. National World War II Museum, "Fun Facts About Victory Gardens."
374. *Brunswick Record*, May 4, 1943.
375. *Boothbay Register*, April 9, 1943.
376. Ibid., March 19, 1943.
377. Examples from the author's collection.
378. *Brunswick Record*, June 4, 1942.
379. Ibid., July 15, 1942.
380. Ibid., August 5, 1943.
381. Ibid., October 7, 1943.
382. Universal Picture Company, "Prices Unlimited."
383. Jeffries, *Wartime America*, 31.
384. Geraldine Coombs interview, 2014.
385. *Lowell Sun*, "End of Sugar Rationing Complete," July 28, 1947.

Chapter 13

386. Radio Days, "Gabriel Heatter"; RUSC, "Gabriel Heatter."
387. Calvin and Marjorie Dodge interview, December 7, 2016; Dodge and Dodge, "War Years Seen through the Eyes of Young Children."
388. Chenoweth, "Out of the Past."
389. As told to the author when she came to Brunswick in the mid-1990s and asked a historical society staff member why there were two Catholic churches so close to each other.
390. Brewer, *Southport*, 233.
391. Chenoweth, "Out of the Past."
392. *Brunswick Record*, October 21, 1943.
393. Ibid., March 4, 1943.
394. Ibid.
395. Ibid.
396. Ibid., July 8, 1943.
397. Ibid., July 22, 1943.
398. Ibid., February 4, 1943.

399. Ibid., December 2, 1943. For a list of Brunswick USO volunteer hostesses, see Table V.
400. Ibid., November 25, 1943.
401. *Boothbay Register*, December 4, 1942.
402. *Brunswick Record*, August 8, 1942.
403. *Boothbay Register*, October 15, 1943.
404. Ibid., November 20, 1942.
405. Ibid.
406. Brewer, *Heroes Among Us*, 498.
407. *Brunswick Record*, June 25, 1942.
408. *Boothbay Register*, December 2, 1943.
409. Topsham Directory. 1942–43.
410. Rivest, *Rivest's Ultimate List of Movie Theaters*.
411. Calvin and Marjorie Dodge interview, December 7, 2016.
412. Ibid.
413. Topsham Directory, 1942–43, 8.

Chapter 14

414. National Archives and Records Administration, Maine State Summary of War Casualties.

BIBLIOGRAPHY

A&E. *Sea Tales: The Hooligan Navy (the Corsair Fleet)*. A&E Television Networks, 1997. Online video 5:23 p.m. October 7, 2016. www.nshof.org/index.php?option=com_content&view=article&id=314.

Adjutant General Military Records of the Adjutant General of the State of Maine 1631–1976. search.ancestry.com/cgi-bin/sse.dll?indiv=try&db=adjgenmilrecUS1890&h=1082362.

American Red Cross. "World War II and the American Red Cross." www.redcross.org/about-us/history/red-cross-american-history/WWII.

Ancestry.com. "UK, Army and Navy, Birth, Marriage and Death Records, 1730–1960." www.ancestry.com/search/categories/39/?keyword=UK,+Army+and+Navy,+Birth,+Marriage+and+Death+Records,+1730%E2%80%931960&keyword_x=1.

Bales, James J., Jr. "Lawrence County Memoirs, Historical Recollections from Lawrence County Pennsylvania and Surrounding Areas, War Rationing Efforts 1941–1945 New Castle, PA." 2011. lawrencecountymemoirs.com/lcmpages/432/war-rationing-efforts-1941-1945-new-castle-pa.

Bellafaire, Judith A. *The Women's Army Corps: Commemoration of World War II Service.* U.S. Army Center for Military History, CMH Publication 72-15. www.history.army.mil/brochures/WAC/WAC.HTM.

Brewer, Sarah Sherman. *Heroes Among Us.* Southport, ME: Cozy Harbor Press, 1999.

———. *Southport.* Southport, ME: Cozy Harbor Press, 1996.

Brunmier, Megan. "Intrepid Idealism and a Hard Practicality: Bowdoin College during World War II." Bowdoin College. www.bowdoin.edu/mckeen-center/about/peculiar-obligations/images/panels/panel5-final.pdf.

Burden, Dr. Charles E. "Bath's North End Grocery Stores." Presentation to Bath Historical Society, date unknown. DVD courtesy of Sagadahoc History & Genealogy Room, Patten Free Library.

———. "Memories of Bath, 1949." Presentation to the Bath Historical Society, 2011. DVD courtesy of Sagadahoc History & Genealogy Room, Patten Free Library.

Chenoweth, Jean Huskins. "Out of the Past." *Boothbay Register*, August 31, 2016. www.boothbayregister.com/article/west-boothbay-harbor-1940s-and-1950s-part-i/75116.

Cohen, Stan. *V for Victory: America's Home Front During World War II.* Missoula, MT: Pictorial Histories Publishing Co., 1993.

Cross, John C. "Whispering Pines: Eleanor Roosevelt's Day—December 12, 1942." *Bowdoin Daily Sun*, November 26, 2014.

Dodge, Calvin, and Marjorie Dodge. "Damariscotta and Newcastle Played an Active Part in WWII." *Lincoln County News*, December 29, 2011.

———. "War Years Seen through the Eyes of Young Children 1941–1945." *Lincoln County News*, December 27, 2012.

Duncan, Roger. *Coastal Maine.* Woodstock, VT: Countryman Press, 1992.

Fairchild, Lenny. "Honoring Our Veteran Mothers' Courage, Strength and Patience." *Boothbay Register*, May 11, 1995.

Farnum, Col. Francis H. *History Maine Civil Defense Corps 1941–1944.* N.p.: Maine Office of Civil Defense, 1945.

Federal Security Agency, Public Health Service. "The United States Cadet Nurse Corps and Other Federal Nurse Training Programs." 1950. ia902302.us.archive.org/12/items/CadetNurseCorps1943-1948/CadetNurseCorps1943-1948.pdf.

Grigg, Bob. "Air Spotters of WWII." Colebrook Historical Society. www.colebrookhistoricalsociety.org/PDF%20Images/Air%20Spotters%20of%20WWII.pdf.

Jeffries, John J. *Wartime America.* Chicago: Ivan R. Dee, 1996.

Kansas Collection, University of Kansas. "Global World War II Rationed Items List and Timeline." www.kancoll.org/voices/1997/0597ratm.htm.

Kearney, Caitlin. "A Taste of Wartime Rationing in 1940s Cookbooks." O Say Can You See: Stories from the National Museum of American History, Smithsonian Institute. americanhistory.si.edu/blog/taste-wartime-rationing-1940s-product-cookbooks.

Larson, C. Kay. National Historian, U.S. Coast Guard Auxiliary. "Bravo Zero: The Coast Guard Auxiliary in World War II." wow.uscgaux.info/Uploads_wowII/I-DEPT/pdf_files/AuxHx.pdf.

Lingeman, Richard. *Don't You Know There's a War On.* New York: Thunder Mouth's Press, 1970.

Long, Tony. "December 1, 1942: Mandatory Gas Rationing, Lots of Whining." Wired. www.wired.com/2009/11/1201world-war-2-gasoline-rationing.

Maine Registers 1942–43, 1943–44, 1944–45. Portland, ME: Fred L. Tower Companies.

Martin, Kenneth R., and Linwood Snow. *Maine Odyssey: Good Times and Hard Times in Bath 1936–1986.* Bath, ME: Patten Free Library, 1988.

Morison, Samuel Eliot. *History of the United States Naval Operations in World War II.* Vol. 1, *The Battle of the Atlantic September 1939–May 1943.* Annapolis, MD: Naval Institute Press, 1947.

Myers, Chief Jessica. Office of Women's Policy, Navy News Service. "America's Navy: The Navy's History of Making WAVES." www.homefrontheroines.com/exhibits/uniform-identity/design/the-designer.

National Archives and Records Administration. State Summary of War Casualties from World War II for Navy, Marine Corps and Coast Guard Personnel from Maine, 1946. Department of the Navy. www.archives.gov/research/military/ww2/navy-casualties/maine.html.

National World War II Museum. "Fun Facts About Victory Gardens." www.nationalww2museum.org/learn/education/for-students/ww2-history/at-a-glance/victory-gardens.html.

Naval History and Heritage Command. "Women in the U.S. Navy." www.history.navy.mil/browse-by-topic/diversity/women-in-the-navy.html.

Nelson, Kerry. "Bath's South End Grocery Stores." Presentation to the Bath Historical Society, date unknown. DVD courtesy of Sagadahoc History & Genealogy Room, Patten Free Library.

Newman, Caitlin. "Armed Services Edition: A Few Square Inches of Home." History.net, October 30, 2016. www.historynet.com/armed-services-editions-a-few-square-inches-of-home.htm.

Noble, Dennis. "The Beach Patrol and Corsair Fleet: The U.S. Coast Guard in World War II." 1987. www.uscg.mil/history/articles/BeachPatrolCorsairFleet.pdf.

Noddin, Pete. "State of Maine Military Aircraft Crash List 1919–1989." www.mewreckchasers.com/listnote.html.

Office of War Information and War Production Board. "Food and Magic, Wartime Rationing." N.d. Ella's Archives. www.youtube.com/watch?v=k9rDDFTNQik.

———. "Wartime Nutrition." N.d. but probably 1942. Historia-Bel99TV. www.youtube.com/watch?v=YX4RyOk7lM0.

Pejepscot Historical Society. "Brunswick Women's History Trail, Loop B." bwht.pejepscothistorical.org/ContentB4.html.

———. "Women's History Trail." bwht.pejepscothistorical.org/ContentA1,A2.html.

Radio Days. "Gabriel Heatter." www.otr.com/heatter.html.

Rivest, Mike. *Rivest's Ultimate List of Movie Theaters and Drive-Ins.* "History of Maine's Movie Theaters and Drive-Ins, January 2, 2012." (1891 De Villiers, Montreal QC H4E 1K9). movie-theatre.org/usa/me/ME%20 Maine.pdf, 11/17/16.

Rockoff, Hugh. "Keep on Scrapping: The Salvage Drives of World War II." Working Paper 13418. Cambridge, MA: National Bureau of Economic Research, 2007.

Romm, Cari. "The World War II Campaign to Bring Organ Meats to the Dinner Table." *The Atlantic*, September 25, 2014. www.theatlantic.com/health/archive/2014/09/the-world-war-ii-campaign-to-bring-organ-meats-to-the-dinner-table/380737.

Rumsey, Barbara. "The January 1944 Storm." *Boothbay Register*, January 11, 2014.

———. "Scrap Drive 1942." *Boothbay Register*, April 8, 2010.

RUSC. "Gabriel Heatter." www.rusc.com/old-time-radio/Gabriel-Heatter.aspx?t=3219.

Ryan, Kathleen, et al. "The Designer." Homefront Heroines: The WAVES of World War II. www.home frontheroines.com/exhibits/uniform-identity/design/the-designer.

Snow, Ralph Linwood. *Bath Iron Works: The First Hundred Years.* Bath: Maine Maritime Museum, 1987.

Sundin, Sarah. "World War II War Bonds." Sarah's Blog, December 3, 2012. www.sarahsundin.com/world-war-ii-war-bonds.

Trex, Ethan. "The Surprisingly Interesting History of Margarine." Mental Floss, August 31, 2010. mentalfloss.com/article/25638/surprisingly-interesting-history-margarine.

Universal Picture Company. "Prices Unlimited." For the OPA and Office of War Information, 1944. www.youtube.com/watch?v=7 D8sRGzeqag.

U.S. Army Film Misc.-958. "It's Your War, Too." 1944. www.youtube.com/watch?v=kxNnG7aPAfg.

U.S. Coast Guard. "The Coast Guard Auxiliary: A Brief History." Insert to *Coast Guard*, January 1997. www.uscg.mil/history/articles/CGAuxiliary.pdf.

U.S. Department of Agriculture. *Family Food Consumption in the United States.* U.S. Department of Agriculture Miscellaneous Publication No. 550, 1944. www.ars.usda.gov/ARSUserFiles/80400530/pdf/hist/bhnhe_1944_misc_pub_550.pdf.

U-S-History.com. "WAVES." www.u-s-history.com/pages/h1708.html.

Walt Disney Studios. "Out of the Frying Pan into the Firing Line." War Production Board, 1942. archive.org/details/OutOfTheFryingPanIntoTheFiringLine.

Ward, Barbara McLean, ed. *Produce & Conserve, Share & Play Square: The Grocer & the Consumer on the Home Front Battlefield During World War II.* Portsmouth, NH: Strawbery Banke Museum, 1994.

Weatherford, Doris. *American Women and World War II.* Edison, NJ: Castle Books, 2008.

Wilde, E. Andrew, Jr. *The U.S.S. McFarland (DD-237/AVD-14) in World War II: Documents, Recollections and Photographs.* Privately published by the author, 1994. Revised 2001. destroyerhistory.org/assets/pdf/wilde/avd014mcfarland_wilde.pdf.

Winkler, Allan M. *Home Front U.S.A.: The American History Series.* Wheeling, IL: Harland Davidson, Inc., 1996.

Woofenden, Todd. "Mrs. Anita Sturges Dole, 1889–1973." Obituary provided to the author, January 15, 2017.

Yellin, Emily. *Our Mother's War: American Women at Home and at the Front during World War II.* New York: Free Press, 2004.

INDEX

C

D

I

J

K

L

M

N

O

P

R

S

T

U

V

W

Y

Z

ABOUT THE AUTHOR

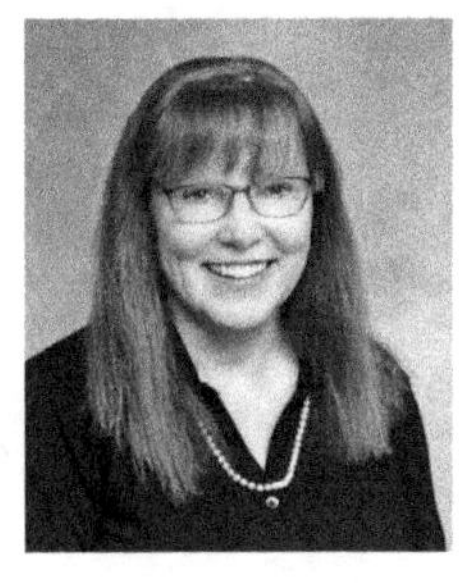

Margaret Shiels Konitzky grew up in Glen Ridge, New Jersey. She graduated from the Georgetown University School of Foreign Service and earned an MBA from New York University's Stern School of Business and a museum studies certificate from Tufts University. Peggy escaped from the business world in 2001 to pursue her true passions of history and museums. She currently manages several historic house museums for Historic New England and lives with her husband, Gus, and their mischievous cat, Raffi, in an 1830 house in Topsham, Maine.

www.ingramcontent.com/pod-product-compliance
Lightning Source LLC
LaVergne TN
LVHW010936100826
845153LV00001B/61
9781540228918